Teachers Are Researchers: Reflection and Action

Leslie Patterson, *Sam Houston State University*, Huntsville, Texas

Carol Minnick Santa, *School District #5*, Kalispell, Montana

Kathy G. Short, *University of Arizona*, Tucson, Arizona

Karen Smith, *National Council of Teachers of English*, Urbana, Illinois

Editors

International Reading Association
Newark, Delaware 19714, USA

The International Reading Association attempts, through its publications, to provide a forum for a wide spectrum of opinions on reading. This policy permits divergent viewpoints without assuming the endorsement of the Association.

Every attempt has been made to protect the privacy of the students described and discussed in this volume. All names are pseudonyms.

Director of Publications   Joan M. Irwin
Managing Editor   Romayne McElhaney
Associate Editor   Anne Fullerton
Assistant Editor   Amy Trefsger
Editorial Assistant   Janet Parrack
Production Department Manager   Iona Sauscermen
Graphic Design Coordinator   Boni Nash
Design Consultant   Larry Husfelt
Desktop Publishing Supervisor   Wendy Mazur
Desktop Publishing   Anette Schuetz-Ruff
                        Cheryl Strum
                        Richard James
Proofing   Florence Pratt

Cover Photos   Mary Loewenstein-Anderson (top left)
                   Super Stock (top right and bottom)

Copyright 1993 by the
International Reading Association, Inc.

Library of Congress Cataloging in Publication Data
Teachers are researchers: reflection and action/Leslie Patterson...(et al.), editors.
    p. cm.
    Includes bibliographical references and index.
    1. Action research in education—United States. I. Patterson, Leslie. II. International Reading Association.
LB1028.24.T425   1993   93-6691
370'.82—dc20   CIP
ISBN 0-87207-748-9

Contents

Part Three   Middle and High School Teachers
                  Are Researchers

Foreword

*I*n spite of shrinking budgets and reductions in staff in many of our schools, on the level of personal satisfaction I don't think there could be a better time than right now to be a classroom teacher. The teacher-research movement has made it possible for teachers to make a difference both within the walls of our classrooms—in the lives of the children we teach—and among a world of colleagues who are ready to hear the stories of what we have learned and to reflect on these stories' meanings for the children they teach.

Educators who learn in their classrooms, who conduct research and write about their observations, become the best possible teachers, thoughtful about how students learn and how they can help. They understand that real learning is always active and collaborative, for children *and* for adults. And they find their voices. They reject the role of teachers as mere technicians, people easy to bypass or blame, and redefine professionalism. They turn teaching into work that is real.

In 1974, when I became a teacher, the work was not real. I was the classic teacher-technician, and my work was classroom management. I managed the kids, the programs, and the paperwork. I viewed academics as the experts who were going to manage me, and I looked to them to be the "someone elses" who would tell me what to do with my students in my classroom. When the methods didn't work or didn't work with everyone, I blamed the experts. Or worse—I blamed the kids. Then I looked around for new gurus and recipes.

In truth, no expert could give me the two kinds of knowledge I lacked for all my management skills. I was a teacher of writing and reading who did not know what writers and readers actually do when they use language to make meaning; nor did I know the individual writers and readers who passed in and out of my classroom all day long. I was barricaded behind the big desk at the front of the room, orchestrating assignments, talking nonstop, and never getting my hands dirty with the real work of teaching: observing kids, asking them questions, and reflecting on their—and my own—behavior so I could teach them what they needed to know.

Two teachers helped me come out from behind my big desk, learn in my classroom, and help students sit behind big desks of their own. One was Donald Graves of the University of New Hampshire. I was floored when Graves, with Lucy Calkins and Susan Sowers, began to publish the results of studies of children's writing abilities (1978-1981). I had never before seen research reports filled with pieces of student writing, classroom conversations, and stories about students and teachers at work. The data were grounded in real children, and, perhaps even more astonishing, the reports were written in English.

This new research paradigm challenged the only educational research model I knew: controlled experiments reporting statistics that had been gathered in absentia. Graves (1983) argued that educators must stop pretending that we can transfer scientific procedures to what are essentially social events and processes. Research that ignores context—real episodes from real classrooms in real communities—does little to help us become better teachers to the various and unpredictable bodies that fill our rooms on Monday mornings. But process-observational research, conducted in the full, messy context of the life of a classroom, gives us rich descriptions of people in action. It illuminates the patterns of behavior as well as the episodes of idiosyncrasy that good teaching must allow for. I could see and hear the students that Donald Graves wrote about. He made me want to see and hear my own students.

The other teacher who influenced the change in my role in the classroom was Dixie Goswami of the Bread Loaf School of English at Middlebury College, Vermont, where I spent three summers. Dixie insisted that we teachers should act as researchers in our classrooms in order to understand the processes we teach, the students we teach, and our own actions in relation to students. I saw that the lockstep of classroom management—of set-it-up-and-evaluate-it—made it impossible for me to observe and learn from my students. I could not observe when I was up at the front of the room talking at the whole group, and I could not learn from what my students did as writers and readers because they so seldom initiated anything. All the ideas and intentions were mine.

Slowly, painfully, I emerged from behind the big desk. The day I filed away the programmed materials and invited eighth grade writers to develop their own topics, purposes, audiences, pacing, and processes was the birthday of my professionalism. I ventured out among my students to follow their leads, observe their learning, and ask them genuine questions. I talked with my colleagues and wrote about what I saw and heard, and I revised and revised my behavior as a teacher.

I had a hundred questions: Why will my students write? For whom? What topics will they develop? Which genres? Are there patterns of growth in the writing of adolescents? What conventions or skills will these writers need, and how do I best teach them? What kinds of record-keeping will serve my needs? Their needs? How will students talk to one another about their writing, and how do I talk with writers in ways that will move them forward? Will their reading affect their writing? What are the implications of writing workshop approaches for learning-disabled students? For instruction in reading? For the uses of writing across the disciplines? These were not hypotheses to test. I had no pet treatment to bestow on some of my classes and withhold from others. Bissex has called the questions that a teacher researcher poses less hypotheses to test than "wonderings to pursue" (1987). I began to wonder systematically.

I called the notes, tapes, and writing samples I collected by way of response my data. In this interactive community where an adult and a group of students spent their time discussing, interpreting, analyzing, informing, criticizing, collaborating, and inventing, my teaching and research went hand in hand. My admittedly subjective role as provider for and teacher of these students, which I was careful to describe, did not negate my findings. My role as teacher made my findings possible, it made them specific and context rich, and it made them valuable to many of the teachers who read about them.

I began to write. A systematic gathering of data was not enough. Although I did learn through collecting pieces of writing and making transcripts of student talk, the most significant lessons came from rereading the data and reflecting on it through writing, whether for an audience of educators or for my own benefit as the teacher of these students. Writing fuels my best insights. It makes me understand things I did not know before I wrote. And while my research gave me a voice as a writer, it also allowed me to read research with a different voice. I began to understand my own theory of language learning through articulating it, but I also wanted to understand the theories of others. So I read, trying to relate my work to the disciplines that could inform my inquiries: composition and literacy studies, but also linguistics, literary criticism, psychology, and anthropology. I needed scholarship because my research required me to begin acting as a scholar. And I needed teaching because only first-hand experience in a classroom gave me opportunities for learning this rich.

Many of my new mentors, whose writing I read and whose sessions I attend at professional conferences, are other teachers who conduct classroom inquiries at different grade levels in different cultures and communities and who share their findings. They have made distinctive roles for themselves in the larger educational community by going against the stereotype that says that the only way a teacher can grow professionally is by being promoted out of the classroom. And they achieved their status by being unafraid to ask the big questions about teaching and learning. They determined to make their real work in classrooms mean something.

This volume invites us to honor the wisdom of teachers and the stories they tell of their classrooms. It speaks the language of community and energy that is heard whenever teachers learn together. *Teachers*

Are Researchers celebrates the power of teachers to transform their world.

Nancie Atwell
Center for Teaching and Learning
Edgecomb, Maine
February 1993

References

Bissex, G.L. (1987). What is a teacher-researcher? In G.L. Bissex & R. Bullock (Eds.), *Seeing for ourselves: Case-study research by teachers of writing*. Portsmouth, NH: Heinemann.

Graves, D.H. (1978-1981). *A case study observing the development of primary children's composing, spelling, and motor behaviors during the writing process*. Washington, DC: National Institute of Education.

Graves, D.H. (1983). A new look at writing research. In D.H. Graves, *A researcher learns to write*. Portsmouth, NH: Heinemann.

Acknowledgments

This volume would not have been possible without the support and guidance of the Teacher as Researcher Committee of the International Reading Association, 1989-1990, 1990-1991, and 1991-1992. We also appreciate the support of IRA's Publications Committee and Headquarters staff.

Thanks also go to the following teacher researchers who invested considerable time to review the manuscripts: Pam Clark, Sunnyslope School, Phoenix, Arizona; Sue Daily, Linderman School, Kalispell, Montana; Lynn Davey, Machan School, Phoenix, Arizona; Diana Doyle, Sunnyslope School, Phoenix, Arizona; Kelly Draper, Machan School, Phoenix, Arizona; Maryann Eeds, Arizona State University, Tempe; Mary Glover, Awakening Seed School, Tempe, Arizona; Yetta Goodman, University of Arizona, Tucson; Jerome C. Harste, Indiana University, Bloomington; Dottie King, Research and Training Associates, Inc., Flagstaff, Arizona; Ann McCallum, Fairfax County Public Schools, Virginia; Joy Monahan, Orange County Public Schools, Florida; Judith Newman, Mount St. Vincent University, Halifax, Nova Scotia; Mary W. Olson, University of North Carolina at Greensboro;

E. Bess Osburn, Sam Houston State University, Huntsville, Texas; Lynn Rhodes, University of Colorado, Denver; Deborah Rowe, Vanderbilt University, Nashville, Tennessee; Wayne Serebin, University of Winnipeg, Manitoba; Irene Serna, Arizona State University, Tempe; Linda Sheppard, Washington School District, Phoenix, Arizona; Diane Stephens, University of Hawaii-Honolulu; and Jane White, East Texas State University, Commerce. Their insights and suggestions fueled our editorial process.

Finally, our deep appreciation goes to all the teacher researchers who submitted manuscripts. Space limitations meant that we had to make some difficult choices. We were consistently impressed by the energy and professional commitment so apparent in all the manuscripts we received, and we encourage each of the teacher researchers who submitted material to us to continue the important work they have begun.

LP
CMS
KGS
KS

Introduction

This book had a social life before it was published. As with most social life, some of it was cheerful and upbeat, and some of it was not.

The idea for the book was spawned during a Teacher as Researcher Committee meeting at an IRA convention. Committee members at that meeting were struck by the energy with which teacher researchers discussed the context and conclusions of their investigations of their practice, the ways in which their students learned, the opportunities and constraints that curricula and materials afford their classes, and the various means by which policy becomes practice in schools. We found our experience researching our practices in and out of classrooms to be fulfilling, also. We decided that one useful activity we could undertake as a committee was to seek ways in which teacher researchers could share their excitement and studies with wider audiences. We proposed preparing an annual edited volume of teacher research that would cut across the traditional levels of schooling (elementary, secondary, and postsecondary) in order to bring IRA members and other educators closer together.

You see, at its inception, our vision for this book was pure, and we eagerly submitted a proposal to IRA's Publications Committee. We were turned down. The reviewers' response was that IRA had a sufficient number of outlets for teacher researchers' writing and that to publish a yearbook solely for teacher research would suggest that teacher researchers are not able to compete with other writers who attempt to publish in the established IRA journals. In short, the reviewers informed us that a yearbook would contradict our expressed purpose of acknowledging the fine work of teacher researchers.

Although we appreciate the IRA journals, enjoyed the column devoted to teacher research that appeared in *Reading Today,* and recognize the remarkable service that these publications provide to teachers and researchers, we believe that the response to our proposal exposed a certain naiveté among Publications Committee members about the politics of publishing in journals and about teacher research itself. One way to discuss the politics of journal publishing is to take a look at how much teacher research has been published in IRA's journals. Our survey of *The Reading Teacher,* the *Journal of Reading,* and *Reading Research Quarterly* reveals that IRA has published virtually no teacher research as of the end of the 1991-1992 volume year. When teachers do appear as authors in these journals, they suggest methods and materials to improve teachers' performance or student learning. Although these suggestions may be based on teachers' research, they are never presented as such. Of course, ours was not a complete analysis of IRA outlets for possible publication of teacher research. But it suggests that teacher researchers will not find models to emulate in IRA publications and may not look on these journals as

likely places to publish their studies.

We can only speculate about the reasons why so few teacher researcher articles are published in IRA journals. Our own modest attempt to solicit manuscripts for this book brought over 90 offerings from teacher researchers. It could be that few teacher researchers submit manuscripts to IRA journal editors for consideration; it could be that the quality of those submitted is indeed low; it could be that these journals are the domain of university professors who seek to build teachers' professionalism through explanations of theory, research, and practice. If the latter is, in fact, the case with IRA journals, then this book does indeed have a different aim. This book is intended to acknowledge the work of teacher researchers and, more important, to provide a forum through which teacher researchers may participate in the collective theory-building that has traditionally been dominated by university researchers.

In the past decade, many of us have eagerly rallied around the growing teacher-research movement. We who served on the Teacher as Researcher Committee believe in the potential for teacher research to change the way teachers see their students, their work, and themselves. We believe in the power of critical reflection to change classrooms, campuses, and communities. Not only have we conducted research in our own classrooms, we have also invited and encouraged other teachers to do the same. We have tried to make teacher-research reports available to wide audiences through presentations and publications. In fact, this book is one result of that work. We were honored to participate in this project, an entire volume meant to celebrate teachers and their reflective decision making. Through publications like this, we believe that teacher researchers will come into their own.

The first section of this book, edited by Leslie Patterson, addresses general issues about teacher research: its definition; its historical foundations; its challenges and rewards. The second section, edited by Karen Smith, presents the work of teacher researchers in elementary classrooms. The third section presents studies by secondary teacher researchers and was edited by Carol Santa. The final section, edited by Kathy Short, presents reports by teacher researchers who are working in teacher-preparation programs.

The title of this book, *Teachers Are Researchers: Reflection and Action,* served as a focus for us throughout the project. All the authors included here are reflective teachers who make critical decisions to support their students' learning. These teachers, and many others like them, lead courageous professional lives. They deserve to be heard; their stories, told so powerfully here, can change the lives of all our students.

We offer this book as a testament to teachers' expanding participation in collecting data and building theories about teaching, learning, curriculum, and assessment. Professionals are full participants in the structure and conduct of their work, and teacher research is a sign of professionalism in literacy education. The chapters in this book demonstrate that there are significant similarities in teachers' concerns in spite of the obvious differences that exist across grade levels—we *all* struggle to understand and improve our work so that students at all levels can learn. Moreover, these chapters present content, conclusions, and emotions about literacy education that can be found in no other IRA source. Now that it's published, we hope the social life of this book will beget yearly offspring.

Patrick Shannon
Chair, 1990-1992
Teacher as Researcher Committee

Part One

Teachers Are Researchers

Chapter 1

Reflection, Inquiry, Action

Leslie Patterson and
Patrick Shannon

Patterson, an editor of this volume,
teaches at Sam Houston State University in Huntsville, Texas, and has a particular interest in collaborative learning.
Shannon teaches in the Department
of Curriculum and Instruction at The
Pennsylvania State University in University Park and coordinates the undergraduate teacher-education program.

Reviewing the manu-
scripts submitted for this volume was a
learning experience. We were pushed beyond our comfortable position as advocates
of teacher research to the uncomfortable
role of having to judge widely diverse manuscripts submitted in numbers that far exceeded the fixed number of available article
slots. We had to ask ourselves some difficult
questions: How can we develop appropriate
criteria for evaluating reports of teacher research? What is it about teacher research
that makes it different from other research?
How do teacher-research reports support
other researchers' investigations? Our
search for answers led us to new places in
our understanding of teacher research and
to some new questions.

We are convinced that teacher research
is a unique genre of research. Experimental
researchers strive for valid and reliable
measures in order to assume generalizabili-
ty of their results; naturalistic researchers
seek trustworthiness and authenticity in order to uncover the social rules for the situations they describe. In contrast, teacher researchers seek to understand the particular
individuals, actions, policies, and events

that make up their work and work environment in order to make professional decisions. They engage in moments of reflection and inquiry in order to take action that will help their students learn better. In a sense, then, all good teachers participate in teacher research because they reflect about students' learning (and their own), inquire through multiple data sources (observation, analysis of artifacts, conferences, and the like), and then act on their new conclusions.

Schon (1983) provides a useful definition of reflection when he describes the need to look beyond the pat answers and formulas that come to teachers as instructional materials and curriculum kits in order to understand the particular demands of an actual situation:

> With the emphasis on problem solving in most professions, we ignore problem setting: the process by which we define the decisions to be made, the ends to be achieved, the means which may be chosen. In real-world practice, problems do not present themselves to practitioners as givens. They must be constructed from the materials of problematic situations which are puzzling, troubling, and uncertain (p. 40).

Although the routines and findings of generalized research might offer a direction, teaching professionals must recognize that problems don't come to them fully formed, ready for application of generalized solutions; rather, professionals must reflect on the particulars of their situations in the classroom or school or community in order to identify and define the areas that present problems. Here are a few suggestions (there are certainly many others possible) of questions teacher researchers might ask to help them reflect on their classroom practice:

- What specifically am I doing in my classroom?
- What does it mean that I choose to do it this way?
- How are the students responding?
- What does it mean that they respond in these ways?
- How did I come to do and see things this way?
- What do I intend to change? How? (adapted from Smyth, 1989, p. 2)

As you can see from these questions, the moments of inquiry and those of reflection overlap as the teacher researcher articulates a conceptual framework to direct investigation, collect and analyze data, and draw tentative conclusions and plans for action. At times decisions about how to proceed are made with little reflection because teachers must use whatever is at hand to accumulate information about a particular topic. At other times teacher researchers read other researchers' attempts to address similar general issues in order to be more deliberate in their investigation of the particular. In any case, teacher researchers proceed according to their unconscious or conscious assumptions about the reality of their situations to make decisions about data sources and types of analyses that will fit their purposes and social circumstances (Shannon, 1990). That inquiry always requires at least some degree of reflection.

Effective inquiry also requires an explicit focus and plan of action for the study. After a period of observation, reflection, and reading, teacher researchers develop a clear focus about what it is they want to know about a topic. They work hard to hone the question so that it is possible to answer it within the usually limited means available and so that it will serve the purpose of furthering their understanding of their work and their students' learning. For example, a question like "Which method is better for teaching reading?" will not yield useful results because it is too general and unfocused. Many aspects of the question are left undefined: What do I mean by reading? What do I mean by teaching? Who is being taught? Are all the students alike?... Focused questions on teaching place a teacher's concern within the particulars of his or her situation: Why are my students reading? What are they reading? Do they think of themselves as readers?...

Methods of inquiry need not be sophisticated, but they must be systematic. It must be possible to spell them out in detail when teacher researchers report their work to others. For example, in an investigation centered on students' ideas about reading, will the researcher rely on audiotapes, students' journals, or field notes? For descriptions of students' actions, will the researcher work from videotapes, field notes, or personal recollections? How long did the inquiry last? Were tentative conclusions checked with colleagues and students? Answers to such questions make it easier for teacher researchers to track their decisions across time and to ensure that those decisions were based on firm evidence.

Action based on the new knowledge developed through reflection and inquiry is the ultimate goal of teacher research. This action is altogether different from the instinctive reaction professionals often make in the short term when confronted with a problem. Teacher research is aimed at informed action produced and understood simultaneously. Through this action, teacher researchers synthesize and alter the conditions of the classroom and thereby make the familiar unfamiliar and problematic. Teacher researchers see schooling as full of puzzles, paradoxes, anomalies, injustices,

reasons for action, and opportunities for inquiry. Through this action, the research participants are also changed because they now see all events, behaviors, institutions, and intentions as open to teacher research and, therefore, changeable. The teacher researchers whose work appears in this book have taken that kind of action.

Teacher research is not always respected within the educational community because it does not appear to offer the certainty claimed by experimental research or the lengthy teasing out of rules of behavior and intention that comes with ethnographic studies. These sorts of studies seem completely planned, straightforward, and well managed, while teacher researchers' reflection, inquiry, and action do not. Teacher research is instead organic, sometimes messy, unpredictable, and generative—just like teachers' lives in and out of school. Concerns about teacher research seem to center on issues of rigor and theory building and are most often voiced by those outside of classrooms and the immediacy of teachers' and students' work.

The concern for rigor is a fetish among most educational researchers, perhaps because others within academia see educational research as at best an "applied science." To avoid this pejorative label, some educational researchers attempt to make their work look like that of a chemist or biologist. This group suggests, for example, that the ideal design for testing instructional treatments would be the double-blind format used in medical research. Practical considerations preclude teachers from engaging in double-blind studies. Moreover, few of the problems teachers pose fit the designs or purposes of chemical or biological studies. For teacher research, rigor cannot come from following rituals of research methodology in order to confirm hypotheses, nor can it come from ignoring the unique nature of specific problems in order to use someone else's observational checklist. Rigor in teacher research comes instead from an explicit and well-developed philosophical point of view that guides reflection, creativity and responsiveness in gathering information and refining inquiry, and the quality of the action taken.

Traditional conceptions of rigor expect teachers to find relevance in research in which they have no immediate stake. Teachers' apparent conviction that most education research is practically irrelevant could be a direct consequence of the typical standards of rigor in scientific research. If this is true, then each traditional educational study perpetuates its own irrelevance. In teacher research, a different kind of rigor has developed from the struggle to avoid research designs and methods that separate researchers from their research and perceptions about the data collected. This redefined rigor requires teachers to take responsibility for their work and to be changed by their research.

This new expanded view of rigor, and the consequent acceptance of the validity of teacher research that results from it, challenges the formality of traditional relationships among teachers and researchers. Traditionally, the relationship between theory and practice in education has directed the relationship between theorists (researchers) and practitioners (teachers) in schools. Because many educators assume that fully formed theory should result in fully formed practice, hierarchical and dependent relationships have formed between researchers and teachers. In this sort of relationship teachers simply implement researchers' plans, at times through the mediation of curriculum designers. (Of course, it is only fair to point out that this arrange-

ment is not peculiar to education.) When teachers engage in research, these three roles are combined: teachers themselves build theory concerning the particulars of their circumstances through reflection, inquiry, and action; they perform the role of curriculum designer based on their research (perhaps consulting with other teachers and students); and they adjust their practice based on their conclusions from the study.

Reflection, inquiry, and action are interrelated in teacher research because teachers act as thinkers, learners, and practitioners throughout their studies. Each study integrates these processes differently—depending on its purpose, audience, the investigator's beliefs, and the context—and may feature one aspect over others. For example, a teacher researcher may have found his or her process of reflection to be the most compelling part of a particular investigation and may choose to write a personal narrative to describe why. Another teacher may have become interested in data-gathering procedures and may choose to write a technical explanation of the inquiry itself—the instrument designed, analysis, and procedures involved in coming to a conclusion. Still another may choose to focus on plans to act differently or on the consequences of actions taken. Regardless of the way teacher research is written up, reflection, inquiry, and action are found in all teacher research. Diversity is a powerful characteristic of teacher research, but all researching teachers share a common process of reflecting on their practice, inquiring about it, and taking action.

Teaching, literacy, learning, and schooling are cultural, social, aesthetic, historical, emotional, political, and psychological endeavors that chase after meaning and understanding. Too often we look only at the psychological and try to use an almost mathematical logic to ask questions. Too often we disregard the uniqueness of particular teachers, students, and contexts. Recently, concerns about social and cultural aspects of education have introduced the methods of inquiry of anthropology into educational research. Readers of such reports learn vicariously what it's like to be those teachers or those students, but we need to know more. What about the artistic, emotional, historical, and political modes of reasoning and investigation? What do these other ways of looking at the world have to teach us about our work, our students, and ourselves? We wait for teachers' reflection, inquiry, and action to tell us.

References

Schon, D. (1983). *The reflective practitioner: How professionals think in action.* New York: Basic.

Shannon, P. (1990). Commentary: Teachers are researchers. In M.W. Olson (Ed.), *Opening the door to classroom research* (pp. 141-154). Newark, DE: International Reading Association.

Smyth, J. (1989). Developing and sustaining critical reflection in teacher education. *Journal of Teacher Education, 37*(2), 2-9.

Chapter 2

Historical Perspectives

Katherine P. McFarland and
John C. Stansell

McFarland is a teacher educator at the
Region VI Educational Service Center in
Huntsville, Texas, with a concentration in
the areas of language arts, ESL, and mi-
grant education. Stansell teaches in the
Department of Educational Curriculum
and Instruction at Texas A&M University
in College Station and is active in helping
preservice and inservice teachers with
their research.

During the last decade, it
has grown increasingly difficult to attend
professional conferences or read professional journals, especially in the field of literacy
education, without encountering the phrase
"teacher as researcher." Many individuals
in our field have become involved in the
teacher-research movement that is gaining
prominence throughout education. Literacy
organizations such as the International
Reading Association are providing important support: teacher researchers are beginning to publish in IRA journals and present
their work at IRA conventions; the Teaching as a Researching Profession Special
Interest Group of IRA is becoming an international network for teacher researchers
and a forum for discussion of their work;
IRA's Teacher as Researcher Committee organizes convention sessions and developed
this volume.

As teacher research flourishes and
more and more teachers begin to share their
work, teacher research is increasingly being
hailed as a new idea with great promise for
staff development, teacher empowerment,

and the linking of theory and practice. Yet this "new" idea is not new at all. Teacher research has a long history in the teaching profession, in educational theory, and in Western thought. The roots of teacher research could, for example, be traced back to Aristotle's fourth-century BC notions of the observer's role in constructing reality and to his emphasis on morally informed action as a distinct and elevated form of thought that clarifies belief and deepens understanding. These ideas are central to the naturalistic inquiries that many teachers are engaged in today (Atkin, 1989).

Piaget (1967) stated that child-centered observation might have started with the work of Comenius (1592-1670), an advocate of teaching methods based on child psychology and observational research. In *The Great Didactic,* Comenius's treatise on education, several pedagogical principles based on observation are outlined. In the Ninth Principle, Comenius states that only applications that are easy to demonstrate to children are worth teaching. Such insights were the result of his empirical observations of how children learn.

Perhaps we could also say that the teacher as researcher idea exists in the work of Rousseau (1712-1778), whose *Emile* helped advance the notion that child development must be observed in the same way as we observe nature. Rousseau also believed that sound educational principles come from naturalistic methods of observation, and he placed heavy emphasis on the discovery method of learning.

Pestalozzi (1746-1827) probably came closest to the contemporary notion of teacher research. After reading Rousseau's *Emile,* Pestalozzi was determined to apply naturalistic methods of observation to a study of his own son and, later, to other children. In his subsequent work with under-privileged children, he began to develop and test his ideas of child-rearing. Still later, as director of an orphanage, he applied his pedagogical ideas. Pestalozzi used and encouraged inquiry methods of observation to enable teachers to understand and address the needs of their students.

Herbart (1776-1841) knew well the writings of his contemporary Pestalozzi, and took seriously the naturalistic methods Pestalozzi described and advocated. Yet Herbart developed his own methods of observation that he saw as more compatible with the established scientific principles of his time, methods that relied both on direct observation of children and on experimentation with them. From his investigations, Herbart formulated a series of pedagogical principles that are still visible in classrooms today, including the idea that learning should take place through the developed interests of the child and that new learning needs to build on what is already known.

A more contemporary influence comes from the work of Maria Montessori (1870-1952), who used experimentation and special methods of observation in school settings and trained teachers in observation methods. Today her work would be considered naturalistic in that she recorded teachers' methods and their effects on students. About her own school Montessori stated as follows:

> I placed no restriction upon the teacher and imposed no special duties...I merely wanted to study the children's reactions. I asked her (the teacher) not to interfere with them in any way as otherwise I would not be able to observe them (quoted in Kramer, 1976, p. 89).

Her work, although virtually unknown at the time, eventually made major contributions to 20th-century educational thought.

Early Teacher Research in the United States

Francis W. Parker was the first well-known American educator to promote research by teachers. Parker saw observational research as a basis for the child-centered pedagogical practices he advocated. Beginning in 1875, he led a reform movement for a more relevant secondary school program in Quincy, Massachusetts, which became widely known as the "Quincy System." In 1879, Parker wrote of his work, "I am simply trying to apply well-established principles of teaching...the methods springing from them are found in the development of every child" (quoted in Cremin, 1961, p. 130). In 1882, Parker became principal of the Cook County Normal School in Chicago; soon after, teachers in Cook County began conducting classroom studies and publishing their work in *The Elementary School Teacher and Course of Study*.

The dawn of "Progressive Education" rose at the end of the 19th century. Progressivism was a reaction to the reliance on memorization and recitation of facts that characterized American education. The focus of Progressivism was on the child rather than the subject matter, on active rather than passive learning, and on the classroom as a laboratory where students experimented in order to learn things relevant to their lives. John Dewey gave the Progressive movement its philosophical foundation and much of its energy. With his wife, Alice, Dewey founded a laboratory school in Chicago in 1896 that drew national attention by putting his theories into practice. Katherine Camp Mayhew and Anna Camp Edwards were active researchers and teachers at the school; together they wrote *The Dewey School: The Laboratory School of the University of Chicago* (1936). Dewey helped establish the Progressive Education

Association in 1919, became its president in 1927, and established the *Progressive Journal* in 1924. In 1929 he wrote that the development of a science of education depended on the involvement of teachers in research, and in 1933 he called for "reflective action" (quoted in Zeichner, 1983) as part of the role of each teacher.

Lucy Sprague Mitchell, a close friend of Dewey's, wrote that in the lab school "we were looking at little children learning, and intentionally facilitating the process every day" (quoted in Greenberg, 1987, p. 75). To do this, she said that it was necessary for those in the lab school "to make an unbiased, scientific study of children, their nature and their growth" (Greenberg, p. 81). In 1916, Mitchell founded the Bureau of Education Experiments (BEE) to support the research of teachers and the dissemination of their findings; in 1930, BEE became the Bank Street College of Education. Mitchell, Dewey, and others within the Progressive movement clearly provided much encouragement and many opportunities for American teacher researchers.

Action Research

The work of teachers engaged in observational research in classrooms had little effect on the larger community of researchers until the 1940s and the work of Kurt Lewin. Lewin is often credited with coining the term "action research" to describe work that did not separate investigation from the action needed to solve problems. As a social psychologist, Lewin sought to "bring researchers and practitioners together in a collaborative relationship to engage in a variety of applied research projects designed to address pressing problems" (quoted in Simmons, 1985, p. 9). Lewin also made a major distinction between traditional research that involves quantitative data and qualitative research based on observation.

The advent of action research brought other social science researchers to naturalistic inquiry. Action research gained a foothold in education largely through the Horace Mann-Lincoln Institute at Teachers College, Columbia University. Founded in 1943, the institute became a research laboratory working to effect curriculum changes and serve as a link between Teachers College and the schools. By 1948, the institute's Study Group assumed not only that "every teacher is a potential researcher," but that engaging in group research was a "must for good teaching" (1948, p. 113). The Study Group viewed teaching and researching as enterprises that involved the same essential steps—namely, defining a problem, developing a hypothesis, testing, and generalizing—and stated:

> Probably most teachers take many or all of these steps without recognizing that they are researchers. Sometimes they take some of the steps without following through to completion. When teaching is organized and its entire potentiality realized, it comes close to being research (1948, p. 108).

Stephen Corey of Teachers College described action research as "the process by which practitioners attempt to study their problems scientifically in order to guide, correct, and evaluate their decisions and actions..." (1953, p. 6). He quoted teachers who had undertaken classroom action research as follows:

> We are convinced that the disposition to study, as objectively as possible, the consequences of our own teaching is more likely to change and improve our practices than is reading about what someone else has discovered regarding the consequences of his teaching (1953, p. 70).

Corey, like Lewin, emphasized the need for researchers and teachers to work together as collaborators in research, and the collaborative efforts we see today reflect their influence. Between 1953 and 1957, however, interest waned and action research methodology was attacked (Smulyan, 1984). In 1957 Hodgkinson wrote, "Perhaps it would be better to describe action research as quantified common sense rather than a form of scientific, empirical research" and concluded that "research is no place for an amateur" (p. 146). Much more criticism of this sort came from researchers interested in "model building" paradigms and experimental research designs characteristic of the 1960s (Smulyan). As a result, more collaboration among university researchers and classroom teachers began to emerge.

In the 1970s, action research in education resurfaced in Britain, where there had been continued interest in it in other fields. Researchers in education "began to question the applicability of quantitative, experimental methodologies to educational settings and problems" (Smulyan, 1984, p. 8). The work of Lawrence Stenhouse during this period involved many British teachers and university faculty in collaborative research projects. Stenhouse endorsed research by teachers as a means of professional development and argued that the goal of educational research was to help teachers solve the problems of practice (Stenhouse, 1975).

In 1974, Stenhouse's associate John Elliott founded the Cambridge Institute of Education as a network for teacher researchers. That year, 40 teachers were involved through CIE in a search for appropriate methods to help them solve classroom problems. They participated in naturalistic inquiry by observing other classrooms, taking notes, and interviewing other teachers. Many methods of data collection were studied. After a decade of research and reflection, Elliott and his colleagues arrived at a view of teacher research that many subscribe to today:

> Elliott and his co-workers do not see classroom action research as a way to provide generalizable empirical research findings but rather as a way to help teachers generate and examine explanations for their own teaching behavior (Torney-Purta, 1985, p. 73).

Teacher Research in Reading Today

Qualitative research, emphasized earlier by Kurt Lewin, became the paradigm of choice for many reading researchers during the late 1970s. The republication in 1968 of E.B. Huey's classic 1908 work *The Psychology and Pedagogy of Reading* led many to reflect on how current Huey's work seemed and how little had apparently been learned through sophisticated experimental research in the intervening 60 years. As dissatisfaction with the fruits of experimental research was growing, the whole language movement also began to gain momentum and advance its view of language use and learning as a personal and social process inseparable from context. Whole language researchers began to explore ethnography and other qualitative, naturalistic approaches as frameworks that were consistent with their view of language. Whole language teachers began to rely on "kid watching" (Goodman, 1978) rather than test scores to understand learners' strengths and needs. For many, kid watching became both a springboard to and a vital method for naturalistic classroom research.

During the 1980s, teachers from many nations embraced the role of researcher in growing numbers. Though not immune to the criticism that they are "imperfect re-searchers" (Applebee, 1987), contemporary teacher researchers are also described as theory builders with crucial roles to play in developing the profession's knowledge base as well as its practice (Patterson, Stansell, & Lee, 1990; Stansell & Patterson, 1987). A substantial portion of their work involves scholarly reviews and use of existing research literature, employs sophisticated research designs and data-analysis procedures, and appears on conference programs and in journals where it successfully competes for space with the work of other researchers.

Collaboration between teachers and outside researchers is also thriving. Though this collaboration may have begun because of the criticisms university researchers leveled at teachers' investigations, it now promises to unite professionals too long separated and too often stereotyped in their roles. The Texas A&M School/University Partnerships is just one example of a growing number of organized groups that bring classroom teachers and university professors together as colleagues to work on research of mutual interest. These partnerships involve teachers, university faculty, and undergraduate students who teach and research together in schools to develop and study curricular innovations and preservice teacher-education programs. The partnerships support teachers as well as the university personnel in disseminating findings. Teachers within the partnerships have been encouraged and helped to present their work at conferences and to submit manuscripts for publication.

Other promising opportunities for collaboration among researchers in schools and universities are offered by the Professional Development Schools (PDS) now being developed by Holmes Group universities and schools. The PDS concept includes research as an integral, ongoing part of the school's function, and supports the idea of school and university faculty working as colleagues in teaching, curriculum development, research, and teacher education.

Persistence, Prominence, and Potential

Teacher research has a long and distinguished history, and although it has been more prominent in some periods than in others, it keeps coming around again and again. No longer just another movement on the fringes of the profession, it has become in recent years a worldwide activity that makes major contributions to both knowledge and practice. Today's teacher researchers are gaining attention and respect for what they have shown they can do: develop theory in settings that reflect authentic language use and learning rather than in contrived, artifical experiments that distort the nature of language; develop ideas that will not need to be adapted to practice because they come from practice; eliminate the theory-to-practice gap; gain for themselves the respect they deserve; and, perhaps most important, use what they learn from research to provide better learning opportunities for their students.

Despite teacher researchers' many accomplishments and the current excitement about teacher research within the profession, however, there may well be cause for concern. While teacher research flourished in the 1980s, there is clearly reason to wonder whether it can continue to do so. Powerful groups in many nations are now at work on various educational reforms, including national curricula and national tests, which presume no need for further inquiry among teachers and which cast them as mere technicians who will have no role in building curricula from their research in the classroom. Quite possibly, teacher researchers will face serious challenges in the 1990s, challenges that will severely test their commitment as well as the theory, curricula, and teaching practices they have developed.

If we see teacher researchers as "new kids" on the professional block, born in the 1980s into a doting and admiring extended family and aglow with the enthusiasm and naiveté of youth, we may well doubt that they will survive these challenges. What we should see, though, are the heirs to a professional and intellectual tradition that has very deep roots and has persisted in spite of many challenges in the past. Perhaps this means that their time has finally come. Teacher research has certainly come around again; maybe this time, it will stay.

References

Applebee, A.N. (1987). Musings: Teachers and the process of research. *Research in the Teaching of English, 21,* 5-7.

Atkin, J.M. (1989). Can educational research keep pace with educational reform? *Phi Delta Kappan, 71,* 200-205.

Corey, S.M. (1953). *Action research to improve school practices.* New York: Teachers College Press.

Cremin, L.A. (1961). *The transformation of the school: Progressivism in American education 1876-1957.* New York: Vintage.

Goodman, Y.M. (1978). Kid watching: An alternative to testing. *National Elementary School Principal, 57*(4), 41-45.

Greenberg, P. (1987). Lucy Sprague Mitchell: A major missing link between early childhood education in the 1980s and Progressive Education in the 1890s-1930s. *Young Children, 42*(5), 70-84.

Hodgkinson, H.L. (1957) Action research: A critique. *Journal of Education Sociology, 31*(4), 137-153.

Horace Mann-Lincoln Study Group (1948). Recommended: Group research for teachers. *Teachers College Record, 50*(2), 108-113.

Kramer, M. (1976). *Maria Montessori.* Chicago, IL: University of Chicago Press.

Mayhew, K.C., & Edwards, A.C. (1936). *The Dewey school: The laboratory school of the University of Chicago.* New York: Appleton-Century.

Patterson, L.A., Stansell, J.C., & Lee, S.C. (1990). *Teacher research: From promise to power.* Katonah, NY: Richard C. Owen.

Piaget, J. (1967). The significance of John Amos Comenius at the present time. *Classics in education #33.* New York: Teachers College Press.

Simmons, J.M. (1985, April) *Exploring the relationship between research and practice: The impact of assuming the role of action researcher in one's own classroom.* Paper presented at the Annual Meeting of the American Educational Research Association, Chicago, IL.

Smulyan, L. (1984, April). *Collaborative action research: Historical trends.* Paper presented at the Annual Meeting of the American Educational Research Association, New Orleans, LA.

Stansell, J.C., & Patterson, L.A. (1987, December). *Beyond teacher research: The teacher as theory builder.* Paper presented at the 37th Annual Meeting of the National Reading Conference, St. Petersburg, FL.

Stenhouse, L. (1975). *An introduction to curriculum research and development.* London: Heinemann

Zeichner, K.M. (1983). Alternative paradigms of teacher education. *Journal of Teacher Education, 34*(3), 5-6.

Chapter 3

Finding and Framing a Research Question

Ruth Shagoury Hubbard and
Brenda Miller Power

Hubbard teaches at Lewis and Clark College in Portland, Oregon, where she is pursuing her interest in different forms of literacy including art, dance, and dreams. In her work at the University of Maine, Orono, Power studies ways to establish integrated curricula and to promote collaboration among teachers.

Teachers who are just beginning their own research often feel overwhelmed; there is so much to study in their classrooms that they wonder how other teachers have ever figured out how to start. As Bissex writes, "A teacher researcher may start out not with a hypothesis to test, but with a wondering to pursue" (1987, p. 3). All teachers have wonderings worth pursuing. Transforming wonderings into questions is the start of teacher research.

In qualitative research, the questions come from real-world observations and dilemmas; for teacher researchers, questions arise from classroom queries and are important for their teaching. Here are some examples of questions teacher researchers we know are pursuing:

- What procedures or activities promote or encourage students to revise their writing?

- How does a writing workshop approach affect the growth of students' skills in the mechanics of writing?

- How does a whole language, process approach affect a learning-disabled child?

- What problems do preservice teachers encounter when they begin to teach without their mentor teachers?
- What happens when eighth graders choose their own reading material in a reading workshop?
- What sort of language is used in math class and what role does it play?
- What can my eighth graders and I learn about writing if I ask them to respond to a paper I've written?
- How do writing teachers change their instruction after they've participated in a writing institute?
- How can Inuit students establish a stronger writing voice?
- What is the difference between the genres of writing used by students on a class message board and those attempted in writing folders?
- How do students evaluate the reading and writing of their peers?
- What strategies do students use to help their peers during whole-class discussions of writing?

Such questions often develop gradually as teachers try to figure out why certain things are happening in their classrooms. Here are two examples of how a question can emerge. Kimberly Campbell, a high school teacher from Estacada, Oregon, struggled with the role of conferences in her classroom. In her teaching journal, Kim wrote as follows:

I find that as I move around the room to ask "How's it going?" I get very few responses. Often I end up feeling like an intruder, an interruption in their process.... I also find myself struggling with the hows and whens of holding conferences. For example, to-day I had five students ready for editing conferences but time only for two. I was interrupted three times during one conference by other students. And I had no time to do brief content conferences. I'm feeling confused and overwhelmed.

As the term progressed, Kim was able to focus her concerns into questions for research: What is the role of the conference in a high school writing workshop? How do peer conferences differ from teacher conferences?

Christina Randall, a first grade teacher in St. Albans, Maine, also used her writing to focus her concerns about interactions with students, but her observations led to much different questions:

Last week when I took my class from our portable to the main building for lunch, the children spied the salt-water aquarium. "What's that?" "Is that a starfish?" "What's that starfish doing on top of the clam?" "Lookit! I just saw that clam thing open its shell." Questions were being asked faster than they could possibly be answered. I reluctantly pulled myself back from the tank with "Let's go, gang. We can come back later to look at the aquarium." The questions continued after lunch and throughout the rest of the day. Within days the aquarium began to show up in writing.

To add to our classroom's language-rich environment, I capitalized on interest in the salt-water aquarium. We wrote a group story, found some reference materials, and returned to the main building with observation logs in hand. A teachable moment? As a teacher in search of stimulating topics, I could hardly pass it up.

Teachable moment. Developmentally appropriate practice. Process approach. Cooperative learning. Least restrictive environment. Whole language.... Buzz words suggest that a transition should be made from focusing on how the child succeeds with the curriculum to how the curriculum succeeds with the child. But is success determined by test results or the processes observed and documented? If the curriculum is rich and diverse in language-building activities, what about remedial services like speech and language therapy? Do children need to be pulled out for remedial services to work on specific skills?

Many teachers have to do some wandering to get to their wonderings. Often questions for research start with a feeling of tension. Christina wanted to go beyond faddish buzz words and haphazard implementation of new teaching methods to try to figure out what was really going on with her students' language development and to determine what this meant for the intervention systems in place in her school. This became her focused topic for research.

Teacher researchers look for questions to research that can lead to a new vision of themselves as teachers and their students as learners. These questions often involve seeing their students in new ways. Jack Campbell, a teacher researcher from Fairbanks, Alaska, realized he needed to take a closer look at his predominantly Inuit students and their culture if he wanted to help them become better writers. He wrote as follows:

> This past year, I've watched Native writers become confused because of the way their writing has been edited. When they receive feedback, either from their response groups...or from me, sometimes they lose confidence because they take the criticism personally. When these criticisms occur in their experience-based writing...they seem to interpret their writing as being ineffective. When novice writers offer an essay on personal experiences and these in turn are criticized—perhaps for legitimate technical reasons—their writing voic-

es lose authority and direction. The critiques, without explanations, become forms of cultural tyranny.

As Jack thought about changing his teaching to meet the needs of his Native students, he decided that he wanted to document the effect of particular strategies. He transformed his teaching dilemma into the following question: How can experience-based writing be expanded to develop other written viewpoints in Native students enrolled in my intermediate exposition class?

Goldberg (1990) stresses that the best way to create a vivid and true picture with words is through specific, tangible, concrete images:

> Not car, but Cadillac. Not fruit, but apple. Not bird, but wren. Not a co-dependent, neurotic man, but Harry, who runs to open the refrigerator for his wife, thinking she wants an apple, when she is headed for the gas stove to light her cigarette.... Get below the label and be specific to the person (p. 3).

Goldberg advises writers to be specific; we advise the same thing for teacher researchers. Kim, Christina, and Jack started with specific instances of tension in their classrooms—a lack of rapport in conferences, a moment of confused excitement on the way to lunch, hurt feelings when suggestions for revision were made. As these teacher researchers thought about this tension, they were able to move into larger issues of culture, learning, and school structure. Their research questions weren't aimed at quick-fix solutions to errors in classroom technique. While their answers might indeed help these teachers with their methods, the questions have greater implications: all involve understanding students and teaching in profound ways.

This sort of attempt at new and deeper understanding often leads beyond the classroom door. Joan Merriam, a fourth grade resource-room teacher in Bucksport, Maine, was happy with the successes of her students. But her case study of Charles started when she realized that not everyone involved in Charles's schooling shared her definition of success:

> On Parent Conference night, Charles's entire family arrived in my room at the appointed time. Charles chose some poetry books and took his younger sister to the couch and read to her while I talked with his parents.
>
> They had just come from a conference with Charles's classroom teacher and concern was on their faces. Fourth grade is the first level in our school when letter grades are assigned, so letters on the card were a new experience for them. Charles had received Cs in science, social studies, and spelling. Although his teacher had tried to assure them that C was average, they were not convinced. My glowing report of Charles's progress in reading and his grade of A did little to allay their fears. They were all too aware that *The Boxcar Children*, the book Charles was reading so well, was written at a third grade reading level.
>
> While Charles's mom assured me that he felt successful in my room, she was worried about what to her was his lack of success. She asked me to predict when Charles would catch up with his peers and work at grade level. When he goes on to fifth grade, Charles will rotate among four teachers for classes. Both parents expressed concern that Charles might have difficulty keeping up with the rest of the class next year. While I did my best to reassure them that Charles was progressing, it was evident that they left the conference with some lingering doubts.

> That conference left me with some doubts as well. Charles's parents and I had been operating from different premises. I was excited about how far Charles had come, while they were very worried about how far he had to go. When writing Charles's progress report I had only considered his success during the one hour a day he worked in my room. I needed to look beyond my room to find ways to help him succeed in his classroom and at home.

As a result of that conference, Joan established two research questions worth exploring: (1) How could she help Charles attain a higher level of success in his regular classroom? and (2) How could she better communicate with his parents about his progress?

Joan was willing to look beyond the one hour Charles spent daily in her classroom to understand his needs. Jack's research question would take him into a culture different from his own so he could better understand what criticism meant to his students. The answers to these teachers' research questions won't necessarily validate their teaching practices; rather, it is likely that from the answers these teachers will realize they need to change how they work with and view young learners.

Nancie Atwell, a well-known teacher researcher, remembers how over time her research questions changed with her views of her own teaching:

> For six years I studied the writing of eighth graders. Over these six years, the nature of the questions I asked in my classroom changed, as my understandings of research have changed. In the beginning I wanted to know, What should I do in my classroom? What will happen when I do it? I wanted to measure the effects of my teaching and prove my methods. My research was inevitably some variation of the same question: When I

perform—say, write in my journal when I tell students to write in theirs—what wonderful things will my students do?... The focus was on my methods. The focus was on me. It was a truncated version of classroom research.

Then, as I started looking—really looking, through the prism of the stunning naturalistic studies of children's writing of the last decade—my teaching methods took a back seat. My students climbed up front and became my focus. I conducted research to learn from them about their uses and views of written language (1991, p. 316).

Atwell's evolution as a researcher involved a willingness to change; Kim, Christina, Jack, and Joan were also unthreatened by change. They all could have easily developed questions from a defensive stance, a determination to maintain the classroom status quo. Kim could have asked, "How can I make my students understand the importance of my conferences with them?" Christina could have asked, "How can I get students to spend more time on task?" Instead the research questions they developed would lead to change on the teachers' parts—not merely in methods, but in teaching philosophies and attitudes toward students.

Framing the Question

One purpose of qualitative methods of research is to *discover* important questions, processes, and relationships—but not necessarily to test them (Marshall & Rossman, 1989). In order to keep the research process open to continual discovery, the framing of research questions is critical. The first consideration when framing a question is to make sure it is open-ended enough to allow possibilities to emerge. This rules out the kind of closed, "yes or no" questions that are developed in experimental studies to test the differences between control and experimental groups.

Look again at some of the sample questions we presented earlier. You'll notice that they are posed in a way that will generate descriptions and observations as answers. The key words are most often "how" or "what," which encourage describing the process and changes as they emerge. Framing the questions in this way helps make the research doable in the midst of teaching; there is no rigid procedure that may interfere with the flow of the classroom and with the changing needs of students.

When posing your first research question, come back to what intrigues you in your classroom, what you wonder about. We often find ourselves thinking about how we can help a particular university student who isn't responding. What *does* work for her in the classroom? What specifically is causing him problems? For one of our students, poetry seemed to be the only avenue that helped her make meaning in her writing. What was it about poetry that made writing work for her? In this case, the question was framed to follow and describe the writing behaviors of this student—and peripherally of others in the classroom in relation to the poetry that they read, wrote, and heard.

Instead of framing your question into a case study of one student, you might want to investigate broader teaching dilemmas that have arisen—as Kim did in her question about the conferences in her high school writing class, or as Jack did to find ways to help his Native students retain their voices in their writing. What puzzles you in your classroom? Teachers often need to rely on their intuitive hunches. Trust these hunches to guide you in developing your research question. Remember that research is a process "that religiously uses logical analysis as a critical tool in the refinement of ideas, but which often begins at a very different place, where imagery, metaphor, and analogy, intuitive hunches, kinesthetic feeling states, and even dreams and dream-like states are prepotent" (Bargar & Duncan, 1982, p. 3). Your questions should also take into account the time you'll need for observations to take shape and for the questions to shift in focus. The questions we pursue evolve and become richer when we allow our ideas and observations to incubate.

Harry Matrone, a teacher researcher from Anchorage, Alaska, found his questions and research going through the same early evolution that Atwell (1991) describes. He urges new researchers to give themselves the gift of time:

> As a result of my experience I'm wondering, "Shouldn't the first year of a teacher-research study be just doing observations—with the eye of the researcher—on things going on in one's classroom? Then, after making these general observations, a teacher researcher could identify an area to study during year two. I think my original question is being considered too soon. What I should really be looking at this year are the changes in topics that kids in my workshops experience over the course of a semester or two. Kids invest themselves in learning to the degree that their emotions allow them to. I realized a month or so into the school year that I had put my eye on the cognitive sight before I had considered the emotional.
>
> As far as discoveries related to my original question, while I may have set out in the beginning to check out the strategies kids develop when their instruction is less structured and directed, what I've really done is check out how well they can apply the procedures that I teach. The reality is

that the choices my students have are much more limited than my original question implies. At this point, I'm less taken with the idea of trying to write on my original question than I am to write on some other area I've become more aware of. I feel good about the effort. I'm learning a great deal.

Teacher researchers know that when it comes to research, the joy is in the doing, not in the done. Finding and framing questions takes time, and it may involve lots of wandering through wonderings. But as Harry notes, much can be learned along the way.

The benefits of teacher research begin with finding and enjoying the possibilities in your questions, not with analysis of research results. And the research cycle continues with new questions as well as possible answers.

Suggestions for Getting Started

Keep a teaching journal for at least a week, and preferably longer. Set aside some time each day to write in this journal, reflecting on what you've noticed in the classroom. There is no prescribed format for this kind of writing—make it simply a personal record of observations. If keeping this kind of record is new for you, practice with about 10 minutes of timed writing: put your pen to paper and just keep your hand moving. If you get stuck, write, "I remember in class today..." and go on from there.

After several days of this kind of reflection, reread your journal entries and look for what surprises or intrigues you. See if there are some patterns in your concerns or delights that bear further inquiry. Brainstorm a list of things that you wonder about in your classroom, that you think you'd like to investigate. Set a goal of writing down at least ten things, and don't censor your list.

Make an appointment to get together with a colleague to talk about your list. (We suggest meeting away from school—for lunch on a weekend, or at your favorite café after school. Treat yourself to a comfortable and inviting environment to explore your research agenda.) We think you'll find that just airing possibilities with a trusted colleague can help you focus on the area that really intrigues you.

Be specific in your concerns. Many teachers reject their first questions or broaden them needlessly. They don't always believe that their concerns are worthy of study. "What works well in writing workshops?" is a question we've been presented with more than once by teacher researchers. This is a monumental question, too large for anyone to tackle. Sometimes we are shown specific questions by teacher researchers, such as "How are Julie's perceptions of her role in writing response groups changing over time?" followed by "But I know that's not important enough to study." For too long, educational research has tried to answer big questions with short-term, large-scale studies that ignore the complexity of teacher and student interactions. It's all right for your research to start from a different point—individual students and their needs in your classroom. The more specific you are, the easier it will be to develop research procedures.

Once you've narrowed your area, write a first draft of your question. Don't worry about how it's framed—just get it down on paper. Write it as fully as you need to, as a whole paragraph if necessary. Give yourself permission to play with it, writing it in several different ways until you have all the information you want included in it. Now read it again. Does it still intrigue you? Are you still itching to investigate this area? If the answer is no, look over the process and see where you lost enthusiasm. Make sure you get that aspect back into your draft before you move on to the refining stage.

When you're ready to focus your question, look back over the sample questions in this chapter. Try beginning yours in the same way: What is the role of...? How do...? What procedures...? What happens when...? You may find that you need to make adjustments for your own particular question, but these stems are often a good first step.

Our final advice is the most important: give yourself the time you need, and the permission to modify your question as you continue your investigation. Carry poet Rainer Maria Rilke's (1934) words with you as you begin your endeavor: "Be patient toward all that is unsolved in your heart and try to love the questions themselves."

References

Atwell, N. (1991). Wonderings to pursue. In B.M. Power & R. Hubbard (Eds.), *Literacy in process.* Portsmouth, NH: Heinemann.

Bargar, R.R., & Duncan, J.K. (1982). Cultivating creative endeavor in doctoral research. *Journal of Higher Education, 53*(1), 1-3.

Bissex, G.L. (1987). What is a teacher-researcher? In G.L. Bissex & R. Bullock (Eds.), *Seeing for ourselves: Case-study research by teachers of writing.* Portsmouth, NH: Heinemann.

Goldberg, N. (1990). *Wild mind: Living the writer's life.* New York: Bantam.

Marshall, C., & Rossman, G. (1989). *Designing qualitative research.* Newbury Park, CA: Sage.

Rilke, R.M. (1934). *Letters to a young poet: Letter number 4.* New York: Norton.

Chapter 4

Hard Questions about Teacher Research

Marné B. Isakson and
Robert M. Boody

Isakson teaches reading and English at Timpview High School in Provo, Utah. She is interested in sustaining students' questions, facilitating cycles of inquiry, and encouraging personal connections to literature. Boody teaches in the Department of Educational Psychology and Foundations at the University of Northern Iowa in Cedar Falls, where he pursues research in assessment.

I [Marné] have been trying to do research in my own classroom for several years. Other teachers and administrators often ask me questions that go to the heart of my concerns about becoming involved in research. In this chapter, I give my answers to those questions from the perspective of a teacher who is busy surviving the day-to-day demands of teaching but who still finds time to do research. The chapter also includes comments (presented in italics) from my university-based collaborator, Robert Boody, who offers his perspective on these critical questions.

How Did You Get Started?

"My son has read more in the last six weeks than he had in the last six years. I don't know what you are doing in that classroom of yours, but whatever it is, it's working."

This comment, made by a father at a parent-teacher conference in November 1985, started me thinking. Yes, it was true that many of the reluctant readers in my high school reading classes were "turning on" to reading. But why? What was occurring that supported them as readers? What was it about this class that was different from other classes where they had successfully resisted reading? About this same time, I started receiving requests to conduct inservice programs. Other teachers wanted to know what I was doing to convince students to read. What could I tell them? I wanted to answer my colleagues' questions, but, more important, I wanted to find out what was going on in my classroom so I could better support the learners.

I could simply have listed the events that took place in the class by looking at my plans for each day; I could also have listed the techniques, materials, strategy lessons, activities, and other preplanned learning experiences that occupied students' time on any given day. I well knew, however, that these lists would say little about what was really going on, especially from the perspective of individual students. I explained my predicament to a colleague, who encouraged me to start writing down what I was seeing in my classroom and to reflect on the meaning of those events. Consequently, I began recording observations in notebooks. I used a three-part format: overall literacy events in the classroom; observations of specific student actions; and reflections on the meaning of what had occurred. I did not write every day or address all three areas every time I wrote. Nevertheless, I filled three notebooks that first year and have continued writing almost daily since then. Two things that most struck me about the process of writing my observations were how my writing opened up many questions and how dismal a day could feel when I did not write. All I remembered about those days were the discouraging moments, while on the days I sat down to reflect in writing, I would look at my list of students and recall all kinds of learning.

Four years and stacks of notebooks later, however, I felt I was still missing something significant in my observations. In the spring of 1989, I attended a Teacher as Researcher workshop and became convinced that I needed help in making sense of the data in my journals. I found a professor, David Williams, who was excited and somewhat astonished when I asked for an ethnographer to come into my classroom. A graduate student of his, Rob Boody, became my collaborator. He came into one or more of my classes almost every day in the 1989-1990 school year.

Rob's comments: *I think Marné began leaning toward doing research well before she started recording classroom observations. A decade ago she was recognized by her district for her work in helping disadvantaged students improve their reading, but even with that sort of tangible success she realized that these students still hated to read. Over the years she has dramatically changed her approach, but she has always tried to respond to her students' voices. That is the basis of good research. Technique and skill in research can be developed; caring and openness cannot.*

Her movement toward thinking as a researcher is also apparent in her response to the father's comment that opened this section. Instead of simply being pleased, she immediately began asking questions. This started a journey of wondering, searching for insight, and making discoveries.

How Did You Focus Your Inquiry?

At first Rob and I poked around to see what was going on, looking for patterns and themes. I recorded my observations and reflections in my journal every day. Rob took field notes, interviewed students, participated in discussions, and tape-recorded sessions. In addition, we had students' written work to review. We met weekly to discuss what was happening—to try to make sense of our observations, to reflect on their significance, and to sort out our most pressing questions. David Williams met with us occasionally and brought a fresh perspective that facilitated our thinking.

By mid-November it became obvious that several questions had evolved in my mind as being the most interesting. My journal entry for November 14 reads, "The questions I most want to answer are: How do I invite people to read or orchestrate invitations made by others? What are the conditions that lead students to accept the invitations?"

Rob's comments: *Choosing a focus was a little more difficult for me. I am not a classroom teacher, nor do I specialize in reading, so a lot of the things that were apparent to Marné were not to me and some of my concerns were not important to her. This can be a problem in collaboration, but it is also a potential opportunity. I learned about literacy issues; Marné learned about some issues in educational philosophy and the wider research arena that concerned me; and we both obtained a broader view of the situation than either of us would have developed alone.*

The main focus of "invitations to read" was not one I would have come to at that point by myself, but I was happy to let Marné set the research agenda. The topic did seem important, and after a while I saw that it did tie in with two of my major interests: noncoercive education and student construction of meaning.

How Do You Find Time to Do Research?

By the time I had a focus, many of the processes of doing research—namely making observations of classroom events, re-

flecting on the meaning of those events, and deciding what use I would make of this reflection—were a natural part of my day. I had already discovered that keeping a journal was valuable for preparing for the next day. My notes helped clarify things for me: ideas for supporting a particular student would occur to me while I reviewed them, anomalies or unusual occurrences would surface, and significant questions would arise.

So, how do I find time for research? It is no different from the way I find time to teach, because for me they are the same. The questions I ask as a teacher are the same questions I ask as a researcher: What do I know about each student? What do I know about how each one best learns this content or this process? What support can I provide? My research questions are questions about teaching that consume my interest. The aspects of my research that are not part of my teaching—such as writing articles and doing library research—I do in the summers. I read professional literature as a matter of course throughout the year, so when I have a research question, I direct my reading to the topic. I greatly enjoy discussing pedagogy with colleagues, and now I search out people who can help with my research questions.

Rob's comments: *Doing research takes time, but it is an investment in quality teaching and learning in the classroom. For Marné, research is not something added on top of teaching. Doing research has changed how she uses time, however. The time she once spent creating, administering, and grading four-day units on quotation marks is now spent creating an inviting learning environment with students.*

When Do You Make Field Notes?

Usually I sit down at the end of the day or during my planning period and think back on the events that most struck me. Then I try to describe these events as fully as time permits. Sometimes days go by without my making notes, and I just have to accept the fact that many important events are no longer retrievable—but there are always new ones to record.

I have tried a number of ways of making field notes, each with its advantages and disadvantages. Sometimes I have been able to jot down a few notes on paper or in the margins of my journal while students are busy writing themselves; sometimes I have done the same between classes. Another approach I tried was to jot down observations on a chart with a square for each student.

Needless to say, these "shorthand" notes have to be expanded as soon as possible or I find myself staring at a student's name and a cryptic comment that has become meaningless. One way I tried fleshing out my notes was to speak into a tape recorder. This was easy to do, and Rob had access to secretarial help to transcribe the tapes. This was a luxury I could little afford to rely on for the long term, however, and so I continued to use my word-processor or write my thoughts in longhand. I found that I prefer writing to dictating because it is more conducive to reflection for me.

Rob's comments: *Although teacher researchers develop the ability to remember vividly details of classroom situations, recording observations as soon as possible is essential because this provides quality primary data for later reflection. Waiting too long causes details to be lost or changed or covered over by feelings and reactions.*

Is It Hard to Analyze Ethnographic Data?

Yes, and it is also stimulating and fun. After nine months of collecting information for my "invitations" research, we had a great deal of data: my journals, Rob's field notes, students' journals, students' letters, other student writing, tape recordings, and evaluation documents. What to do with it all? Looking, describing, asking questions, and focusing on a problem are important, but gaining insight is the point of all the research.

I went through my journal looking for every example of invitations to read. Then Rob and I met to make sense of all these stories. We decided to use Spradley's (1980) Developmental Research Sequence. This produced a taxonomy—that is, a classification scheme that showed the types of invitations and their relationships to one another. The figure on the next page shows a tree diagram of our classifications (Boody & Isakson, 1992, p. 92).

What did we learn from this? Even the figure alone suggests that I have limited direct impact on the students' selection of books. The broad category "indirect teacher involvement" has many subcategories, and my data revealed that it did indeed encompass the majority of the "invitations" I noted (62 out of 92). This helped me rethink the degree to which I had considered myself responsible for *all* student learning. Many people support these readers, as does the classroom environment itself.

The impact of this finding freed me from feeling that I have to make all learning happen. I know now that I do play a major role in influencing but not necessarily in directing students' reading. Without my expectation that they will read, many of my students would not have accepted the invitations that were offered. They had generally resisted such invitations before.

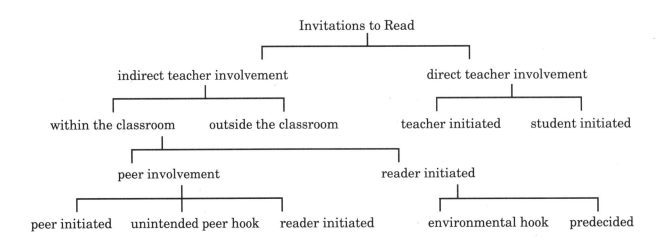

As Rob and I discussed why certain invitations were accepted, several conclusions emerged that were supported by our data. These involved notions of choice, ownership, environment, authenticity, and peer and teacher support.

Rob's comments: *It takes a lot of time to do the rereading and thinking and writing associated with ethnographic data analysis, but the effort puts the researcher in touch with the real people and stories that make up the inquiry. Doing this type of research does not point teachers away from the classroom but, in fact, brings an even deeper awareness of what happens in it.*

How Does a Teacher Researcher Think?

I suppose my thinking about research could be divided into the conscious and the unconscious. My unconscious assumptions, for example, do influence my decisions and actions. I strive to bring these assumptions to conscious awareness so I can assess their worthiness for decision making. I look at my spur-of-the-moment actions and ask myself, "Why did I do that? What was I thinking? What does this action say about what I value?" I ask the same sort of questions when I am preparing for class: "Why am I leaning toward using this teaching strategy instead of that activity? Why do I think it's important to teach this? How can I help Jenny when she tries to make sense of *Jane Eyre*?" These questions help me explore my assumptions about teaching, learning, students, and content. I become a learner in my own classroom by reflecting on what I believe and why I do what I do.

This process has a direct influence on my teaching. Not too long ago, for example, I realized I had been assuming that being on task every minute would lead students to grow in reading proficiency and change their attitude toward reading. This assumption led me to lock horns with one student,

Bo, constantly. He was not about to be co-erced: I could not force him, cajole him, ma-nipulate him, or entice him to read a book. He refused to read outside class and, most of the time, in class as well. He was a senior who felt his whole future was in football, "not in reading some stupid book." When I finally challenged my assumption conscious-ly, I realized it might be wrong and changed my behavior. Fairly quickly things started to change with Bo. One journal entry from that spring shows what I mean:

> Bo came up to my desk to discuss *Go Ask Alice*. "She's suddenly in the hos-pital and it doesn't say what caused it. I've read pages on ahead but it doesn't say. I want to know. I've reread it, too."
>
> We discussed why this hole could be there; it is, after all, a diary. Much goes unexplained in *my* journal; per-haps she didn't write it because she wasn't writing for readers but for her-self.
>
> Bo went back to struggle and look for more clues. As he left class, he said, "I'm going to reread that whole part."

Bo was so involved in creating meaning that he would not be satisfied with confu-sion or incongruity. He formulated the ques-tion he wanted answered; he read on to find answers; when he didn't find what he want-ed, he reread. He even made the unprece-dented move of coming to me for help. When I couldn't help him, he not only continued to struggle on his own but took the book home to reread the entire part. He even wrote the editor, Beatrice Sparks, a letter to ask the questions that were puzzling him and to tell her that he had started his own secret journal.

Rob's comments: *Uncovering and challenging assumptions, as Marné did, is an important aspect of good research. After*

these assumptions have been rethought, though, the new understanding that results must become firmly rooted. In the heat of the moment, one acts from an implicit frame-work of beliefs and knowledge. If the new understandings have not taken hold, they have no power.

Does It Become Easier After a While?

Yes and no. Yes, in that I improved my skills of observation and "kid watching." I am better able to make useful notes that can be fleshed out later. It is easier now for me to invite collaborators into the classroom because I know they are looking at what is happening rather than judging my presen-tation. I have also changed some of my fun-damental assumptions about teaching and learning: I now view teaching as a process of ongoing research rather than as a process of transmitting information; I see myself as a facilitator rather than a taskmaster.

On the other hand, research remains challenging for me because I never reach a sense of closure and certainty. Each re-search project opens up many more ques-tions than it answers. Fascinating areas for study surface daily, and it continues to be hard to ignore the peripheral questions and focus on one interest at a time. Finishing up involves more a conscious decision to stop than arrival at sure answers. As Harste (1991) said, "The function of research is to start new conversations, not to find truth." I never feel sure about what I do in the class-room because each day, each class, each en-counter with content, and each student is unique.

Rob's comments: *Yes, we both know a lot more about how to do research now, and we know how to work together much better. On the other hand, researchers always expe-rience confusion and doubt, even if the area* of concern changes. Teachers also have the extra challenge of being responsible for people, of knowing that their research will have an influence on how their students learn. In these senses, it never does get easier. But if research and teaching ever did become routine, I wonder if anything of value would be occurring.

Good teaching involves reflection, by which I mean both what Schon (1983) calls reflection in action and reflection on action. Reflection on action is essentially retrospective, learning after the fact what might be helpful for the future. Reflection in action, however, occurs during a time when the situation can still be changed. Reflection in action begins with puzzling over the results of a routine action or recognizing the uniqueness of a situation. Past experience comes to mind, the problem is reconceptualized, and an on-the-spot experiment is tried to see if the new way of seeing produces good results. This is essentially a research process, and one which many teachers do frequently. So teachers already are researchers. But teachers can get better at reflection, and undertaking formal research of the kind Marné does can help reflection both in and on action.

Do Your Biases Get in the Way?

Rob's comments: *Yes, of course my biases are an inescapable part of my observations and reflections. Therefore, instead of apologizing for my subjectivity, I try to give as full an accounting of my biases as I can. The word "bias" has a bias: it smacks of prejudice, and prejudice is not a good thing. But if by bias we mean that a particular person with understanding and interests different from other people is doing the research, then the answer to the question is yes, but there is no way of changing this. Individuals have unique ways of understanding things. We can try to put our personal biases aside,* but we can never do so entirely. As Taylor (1987) tells us:

> We cannot turn the background from which we think into an object for us. The task of reason has to be conceived quite differently: as that of articulating this background, "disclosing" what it involves. This may open the way to detaching ourselves from or altering part of what has constituted it—may, indeed, make such alteration irresistible; but only through our unquestioning reliance on the rest [of our background] (pp. 477-478).

Researchers do, of course, have to guard against wild subjectivity. In naturalistic inquiry we are often guided by Lincoln and Guba's (1985) standards:

1. Credibility. *The report of the study should be believable to readers and accurate according to the other participants in the study. Ways to achieve this include using multiple data sources and types of analysis, talking over data and ideas with a colleague, looking for exceptions to conclusions generated, and checking descriptions and interpretations with other participants.*

2. Transferability. *The report of the study should include detailed descriptions of the context, participants, and activities involved so that readers can get a sense of how close the situation is to their own and use what is of value for them.*

3. Dependability. *The researcher's decisions and activities should be consistent and dependable as documented by the research record.*

4. Confirmability. *The data and interpretations should be supported by what the researcher did and recorded in logs or field notes.*

Isakson & Boody

What Are the Ethical Problems You Face?

The ethical problems I face in research are no different from those I face in teaching. I feel it is my ethical duty to do the best I can for each child within the limits of time, money, and my own well-being. My research is always aimed at helping my students. And, of course, I use pseudonyms for my students' names when I describe them in writing or in oral presentations.

With Whom Do You Share Your Research?

My main audience is my students because they are the ones affected by my research through the teaching decisions I make, the type of support I provide, and the increased sensitivity I have to their attempts to learn. I have also shared my research with colleagues. The same person who encouraged me to keep a journal of observations also challenged me to write an article and submit a proposal for a conference. I was stunned at the idea of doing either, but I gathered my courage and took the risk of looking as ignorant as I felt. Both the paper and the proposal were accepted, much to my surprise. Since then I have shared my research and observations with colleagues through presentations at conferences, inservice programs, occasional articles, and informal chats.

What Effect Has Your Research Had on Your Teaching?

I think I have grown more as a teacher since I started looking closely at what was happening in my classroom than ever before in my professional life. I started looking at people instead of at lesson plans. I became involved in the classroom—reading with the students, writing with them, puzzling over difficult questions with them—instead of just directing activities. I started to take risks with my learning. I exchanged the security of familiar notions for challenges by going to conferences, reading professional literature, attending teacher support groups, and reflecting on my teaching. I invited a collaborator into my classroom.

I often try on-the-spot experiments. I see something, puzzle about it, and then try something different instead of carrying on with my lesson plan. For example, when I was talking about books with my class, Patty asked to see a book, then she passed it on. Several students who were not usually interested in reading were enthralled by the book. I passed the other books around, and the students looked at the covers, thumbed through the books, pointed things out to neighbors, and asked where the parts were that I had read aloud. I gained a significant insight: physically handling books helps students become interested in them.

The principles I learned in my "invitations" study were broadly applicable. Bo, for example, was among the hardest of the students I've taught. He read little and wouldn't listen or talk to me at all. When he finally came to me, I was willing to let everything else go and follow this up, even if it meant that Scott was daydreaming in the back of the class. Students not being on task used to irritate me, and before my research I would have marched over to get Scott back on task, thereby leaving Bo to get over his bout of enthusiasm. I've learned that when someone is engaged, supporting them is the most important thing to do. Scott's time will come later. Nagging him won't turn him into an avid reader anyway.

Rob's comments: *During our collaboration I have seen Marné change some of her practices. One example is how much easier it has become for her to talk to the students about teaching and learning—their process-*

es and feelings, the reasons for their actions. She always found it easy to talk to them about the content she was teaching, but this kind of inquiry was new.

How Would You Suggest I Get Started?

My own advice for starting research in the classroom is the same advice that was given to me: start watching, and record your observations. Two rules for observing are (1) record what you see and don't worry about the things you cannot see, and (2) when you see something that interests you, pursue it. Reflect on your observations and ask "What is happening here?" and "What might explain what is happening?" and "What use can I make of this information to support the learners in my classroom?"

I would encourage you to find a support group or someone willing to collaborate with you; either can provide support and insight. And don't forget your students. They are available if you are willing to listen and learn from them. Remember, though, that in the final analysis, you have to make your own sense. This happens for me through dialogue with myself and others. It may happen this way for you, too.

References

Boody, R.M., & Isakson, M. (1992). Inviting the reluctant into the joys of reading. *Contemporary Issues in Reading, 7,* 89-99.

Harste, J. (1991, May). *Teacher research: Inquiring minds want to know.* Paper presented at the Teachers Are Researchers Roundtable Discussion of Work in Progress, the Annual Convention of the International Reading Association, Las Vegas, NV.

Lincoln, Y.S., & Guba, E.G. (1985). *Naturalistic inquiry.* Newbury Park, CA: Sage.

Schon, D.A. (1983). *The reflective practitioner.* New York: Basic.

Spradley, J.P. (1980). *Participant observation.* Orlando, FL: Holt, Rinehart & Winston.

Taylor, C. (1987). Overcoming epistemology. In K. Baynes, J. Bohman, & T. McCarthy (Eds.), *After philosophy: End or transformation?* (pp. 464-488). Cambridge, MA: MIT Press.

Part Two

Elementary Teachers Are Researchers

Chapter 5

Meeting the Challenge of Research in the Elementary Classroom

Karen Smith

Smith, who served as editor of this section of *Teachers Are Researchers*, is Associate Executive Director of the National Council of Teachers of English in Urbana, Illinois. Her main area of interest is response to literature in children from preschool through eighth grade.

O ver the past several years, many elementary teachers have shifted from a transmissive to a transactional mode of teaching. This shift has, in turn, created interest in such things as the processes children use to read and write and the influences context has on learning. Perhaps inspired by this shift, researchers have renewed their interest in alternative research practices, including that of teacher research. Cochran-Smith and Lytle (1990) define this genre of research as systematic and intentional inquiry carried out by teachers. Teacher research by its very nature acknowledges that teachers are capable of carrying out critical inquiry about the meaning of their work and of their students' learning. In increasing numbers, reports of such inquiries are being published in the professional literature. These accounts offer insight into the relationship between teachers' beliefs and their teaching practices; they illustrate the many roles teachers play, the breadth of questions teachers ask, and the various research methodologies they use.

The studies selected for the section of this volume devoted to elementary teachers' research hint at the range of insights offered by teacher research. Jean Clyde, Mark Condon, Kathleen Daniel, and Mary Kenna Sommer share stories of a school-wide research project from the perspectives of the school's faculty, administration, and university-based teacher educators. Both administrators and teachers at a school for children with hearing impairments were attempting to improve their practice by becoming teacher researchers. Groups of researchers collaborated to answer questions about teaching literacy and about teaching teachers of literacy. The similarities in their experiences and in their growth echo the complexity and the importance of this kind of research for those in literacy education.

Caryl Crowell shares her questions about the potential that literature study has for helping students explore persistent problems in our world—specifically, problems associated with the harsh realities of war. Crowell's questions pushed her beyond the use of literature simply as a means of helping children learn to read and write; by transcribing and analyzing numerous audiotaped discussions of literature study groups, she was able to better comprehend literature's potential to deepen students' understanding of moral dilemmas imposed by war. The use of literature for its own sake as well as for teaching reading is a topic of interest to many elementary teachers, and the depth of this study will suggest to these teachers ideas to explore as they examine new ways of using literature in their classrooms.

Adele Fiderer grapples with using literature in the reading program and takes us through a carefully documented journey during which her beliefs and assumptions about teaching reading and talking about books were challenged and changed. Fiderer discusses the data sources she drew on to investigate her questions—transcripts of students' discussions, a research log for recording plans and reflections, students' logs, and conferences with students. She also describes the interactive, recursive nature of the research process: as one research question is answered, another emerges. Her understanding of context in teaching was broadened as she tackled the reasons behind the fact that what works for one group is ineffective for another. Fiderer pushed her thinking about possible answers, and she developed new understanding and theories that moved her teaching in different directions.

Jan Hancock's study is driven by a discrepancy between theory and practice. She declares herself a whole language teacher and does indeed understand the assumptions that undergird this theory of teaching, yet she recognized that her approach to assessment was inconsistent with her beliefs. By recognizing the complexities of reconciling this discrepancy and by formalizing this challenge as inquiry and tracking her efforts to consciously change her practice, she provides for us a model of how this type of challenge can be met. Hancock's tacit knowledge became propositional knowledge over the course of a year, and her shared knowledge adds to our understanding of the role of assessment in whole language classrooms.

Mary Ann Nocerino, a special projects teacher based in a central office, has been a teacher researcher and now works with other teachers involved in research. She says that her own experience as a teacher researcher left her with "a belief that teacher researchers conduct meaningful research because they are living in their laboratory and are most qualified to speak to their everyday world of teaching and learning." Her chapter shows the importance of allowing teacher researchers at all levels the time and space to find their own meaning in their inquiries, and it demonstrates the validity of this genre of research.

The studies chosen for this section also make clear that teacher research is about learning and, consistent with a transactional perspective, that there is no such thing as "pre-research." Teachers bring to their research projects those beliefs and assumptions they hold as individuals at a particular moment within the context of all previous, current, and anticipated experiences. For example, Hancock's study shows us a teacher who has read and thought extensively about her practice and who knows how to carry out an intentional, systematic study in order to make her tacit knowledge explicit. Hancock challenges her current understanding about literacy processes and events and, throughout her study, she uses new understanding to refine both the theory and her practice. On the other hand, the study conducted by Nocerino introduces us to a novice teacher researcher who is conducting her first teacher-research study. Nocerino shares with us this teacher researcher's struggle to identify a question and the worry she experiences as she thinks about whether her research questions are worthwhile and what her colleagues will think of those questions. The honesty of this novice researcher serves to remind us of the risk involved and the courage needed to engage in this form of research.

Time and Support

All the chapters in this section are complex and compelling and add to our shared understanding of the significance of what it means to do teacher research. They also highlight the elements of time and support and how crucial these elements are to the success of this research.

In an article describing their professional growth, Anzul and Ely (1988) assert that teachers know far more than they think they know, and when they are able to think and then think again about a particular phenomenon, it becomes possible to think in purer ways. Unfortunately, many school administrators do not acknowledge the value of reflection in teaching or provide support for this kind of inquiry.

As the teacher-research movement grows, however, things are beginning to change, and more school systems are providing support. Nocerino's chapter, for example, describes a district that funds days for teachers to meet and talk about their research projects. This school system also hires staff whose responsibilities include meeting with the teacher researchers, providing professional development materials, and helping review research data. In addition, this system acknowledges the value of teachers' efforts and results by publishing collections of their studies. This type of support is encouraging.

None of the other studies benefited from this level of central office support, but each of them illustrates other forms of support. The studies by Hancock and by Clyde, Condon, Daniel, and Sommer demonstrate the power of collaboration with other adults. Hancock worked closely with observers; university professors Clyde and Condon, school director Daniel, and classroom teacher Sommer formed a team of researchers, each of whose members shared a common goal yet asked different questions. These collaborations worked to support and challenge the participants. For example, Clyde reveals her surprise when she discovered that the classroom teachers rarely read to their hearing-impaired students. This discovery prompted her to turn to the teachers to learn more about their instructional decision. To support her challenge to the teachers to read to their students, Clyde shared her thinking on the subject which, in turn, prompted several teachers to investigate how reading aloud might work in their classrooms.

The studies by Fiderer and Crowell illuminate how students can provide support in a research project. Both teachers conducted studies during the school year without release time or support from other adults. Nevertheless, they found support from the students who informed their work and participated as critics of their findings. The students sometimes confirmed the teachers' hypotheses; at other times, they offered fresh perspectives.

These studies also show the support teacher researchers find in the literature. Most of the authors tell of reading other teacher-research papers or professional books in order to confirm their findings and challenge their thinking.

These examples are not intended to imply that the support of other adults, students, or texts is enough; on the contrary, they are meant to show that researchers look for support wherever they can find it.

Status and Value

Cochran-Smith and Lytle (1990) contend that teacher research constitutes a legitimate arena of formal knowledge about teaching but that its exact status and value have yet to be determined by school-based teachers. Although this statement is true, it is also true that gains are being made, especially in determining the value of this genre of research. It is unlikely, however, that status and value will be determined concurrently. Teacher research will not be given the status it deserves until education stops privileging a transmissive mode of teaching and learning and begins asking teachers, as part of their daily routine, to reflect critical-

ly on their practices and communicate this to others. However, the lack of respect accorded the transactional mode should not (and does not) prevent the teaching community from determining values about teacher research.

We have seen changes in both the breadth and depth of teacher-research studies over the past 10 years. Many case studies from the early 1980s communicate the worthiness of rich, thick description that reveals and delineates the complexity of classroom life. From these studies we learn that observing, comparing, contrasting, and reflecting are all human processes that can be carried out by teachers in the normal flow of teaching. These narratives validate the relationships among teaching and learning and context. They also confirm the importance of the emic perspective on classroom life—a perspective that generates new understanding as well as new theory. During the mid-1980s, many teachers began examining other aspects of school, from the very specific—such as the discourse structure of students' talk—to the more general—such as the influence of sociocultural factors on classroom practice. These researchers began asking questions about inequities, power, and control, and their studies, along with classroom ethnographies conducted throughout the 1980s, moved teacher research toward interpretative, critical inquiry.

The challenge now facing teacher researchers is to begin structuring this type of inquiry. If this does not occur, it is possible that standards that define it will be generated and imposed from outside the teaching profession. To meet this challenge, teachers will have to ensure that they remain open to negotiation, criticism, and new ways of thinking lest the dynamic process of teacher research become stagnant and contradict the processes of reflecting, inquiring, and acting—the very activities that give impetus to this genre of research.

References

Anzul, M., & Ely, M. (1988). Halls of mirrors: The introduction of the reflective mode. *Language Arts, 65*(7), 675-687.

Cochran-Smith, M., & Lytle, S. (1990). Research on teaching and teacher research: The issues that divide. *Educational Researcher, 19*(2), 2-11.

Chapter 6

Learning through Whole Language: Exploring Book Selection and Use with Preschoolers

Jean Anne Clyde, Mark W.F. Condon, Kathleen Daniel, and Mary Kenna Sommer

Clyde and Condon both teach at the University of Louisville in Louisville, Kentucky; she has a particular interest in early literacy development, and he is active in the field of literacy instruction for learners with special needs. Daniel, now director of the J.W. Peninsula Oral School for the Deaf in Belmont, California, was principal of the Louisville Deaf Oral School when this article was written. Sommer teaches kindergarten at LDOS and works to increase parents' involvement in their children's literacy learning.

"Ten, nine, eight..."— Kathy, D.W., Peter, and Laura begin the countdown that will launch their astronaut friends into space—"...three, two, one, BLASTOFF!"

The small room to the right of the entry has two windows that allow visitors to see the events at "Ground Control." Already this year it has served as a variety of settings for dramatic play, from pet store to circus dressing room to doctor's office. But now the entire school is studying space, a unit that has allowed students in each class to revisit and expand on their understanding of environments, a concept introduced earlier this year.

The three five- and six-year-olds occupying Ground Control are busy scrutinizing the machines, making notes to themselves on clipboards, and placing checkmarks on charts posted in their area. Posters featuring planets, galaxies, and other celestial bodies adorn the walls. Lights indicate that the CB radio on the windowsill overlooking the larger "child development room" is plugged in and ready to go. Beside the radio is some sort of computer simulation, similar to those found in video arcades. Its screen features a spacecraft gliding above a planetary surface, as if about to land.

In a corner of the large room is a child-sized spacecraft, constructed from large building blocks, cardboard, and aluminum foil, that looks much like the one on the video screen. While the lights are on inside Ground Control, the larger room is dark; the spacecraft—and its three pint-sized occupants—are "in space."

Kathy Beam, the child development specialist, calls in a loud voice to one of the ground-crew members overseeing the flight. "D.W.! There's a map of the moon on the wall. Where are they?"

D.W. searches the map, points to a location on it, and yells confidently back to Kathy, "Right here." Kathy encourages him to make a mark on the map and to record the information on his clipboard. D.W. takes this responsibility seriously; he's an astronaut too, but he has been "grounded" due to his inability to pass his "physical."

"Peter," Kathy says, again in a loud voice, "see if the astronauts are okay."

Peter picks up the microphone attached to the CB, which is spewing static and the real voices of nearby users, and checks on the flight crew. "Are you okay?" Muffled replies from the spaceship are taken as an indication that all is well. "They're okay," Peter reports to Kathy.

D.W. is now monitoring the flight simulator. The spaceship is about to land. Kathy crouches beside the capsule, wraps her arms around it as best she can, and begins shaking it; squeals of delight can be heard as the children "experience" the landing. The ground crew applauds in celebration of this historic achievement.

The door of the capsule flies open, and the three young astronauts cautiously emerge. Kenneth is first, air tank on his back, flashlight on and in hand. Just one small detail: he's forgotten his helmet.

"Kenneth," Kathy calls out, "your helmet! Hurry!" Kenneth disappears past Jessica and Cassie and returns with headgear in place. The two girls are already inspecting the "lunar" surface, but Kenneth is not far behind. "Uh oh," Kathy remarks. "You're on the moon. There's no gravity there!" But before she can finish her reminder to the kids, she notices Kenneth, who is walking behind the girls as if weightless. "He's got it," Kathy murmurs to herself, smiling. She turns now to the ground crew, who have their eyes fixed on the simulator. "Ask them what it's like on the moon," she suggests from across the room.

"What's the moon like?" shouts Laura through the CB microphone.

The astronauts shine beams of light around the dark room, as if inspecting it for the first time. "No people," responds Kenneth, "and no buildings."

Kathy nods and smiles at the depth of understanding this five-year-old is displaying. "Good for you, Kenneth!" she says quietly, aloud, but to herself. Her group of children is learning a lot about life and literacy from this dramatic play and she is noting—and celebrating—how Kenneth, D.W., and the others are progressing. Her comments, which go unheard by the children, are characteristic of the internal dialogue that she and her colleagues carry on as they monitor their own teaching.

This is the story of Kathy and her colleagues on the faculty of the Louisville Deaf Oral School (LDOS), a school that happens to serve children from birth to age six who have a wide range of auditory deficits. It relates their attempts to make informed decisions about being better teachers of literacy. The story is important because of what these teachers discover they already know about whole language instruction, what they learn about hearing-impaired children that they thought they already knew, and the process through which they come to their new understandings.

It is also the story of a multilevel collaboration involving two sets of researchers whose coming together encouraged reflection on the assumptions that guided their teaching. One of these groups consists of Kathleen (Kathy) Daniel, the school's administrator, and the school's faculty, represented by Mary Kenna (Kenni) Sommer. The other, initially a "group" of one that was joined later by a second member added for objectivity and analysis, consists of Jean Anne Clyde and Mark Condon, two professors from the University of Louisville.

We believe that the issues addressed in this chapter, though shared through the voices of two unique populations, will be useful to school-based teacher researchers from a wide range of classrooms and to university-based teacher researchers interested in working to become better teacher educators.

Teaching the Hearing-Impaired Child

The goal of the program at LDOS is to develop children's communication potential so they can be mainstreamed by first grade. Language development is obviously a critical component of the program. Deaf children have the same potential ability to develop spoken language as hearing children, but that language is learned much more slowly because of the inability of deaf children to process auditory information (Kretchmer & Kretchmer, 1978). Indeed, this sensory deficit affects all areas of learning for deaf and hearing-impaired children, both in school and at home. They often miss incidental remarks, asides, and idioms, as well as voice-inflected meaning and humor. Even simple cultural myths (such as the tooth fairy) are not shared with young deaf children because of an assumption that their limited language will prevent them from understanding. Deaf children can be further isolated by well-meaning adults who choose to "talk down" to them.

Historically, the accepted method of teaching language to deaf children was to teach high-frequency vocabulary pertinent to each particular unit of study. This approach leads to deaf children's acquisition of a set of labels for things without understanding of a larger conceptual framework. Reading is generally taught with phonics, which clearly puts deaf children at a further disadvantage. Such instructional strategies help explain why most deaf high school students read at a third or fourth grade level (Kretchmer & Kretchmer, 1978).

The faculty at LDOS believes that the limited expressive language skills often possessed by young deaf children do not interfere with cognitive development if those children are given opportunities to think, manipulate objects and ideas, and deal in meaningful ways with abstractions. They have developed what they call a "cognitive curriculum" that is based on the work of cognitive, developmental, and social psychologists (Buckler & Daniel, in press). This curriculum is based on the assumption that each deaf child has the ability to develop literacy skills, regardless of her or his limited language base. Instruction focuses on theme units that connect with a wide range of other themes and ideas. Prior to the events described in this chapter's opening, for example, the youngsters had just completed their unit on the human body. In that unit, they were given "physicals" which led them to create a doctor's office where they used charts and graphs to keep track of health records. Later they revisited their "medical" records to determine who among them was fit for astronaut duty.

In this curriculum, children are active participants in building their own knowledge; vocabulary and ideas are learned together, always in relation to material already encountered. The children are encouraged to establish relationships among words and ideas by comparing and contrasting, classifying, hypothesizing, and so on. Process is valued over product, and the development of independent critical thinking is encouraged. An important fringe benefit of this approach is that it promotes the children's self-confidence. As one teacher remarked, "Self-esteem is so critical for these kids. It convinces them that they actually can communicate and fosters their desire to do so."

Moving to Whole Language

This broad curriculum was firmly in place at LDOS, but the literacy component—how to support these young deaf children in their development as readers and writers—recently became the focus of discussions and study for the staff. Several teachers had begun reading professional literature on whole language and participating in a "support" group of whole language teachers. Their enthusiasm for this approach and its obvious compatibility with their cognitive curriculum had also prompted them to contact Jean Anne Clyde, a university professor specializing in whole language, with the idea that she would "share her expertise" in a traditional inservice program. Jean Anne suggested something different: a collaborative research project in which each of the participants, herself included, would be a learner. She, after all, had no experience with the particular needs of hearing-impaired children; the LDOS faculty, on the oth-

er hand, wanted to learn about whole language. Jean Anne was convinced that involvement in a teacher-research project would help all the participants refine their understanding of whole language and its appropriateness for the hearing impaired. In the spring of 1990, the 10 members of the LDOS faculty, led by the school's director, became involved in this university-sponsored research project.

The Research Project

Jean Anne felt that the framework for the research collaboration itself should be consistent with whole language principles. She believed teachers should have the opportunity to determine the nature of their investigations, interact with colleagues, see whole language instruction demonstrated, and evaluate their own effectiveness as teachers. The collaboration was designed so that each group member would bring a particular strength to the project while at the same time participate as a learner.

In January 1990, Jean Anne began spending one morning a week at the school. To promote a low-risk research environment for the teachers, she told them that she would visit their rooms only if requested and would assume whatever role they deemed appropriate. Some teachers asked for feedback about their instruction; some asked questions about particular children; some wanted to work out a whole language strategy for teaching a specific skill; some wanted to share their successes and seek advice for refining their curricula. At the same time, the faculty began devoting part of the weekly staff meeting to sharing observations, concerns, and questions about the project. Jean Anne participated by identifying the aspects of the existing program that were consistent with a whole language philosophy and highlighting the strengths of the teachers and classrooms she had visited. Her remarks were intended to encourage group members to build on one another's strengths and to provide a frame of reference as they tackled some common concerns.

The most surprising and important discovery made during the study occurred relatively early, when Jean Anne was making initial visits to each of the classrooms. In February, she wrote as follows in her field notes:

> As I get to know the teachers, I marvel at the richness of the experiences each of them provides for her students. Every classroom is filled with objects for children to handle and collections of books about the theme they are exploring. Yet despite the prevalence of books in each classroom, the teachers rarely read to their students. Instead, they "tell" the books to kids or invite kids to identify things in the pictures. This instructional decision runs entirely contrary to the way these teachers usually operate. They all seem so eager to engage children in hands-on experiences with objects and materials; they all encourage the kids in their writing. I suspect the teachers are protecting the kids from concepts and language they fear the kids are not equipped to handle. But the belief that children should not encounter language until it has been "taught" may actually deny them access to the very language the teachers are hoping to teach.

Deciding how to deal with this disconcerting discovery was difficult. The teachers' decision to avoid book language seemed very much akin to the "talking down" to children that they objected to so strongly in parents. Yet the working relationship was so new that Jean Anne was extremely hesitant to be perceived as "criticizing" the teachers.

However, in many ways her lack of experience with hearing-impaired children put her in the perfect position to ask authentic questions regarding the teachers' instructional decisions. She embedded her observations of teachers' uses of books within her usual discussion of what she believed were the wonderful decisions she had seen teachers making that week, as described in this excerpt from her field notes:

> I approached this issue very tentatively...aware that I, too, was operating on the basis of my assumptions of what the teachers' actions suggested. As it turned out, my first hypothesis was confirmed in short order.... They believed it was useless to expose their kids to language with which they had no prior experience. "They haven't got the background experience to deal with the language," teachers would explain. There seemed to be something circular about the argument, and I asked, "How will they ever get experience with it if they're never exposed to it?" The debate was lively and intense...yet each of us understood the other's position.

Following this discussion, two strategies were decided on as vehicles for exploring the feasibility of actually reading to hearing-impaired children. Each teacher researcher would (1) participate in a meeting devoted to discussing Doake's (1988) *Reading Begins at Birth* and (2) consider experimenting with reading text literally to students and adopting a research stance to determine the impact of this reading on them.

The discussion of Doake's work provoked much thought and exploration of deeply-held beliefs about literacy learning and the hearing impaired. Group members took turns quoting from Doake, and they discussed the book's relevance to the teaching of hearing-impaired children, who, they said, brought so little to classroom reading. Jean Anne shared with them something she had discovered in a search of the literature on literacy instruction for hearing-impaired children: while they do bring less prior knowledge to literacy experiences, they learn how to read and write in the same manner as hearing children; the difference is the rate at which they become literate.

As the discussion continued, the teachers offered excerpts from several children's books they were using in their classrooms as evidence that the language was beyond the reach of their students. One such book was Nancy Tafuri's *Have You Seen My Duckling?*, a predictable story about a mother duck in search of her lost baby. The text that accompanies each page's lively illustration is simply "Have you seen my duckling?" Kenni Sommer, who teaches five- and six-year-olds, said, "How can we expect the kids to understand 'Have you seen...' when most of them don't understand the concept of 'where'?" In her field notes Jean Anne recalled the scene:

> I reiterated what seemed so logical to me—the connection between very young children and the hearing impaired. Both have limited experiences as language *users,* but we wouldn't think twice about using adult language around infants or reading to them from books with language that they are incapable of producing themselves. We recognize that it is precisely through such experiences that children come to know and understand the language of books.

At the end of the discussion, Jean Anne and Kathy Daniel encouraged the teachers to become researchers and see for themselves how their hearing-impaired students responded to the language in books. Throughout the rest of the year, the teachers tested their assumptions and met regu-

larly to share stories and field notes, examine samples of children's work, and continue their discussion of the research question. In what follows, they describe what they discovered about book language, their students, and themselves—as teachers and as researchers.

The Project's Impact

Kenni's story is representative of the experiences of the LDOS faculty during the spring of 1990. She wrote as follows in her field notes:

> My previous criteria for selecting books had been to search out realistic and enticing illustrations and rather simple storylines. In light of the language delays of the children, these seemed appropriate to their needs.
>
> Prior to this research project, the value of book language for our hearing-impaired youngsters was completely dismissed. Often "reading" stories meant paraphrasing them with language that was deemed understandable to the children.
>
> One of my first attempts at exposing children to book language involved a group of five-year-olds with no problems in addition to their hearing loss. Toward the end of the school year, the children were having repeated lively discussions about growing up. While looking for a book that would add to the discussions, I rediscovered Bernard Waber's *Ira Sleeps Over*, a book my own son had loved. I knew it could help ease their fears about growing up, but I was reluctant about actually reading it to them. Would the children understand the part about Reggie telling a ghost story? Would they know what it means to say "I changed my mind," "I promise," and "Just a minute"? Would they recognize the sister's remarks as sarcasm? Could they follow the storyline through so much dialogue?

I decided that the potential pluses of reading the story outweighed the minuses, so I took a risk. The children were intent. I slid my finger along the lines of the text and laughed as I mimicked Ira and Reggie's conversation. They appeared to sympathize with Ira when I read the big sister's snooty statements. When Ira discovered that Reggie also had a teddy bear, they seemed to be aware of the implications of this revelation. Once the story ended, the children reacted as if they had just disembarked from a long but exhilarating train ride.

The children requested that I read that story every day for a week. I accommodated their requests and read with the same animation each day, always indicating that I was saying the words written on the page by pointing to them as I read. After a few days, I found one of the girls in a corner with the book during free-choice time. She was nodding her head as if in conversation while she turned the pages. Her verbal expressions duplicated the inflection and mood of each page. Surprisingly, she used language from the book in her own speech. As I watched and listened, I realized how powerful book language can be.

I began taking more risks with books, constantly asking the children for feedback regarding their impressions and understandings. Attractive illustrations and straightforward storylines are still important for these young children, but I now emphasize language and concept development through books. I no longer select books for my students—they select them according to their own criteria.

In October 1990, after a new school year had begun, the research group met for a final time. Many of the teachers' comments resembled Kenni's and reflected the issue of the appropriateness of whole lan-guage for hearing-impaired learners. Interestingly, the issue of book selection that Kenni raised in her field notes was a common area of concern for all the teachers. Cheryl, who worked with three-year-olds, commented, "It's interesting to see their longitudinal progress. They are now choosing books for free time, looking at different books for 20 minutes at a time, and getting something out of it." Trish works with six-year-olds. Like Cheryl's students, they have developed a keen interest in books. "They will now read the same book over and over," Trish commented. "If I try to skip something, they say, 'You missed that part!'" In order to introduce new titles, she tells the students, "I'll read one you pick, but then let me show you a new one."

At that final meeting, Kenni also mentioned a new awareness of the developmental nature of literacy learning:

> Reading and writing are such an avenue for developing language. It's phenomenal what the children can do once they get into it. For the last six weeks of school last year, the children wrote with great enthusiasm. Our discussions of the functions of print led us to publish a newspaper; we wrote directions to parents about field-day activities, made a list of items we needed to take to the zoo, and made posters about what each child wanted to be when he or she grew up; we even wrote messages to each other in autograph books. Those kids had really become confident learners, and they saw themselves as capable of making decisions and evaluating the consequences. It was cyclical. They always wanted more. They were like sponges and I couldn't give them enough.

A lively discussion followed these comments. Mairney, the math specialist, pointed out that students' development in literacy contributed to learning in other areas. She had always used books in her math lab to introduce concepts, but she felt even more comfortable about doing so now. Even though the language of some of the books certainly exceeded the children's language abilities, she recognized that "as the kids get older, they'll fill in." Mairney also noted the children's increased awareness of print and its functions. "Now when we do word problems from the textbook, they ask to see the problem. They want to see the print as part of the problem."

Kathy Daniel congratulated the faculty: "I've noticed that you are much more interested in finding appropriate books and building learning from them. It takes real artistry to read the book, see that the kids are with you, and try to clarify and keep within the flow of the story." She also mentioned how pleased she was at the efforts made to preserve the language of the books shared with students.

Kathy Beam, the child development specialist, responded to the director: "I found myself choosing books at appropriate language levels so I could keep the integrity of the print. If I thought the kids might have a problem with understanding, I'd read the text and then paraphrase—I'd read, 'Have you seen my duckling?' but then I'd look at the kids and say, 'Where's my duckling?'"

"Most of our stories are not one-shot events," said Ronda. "What the kids get out of a book the second time or the third time or next month changes because their world knowledge increases along with their knowledge of language and their familiarity with the book." She now distinguishes between reading to her children and telling them the story: "When I'm in a hurry and it's a long story, I tell the kids, 'I'm not going to read this book— I'm just going to tell you the sto-

ry.' I think they do look for books to be the same over time. Kids would be confused if one time it was 'Have you seen my duckling?', and the next time it was 'Where's my baby duck?'. They may be thinking, 'I wonder how this story got changed from last week?' and they may not know how to ask, 'What's going on here?'"

Vivian and Terri each spoke of her success at finding ways to communicate the richness of the book language to the children. They described how they now use body language, facial expression, and other cues to replace alliteration, tone, and mood that the children miss due to their hearing difficulties. Judy shared some of her observations as well: "One thing I started doing was just making books available to the children. I'd put them out, and they would go to them. Most of the kids were interested in looking at books, and the more consistently I used them, the more time they would spend looking at them." Judy had also been working to educate the parents about the kinds of literate behavior their children were likely to display, the characteristics of texts that support literacy development, and the titles of books children really enjoy. She was excited because "they're starting to bring in appropriate books that their parents bought. So I've seen some good results in terms of parents choosing books."

Reflections on the Research Experience

That final meeting of the project's participants enabled the group members to share and reaffirm their conclusions regarding the value of whole language teaching, but it also provided an opportunity for discussion of the impact this study had on them. Vivian commented, "The project has raised my awareness in terms of reading and writing, and that has helped me stand firm in some of the things I've always kind of known in my heart were important." Mairney indicated that this experience had given her "a better way of looking at things, a better perspective." Ronda discovered that working as a teacher researcher not only caused her to look more closely at her students, but to reflect on herself as a reader and writer. She began to realize that, as for her students, what she derives from reading a particular text changes over time. Kenni described some significant discoveries about herself: "Learning came alive for me in this research project. I used the same investigative model I had always encouraged the children to use. It was a very 'freeing' experience, perhaps because I was encouraged to take a risk. By taking risks alongside the children, I became more convinced that risk-taking is at the heart of learning."

The faculty also commented on the support that Kathy Daniel provided. Her participation helped create a safe environment in which to try new ideas and take risks. She brought the entire staff together with a common agenda that yielded positive results overall. Kathy reflected, "Joining the teachers as an active participant in this research project put me in the role of learner and allowed me to redefine the boundaries of supervision. As a result, the teachers felt they had permission to experiment with ideas, challenge old methodologies, make mistakes, and ultimately succeed."

Jean Anne Clyde also experienced professional growth through her work with the teachers and administrator at LDOS. "Our coming together to share our expertise enabled me to shed my 'expert' role and ask the kinds of questions of my fellow teacher researchers that I was asking myself. Ultimately, we were all able to uncover our assumptions, to give them a hard look. As a result of our collaboration, I am more con-

vinced than ever that those supporting the professional development of teachers must be learners alongside them."

Perhaps the best indicator of the success of the project is that it has resulted in many new questions. During the final meeting while sharing her enthusiasm for the project, Ronda expressed an interest in finding out how children learn language from each other—"But I know that's a different study," she added hastily. Later, Kenni said, "Here's another research project. The children I'm working with this year have multiple handicaps and are so much more needy than the children I had last year. So how does all of the book language stuff work with them?"

It is exciting that these teachers have made a teacher-researcher stance their own. Involvement in this project has shown each of the participants the value and benefits of undertaking research projects. By adopting a research stance, posing questions that challenge their assumptions, and seeking answers for those questions, these group members have learned how to support their students, their peers, and themselves. Their feelings of success mirror their students' feelings of success. That success can surely be experienced by other teacher researchers in collaborative contexts.

References

Buckler, J., & Daniel, K. (in press). *A child views his world: A cognitive-based preschool curriculum.* Louisville, KY: Mimeo.

Doake, D. (1988). *Reading begins at birth.* New York: Scholastic.

Kretchmer, R., & Kretchmer, L. (1978). *Language development and intervention with the hearing impaired.* Baltimore, MD: University Park.

Chapter 7

Living through War Vicariously with Literature

Caryl G. Crowell

Crowell is a whole language teacher in a bilingual (Spanish/English) combination grade two/three class at Borton Primary Magnet School in the Tucson (Arizona) Unified School District. She is pursuing her interests in children's literature and biliteracy through graduate study at the University of Arizona and through continuing classroom research.

On the day American and allied troops began fighting Iraqi soldiers in the Persian Gulf, my third grade students came to school full of questions, comments, hopes, and fears. Our discussion about the war that day lasted more than 30 minutes and, much to my surprise, so did our talks on subsequent days. Many of the children were watching the television news on a daily basis and wanted to share what they had learned. Together we read the newspaper that came to our room each morning. To my dismay, most of the articles concerned technology—the weapons, planes, communications systems—and the perceived superiority of American and allied forces. There was little to give my students a picture of the realities of war: the devastation and death that occur on both sides of the battle lines.

Sensing that some children needed a chance to discuss the war in a more intimate setting, I made available a set of books on war and peace to those children who chose to participate. The books—fiction, nonfiction, and poetry—dealt with the

American Civil War, World War II, the Vietnam War, and aspects of the Arab-Israeli conflict; several recently published books on peace rounded out the set. After the class had had an opportunity to browse through the books, five boys and three girls elected to remain in the group.

In the past, I had used literature study groups to help children learn more about reading and stories. I had a variety of trade books available in my classroom to support our theme studies, although these books were not subject to analysis. Now I was hoping the children in this literature study group would use their discussion times to make connections between the human experiences related in these texts and their own concerns about what was happening in the Persian Gulf. I wanted to know if learning about war and history through literature would be different for students than learning about the same topics through content area activities. I was also curious to see if the situation in the Persian Gulf would have an impact on their reading and discussion of the literature. In other words, my research questions were as follows:

1. What impact does literature have on social studies learning?

2. How do current events affect children's understanding of historical fiction?

3. What kinds of connections do children make between historical fiction and current events?

After several periods of uninterrupted reading over a few days, the group came together for its initial discussion. I was expecting the children to summarize books they had read and perhaps to begin making connections between the books. However, it was immediately apparent that several

books stood apart from the rest and commanded the attention of the group: *Rose Blanche* by Roberto Innocenti, *Faithful Elephants* by Yukio Tsuchiya, *The Wall* by Eve Bunting, *The Butter Battle Book* by Dr. Seuss, and *My Hiroshima* by Junko Morimoto. The children agreed that from this point on, they would meet every few days to discuss a single book that all had agreed was worthy of their time.

The students' behavior during the time set aside for reading was interesting. With only one exception, all of them chose to read with other group members. They talked almost constantly, questioning each other for historical background and commenting on the texts. It wasn't that the words in the books were too difficult for the children, but rather that the ideas expressed were too complex, too compelling, and, at times, too horrific for them to come to terms with on their own. One day, I put a copy of Carole Greene's *Elie Wiesel: Messenger from the Holocaust,* a biography for children, on the table. The boy who picked it up first quickly summoned the others and they clustered around to peer over his shoulder. As he thumbed slowly through the book, the graphic concentration camp photographs produced a shared emotional outcry. This was not the only time they needed each other for emotional support. Several of the books left some of the children visibly teary-eyed. One child, after hearing about *Faithful Elephants* from her peers, remarked, "I don't know if I should read it. I'll start crying." Her reading partner put her arm around her shoulder and said, "That's okay. I'll bring you some Kleenex."

Since it is impossible to facilitate a literature discussion with children and take notes at the same time, I chose to tape-record all of our discussions. Later I transcribed the tapes and analyzed them to develop categories of talk related to my research questions. At first, I concentrated on broad categories of talk—building meaning and expressing personal involvement, for example. By analyzing these broad categories over the weeks of our discussions, more specific types of talk became apparent. I noticed that a great deal of time was spent talking about the books' historical context. The children raised many questions about historical events not directly related to the stories. If I could not answer, we looked for information beyond the books. Without any prompting from me, they began to use what they knew about the Persian Gulf crisis to help them interpret the historical events in the books. The children also carried what they were learning about history into the present to help them understand what was happening in their own lifetimes. In this regard, my expectations about the content of our discussions were met. However, I was unprepared for the depth of their discussions, which included explorations of moral dilemmas, historical questions, and social issues—discussions that consumed this group for almost six weeks. They asked the same hard questions that occupy concerned adults: Why don't some people like others who are different? Why didn't the regular Germans fight back against the Nazis? Why didn't the Americans help the Jews? Why did we have to drop the atomic bomb on a city full of innocent people? Aren't the bombs we're dropping in Iraq hurting innocent people, too?

In addition to making connections to social studies, the group spent a fair amount of time responding to illustrations and the literary qualities of the texts. Although organizing their thoughts on these issues was not always easy for them, they attempted to explain what made certain books so powerful for them. They also displayed a surprising awareness of the workings of their discussions and recognized that the time they spent raising difficult questions was important to their group's success.

The audiotapes were not my only source of data. I also made use of the field notes taken during the discussions and independent reading times by a doctoral student doing dissertation research and by a colleague who was anxious to learn more about literature-discussion groups. My most important collaborators were the children themselves. Their willingness to become participants in my learning was a reflection of our classroom's accepted mode of operation—everyone, the teacher included, comes to school to learn. The students helped me by patiently answering my questions about what they were thinking, by taking on extra assignments, and by editing my transcripts of their conversations.

By coding each transcript for kinds of talk and then grouping together related portions across all of the transcripts, I developed the following categories relevant to my research questions: learning about history, connecting to current events, responding aesthetically, exploring alternate interpretations, and changing thoughts about war. In the remainder of this chapter, I describe these categories in more depth, illustrating each with examples of the children's talk and information gained from field notes and interviews with the children.

"What Is a Nazi?": Learning about History

When children write expository text, they usually have a difficult time being objective. It seems logical to assume that making sense of history texts would be difficult for them, too. Freeman and Levstik (1988) found historical fiction to be effective in presenting history to children. In the context of a story, children can examine history from a personal point of view. In the case of this particular literature study, stories allowed them to explore the worst of human behavior in the safety of a community of peers.

In our first discussion of the books we were reading, David attempted to define the genre of historical fiction with references to Roberto Innocenti's *Rose Blanche*: "It's kind of like one of those books that is kind of like true. It is kind of like not true, but it's telling about it, kind of like a fact book, only it's not true." In their lists of books read that month, David and Eric both categorized *Rose Blanche* as "real," attesting to the power of literature to convey historical information.

We discussed *Rose Blanche* over three days, during which time the children explored the historical context of the Holocaust, deferring to David and me, the Jewish members of the group, as the resident experts. Sara, in particular, asked many questions on behalf of the less knowledgeable members of the group: "How can the mayor tell who is Jewish and who is not Jewish?... What is a Nazi? Did we like Russians or not?" David and my responses to questions such as these helped the children learn about a historical period that was unknown to them within the familiar format of a literature discussion group.

Similarly, a tremendous amount of conversation focused on the historical contexts of *Faithful Elephants, My Hiroshima,* and *The Wall*. We discussed Japan's role in World War II, the bombings of Hiroshima and Nagasaki, the internment of Japanese-Americans, the Cold War, the Cuban Missile Crisis, and the Vietnam War. These discussions often became quite personal. The children wanted to meet my husband, a Vietnam veteran, and hear about his war experiences and the nightmares that invaded his sleep for years after his return. Over and over, Sara asked about my personal connection with the concentration camps and the fate of the European Jews. At first, I regarded Sara's persistent questions as naive; I quickly realized, however, that they sprang from the difficulty she was experiencing in accepting the monstrosity of the Holocaust as within the potential of human behavior. The group also spent considerable time deploring the bombing of innocent people at Hiroshima.

"Saddam's Another Hitler": Connecting to Current Events

Almost without exception, our discussion of the history surrounding the books in the literature set led to discussions of current events. Saddam Hussein was compared to Hitler on several occasions; David wanted to know if Hussein had been abused as a child, as he assumed Hitler had been. A discussion of skinheads, neo-Nazis, and white supremacist groups arose, and we talked about the kinds of people the Nazis had exterminated during World War II. The children also speculated about whether Hitler would have joined the Ku Klux Klan if he had lived in the United States.

The doctoral student doing research in our classroom told the students about the plight of the animals in the Kuwaiti zoo during the Persian Gulf conflict. That knowledge became part of the discussion about *Faithful Elephants*:

> Sara: But you know, in the Gulf War, they had to do this too.
>
> Eric: Yeah.
>
> Sara: They had to kill them in Kuwait 'cause what if the animals got loose and ran all over the city. They'd have to....

Eric: That's why they had to kill them. 'Cause if a bomb dropped on their zoo, the animals would probably get loose. Well, unless they died. But they could have gotten loose and ran away and started knocking down the people's houses just before the bomb.

William: And killing people.

Eric: Yeah, and then they'd get killed by a bomb and that would be a horrible way to die.

William: Yeah, it would.

Eric: Well, it's bad enough they died in a zoo cage.

Sara: But that's mean that they had to kill them and then the Gulf War ended. They killed the animals and then the war ended.

Our discussion of *My Hiroshima* led to talk about the development and testing of nuclear weapons, the arms race, and disarmament treaties. David, who had been writing a report on New Zealand for a geography theme cycle, shared with us that country's policy banning the production and transportation of nuclear weapons within its territory and the United States government's resulting cancellation of defense agreements with New Zealand. Eric was particularly offended at the bombing of Hiroshima. He astutely made a connection between the annihilation of Japanese civilians and the air war in the Persian Gulf: "They could have bombed, like, an air-force base, not where people were innocent. That would be just like Iraq coming over here and bombing us, and we're innocent. Or like us going over there and bombing innocent people, which did happen.... And Iraq bombing Israel."

"The Sadder They Are, the Gooder They Get": Responding Aesthetically

Many articles in the professional literature extol the ability of trade books to bring readers a personal understanding of war (see, for example, Freeman & Levstik, 1988; Kiefer, 1988; Salevouris, 1989; Yolen, 1989; and Zack, 1991). Certainly the books in my literature set touched and moved my students. I was unprepared, however, for the depth of their critical reading and their awareness of the role of illustrations in deepening their understanding.

In our final discussion, I asked the children to identify the books they felt had had an impact on their thinking. Every child put *Rose Blanche* and *My Hiroshima* at the top of their lists. Both of these books focus on a central character, a child of about the same age as my students, with whom the children seemed to identify. Both books are told in the first person, which served to draw these young readers further into the stories. Through these books, the children vicariously experienced history and made it part of their own past. They frequently put themselves in characters' places and explored what their own feelings and actions might have been. In discussing *Rose Blanche,* for example, Eric said, "I'd help David if he was in the concentration camp." About *My Hiroshima,* the following discussion took place:

David: Yeah, but if I knew there was a war near Arizona, then every plane that I heard, I'd probably go look.

Sara: That's what I did during the, when we were having the...

Trent: Iraqi war?

Sara: Uh huh. I always heard a siren, like a police siren. And I thought it was a siren going off that we were going to be bombed.

And about *Faithful Elephants*:

Sara: What would you do if you had to kill those animals?

William: I would send them somewhere else.

Sara: But what if a bomb dropped into the train while you were sending them somewhere else?

The children were very much aware of the way the illustrations influenced their emotional responses to the stories. As they discussed *Rose Blanche,* they consistently referred to the illustrations to clarify meanings and search for clues to aid their understanding of the events. They were particularly moved by the last illustration—a single flower draped across the barbed-wire fence, placed there by Rose Blanche before she was shot:

Lupe: It's real sad at the end.

David: It's real beautiful at the back when....

Trent: Yeah, except for that one little flower.

Myself: That really surprised me. Why do you think the author did that?

David: To make it a little happy and sad. To make it happy.

In *Elie Wiesel,* the children discovered a photograph of a young Jewish boy with hands raised, being marched to the trains by armed German guards. Immediately the children cried, "That's in *Rose Blanche!*" Innocenti's use of a real photograph from the Holocaust to inspire his illustration served to heighten the realness of *Rose Blanche* in the children's minds. The children also compared Innocenti's work to Dr. Seuss's in *The Butter Battle Book.* The children's knowledge of Dr. Seuss as an author of humorous books made it difficult for them to take him seriously as an author on war. They saw *The Butter Battle Book* as "kind of a kids' war book"; as Eric commented, "He writes funny books and the illustrations are way different...some are like play. Like in *Rose Blanche*—there are realistic pictures, not play pictures, and dark colors."

As in *Rose Blanche, My Hiroshima*'s illustrations dominate the small amount of text. Without doubt, the children were moved by the illustrations:

Eric: But there's some really sad pictures in here.

David: She thought the plane was really far away. That's sad. It shows the baby kind of flying away from the mother.

Trent: And all the hands reaching up.

Eric: It's sad, because it shows all these pictures of people with hardly any clothes on, ripped and torn and bombed and bloody.

David: It looks like their skin's peeling off.

William: I'm sure it is.

David, the artist in our class, was especially aware of the artist's conscious choices in making the illustrations: "The author really made the illustrations with a lot of expression.... That author was really expressional."

"There Was Lots of Questions": Exploring Alternate Interpretations

The ways that books can raise questions was central to many of our discussions over the period. At first, the questions focused on sorting out events and historical contexts when it was not immediately obvious what had happened in a book. Two days were spent trying to figure out the change in Rose Blanche's thinking and determining whether she had been shot on purpose. The group valued this questioning and saw it as important to their discussion process. They recognized that the authors who raised questions left room for readers' interpretations and that those interpretations could change over time:

David: This book gives you a lot of questions.

Myself: Doesn't it? I had a lot of questions, too, when I read that book.

David: Every time I read it, I usually have questions about it.

Myself: How many times have you read that book, David?

David: About three times.

Myself: And do you have different questions each time you read it?

David: Yeah.

Eric: Because this book has a lot of questions.... I might write a book about all the questions I have in here.

Many people feel *The Butter Battle Book* raises important questions for young readers. Yet, because of their preconceptions about Dr. Seuss and because of the "play pictures," my students concluded that the unresolved ending was "boring":

William: The only question is what happens.

Eric: And that's a dumb question, I think. In all the other books, it tells you what happens, but there's more questions. Like in *Rose Blanche,* there's more questions. That means they're more interesting.

When pushed to describe what they thought of as a good question, Lisa, who had been silent throughout most of our discussions, gave a clear explanation of their meaning: "What makes a question good is because if the question is real hard to answer it, and you don't really know it, and it takes a long time to find out, that's what makes it interesting."

Using their own criteria—asking good questions and having illustrations and stories that evoked a personal, emotional response—the children unanimously chose *Rose Blanche* and *My Hiroshima* as their favorite books. David and Trent summed up for the group:

David: But these two books are the best.

Trent: Yeah, the sadder they are, the gooder they get.

David: I liked *Rose Blanche* and *My Hiroshima* because they make you kind of really feel it. The author does.

Trent: Me, too. Those were my two favorites. I think we like talked about them the most.

David: The authors made you think.

They really made you feel it.

Trent: And wonder what it was like.

"I Just Don't Play That Way Any More": Changing Thoughts about War

As the mother of two boys, I have worried frequently about our society's romanticized vision of war. Although I have never bought either of my children a toy gun, they make them out of odds and ends. They play elaborate, imaginative games in which they pretend to be movie-type war heroes. My younger son has an extensive collection of war toys, purchased with his own money. My older child wants to attend the U.S. Air Force Academy and become a pilot. I can understand his desire to experience the thrill of flying; I only hope he considers that if there is a war and he is called on to drop a bomb or shoot a missile, people may die as a result of his action.

The children in my class are exposed to the same glorified images of war as my own children. The press coverage of the Persian Gulf conflict did little to present any opposing viewpoint. I do not condemn the appeal to support the troops. After the experience of Vietnam, we have, I hope, learned to separate individual soldiers from what may be our profound disagreement with a war itself. However, I believe we must expose children and adults to the war's personal consequences if we are ever going to make the collective decisions that will avoid wars in the future.

Through the vicarious experiences provided by literature, we can help children build understanding and give them options to consider as they wrestle with the moral dilemmas imposed by wars. The children in this literature study group clarified their understanding about the human costs of war, why wars happen, what constitutes a war, and how its impact is felt on opposing sides:

William: Yeah, because, like one kind of people don't like the way that the other people do things...and so they decide that they want to stop those people.... So they get into a war trying to change the other people's ways.

Sara: I thought in wars everybody got killed. But then, in the Iraqi war, when they were, like, fighting the air war, I didn't believe there was such a thing as air war. I thought there was only a ground war. And then how only 20 people got killed in the air war.

Myself: There weren't many Americans, right?

William: Only about 25.

Myself: I just wonder about the Iraqis.

Sara: That's what I mean.

William: Only 25 got killed, but we killed hundreds, maybe thousands.

On the last day we met as a group, the children shared with me how much they had learned about history and life. The boys in the group surprised all of us with the change in their attitudes about war. With quiet voices, they all admitted that they had given up war games:

Trent: I've changed my thoughts about war. I used to, like, play war, but now it makes me sick.

Eric: Now I think about it a lot more...what's going on, what was going on in Iraq and about other stuff.

William: I felt the same way as Trent did. Now I just don't play that way anymore because I think it's so gross, after I read the books.

David: I did both [play with war toys and act out roles in war games]. But then, when I was reading the books, I didn't play with them that much.

The intense discussion of such important social and moral issues was at times exhausting. I recall one discussion, when Sara and Lupe were sprawled on the floor. "We're tired, Mrs. C.," was their comment.

I am convinced, however, that no newspaper or magazine article, no discussions of current events or TV news program could have had the impact that literature had on these children. At a young age, they experienced the lessons that history has to teach, at a level that had personal significance for them. They were able to bring those lessons into the present to support their changing understanding of society's frequently precarious situation and the role they will play in its future. David said to me one day, "Didn't they say that if you don't...something about Hitler. If you don't remember history and stuff about it that something will happen to you?"

"Are you thinking about that if you don't remember history that you are condemned to repeat it?" I replied.

"Yeah, that's it. I think that's true," he concluded.

I came away from this inquiry project awed by the power of books to influence children and teach them about things other than literature. The first-person narratives, in particular, and our own personal experiences and knowledge were important to the development of historical understanding; the current events connection was made when the Persian Gulf conflict was interpreted within the context of the children's newly acquired historical awareness. These connections were consistently made at an emotional level, as the children responded to the dramatic illustrations and placed themselves within the stories. Not all of the books in the text set had this impact and the children themselves were able to identify the stories that had drawn them in so completely. It does seem clear to me, though, that by carefully selecting books about war and peace and by supporting children emotionally and intellectually through their reading and discussion, a teacher may actually play a small role in the growth of a peaceful society.

References
Freeman, E.B., & Levstik, L. (1988). Recreating the past: Historical fiction in the social studies curriculum. *Elementary School Journal, 88,* 329-337.

Kiefer, B. (1988). Picture books as contexts for literary, aesthetic, and real world understandings. *Language Arts, 65,* 269-271.

Salevouris, M.J. (1989). Warfare and the teaching of history. *History Teacher, 22,* 341-355.

Yolen, J. (1989). An experiential act. *Language Arts, 66,* 246-251.

Zack, V. (1991). It was the worst of times: Learning about the Holocaust through literature. *Language Arts, 68,* 42-48.

Talking and Thinking: Making What We Read Ours

Adele Fiderer

In her work as language arts consultant to the Scarsdale Public Schools in Scarsdale, New York, Fiderer has developed, coordinated, and served as an advisor on numerous teacher-research projects covering a wide range of topics.

T wo fifth graders were trying to come to grips with Matt's dilemma in Rachel George Speare's *The Sign of the Beaver*:

> Li-An: If you were Matt, would you have gone with the Indians?
>
> Pierre: I would have gone. If my father didn't come, then I'd be alone and scared. And I wouldn't have a gun and I'd eat fish all the time.
>
> Li-An: I sort of would have stayed because even if he didn't come, which it seemed like he wouldn't, he promised his father he'd stay. And even if he did come about a year later, well, it seems like you have to stay with your parents if you think that they're alive.
>
> Pierre: Well, there were a lot of times that I thought his parents weren't going to come, 'cause it was a long time.

Li-An: He said it was going to be about seven weeks and he kept on....

Pierre: Cutting notches?

Li-An: Yeah, cutting notches on a stick.

Pierre: And he finally...didn't keep count any more because he was getting scared and worried that his parents wouldn't come.

Li-An and Pierre debated whether Matt should wait for his long-overdue parents or ensure his survival by moving away with the Beaver Clan and asked and answered questions to clarify their feelings and opinions. By working in collaborative groups these students learned to talk and think about a book knowing that there was more than one right answer and opinion about its content.

I decided to try this new approach to teaching reading the year that Li-An and Pierre entered my fifth grade classroom. In previous years, daily sustained silent reading periods during which students read literature of their choice had been supplemented with skills study periods during which students read and completed questions about stories from commercial reading programs. I met regularly with students in individual conferences to discuss the books they were reading and knew how well each could read and understand the stories. Still, I worried that I wasn't spending enough time on systematic instruction in areas such as vocabulary, sequence of events, main idea, and decoding strategies.

My growing understanding of two important ideas led me to change the way I taught reading. The first was my acceptance of the process approach that had transformed the way I taught writing. Our writ-

ing workshop was strongly influenced by the early research of Calkins and Graves. Following their recommendations, I began to teach writing skills in ways that were relevant to the students' experiences. My students learned the mechanics and conventions of writing in the context of editing their own stories, not through isolated practice. After reading Atwell's (1984) article describing how she revised her reading program to make it consistent with the ways she taught writing, I decided to do the same thing. I would give up skills-based support materials and hope that my students would learn about reading by reading.

The second idea that changed my beliefs about teaching reading concerned the nature of response. When my students tried to improve their writing, they turned to their classmates and to me for reactions to their ideas. Collaborative talk was essential to meaning making for writers. Why should it not be the same for readers? My own experiences as a member of a book group taught me that talking about literature could be an enjoyable and important element of the reading experience. I decided to organize a reading workshop that would provide ample opportunities for readers to come together and share their thinking about books.

But what would be the nature of this thinking? What kinds of organizational structures would facilitate both talking and thinking? To find answers to these broad questions, I decided to tape-record groups of students as they talked about books and keep notes of my reactions and resulting teaching. My research began six years ago in Li-An and Pierre's fifth grade and has continued through new assignments to grades three and four. This chapter describes my research and teaching in grades five and three and shows changes in the nature of collaborative groups and what I learned from my students about their thinking and responses. My main data sources were audiotapes of students' talk, a research log for recording my plans and reflections, students' comments in reading journals, and informal student interviews.

Grade Five

My first challenge was to establish a predictable, uncomplicated organizational structure so that students could meet to talk about books. I had seen children accustomed to the constraints of basal reading groups come into my classroom with little enthusiasm for reading. After experiencing the delights of being able to choose a book, to read it at their own pace, and to abandon a book they did not enjoy, many students became avid readers. My plan was to bring readers of the same book together for a conference. To increase the likelihood that readers would choose the same book, I ordered multiple copies of high-quality, popular paperbacks for our classroom library and encouraged students to choose books from home and from community and school libraries. In a "book-sharing time" that concluded each reading workshop, students tried to attract other readers with a one-minute sales pitch written on an index card.

To prepare for a conference, students had to write questions about a book they'd read on cards to be used by future readers of that book. The process of writing the questions and "testing them out" on a partner would, I hoped, encourage the students in their thinking and talking about books. The idea for using questioning as a guide for talking came from Christenbury and Kelly (1983): "Questioning...helps students discover their own ideas; it gives students an opportunity to explore and argue and to sharpen critical thinking skills..." (p. 3). I taught

my students how to create open-ended questions that would promote discussion with words such as *why, how, explain, if you were, what do you think about, what if, what do you suppose*, and others. I also demonstrated how to draw out additional thinking after an initial response with "piggyback questions" such as these: How come? Why do you think so? Can you give me an example of what you mean? What would you have done in that situation?

If students had trouble coming up with thought-provoking questions, we would look together at some question cards prepared for earlier conferences. This would help students think about the setting of the story, a book's characters, and other books by the same author to come up with questions of their own. This procedure also encouraged readers to pose questions that involved a variety of perspectives: literal recall of the text, personal interpretations, and evaluations.

After students had completed a book and drafted their questions, they met with me. The conference began with their responding to their own questions to determine which of them would encourage other readers to "talk a lot" and which needed to be clarified and revised. Then the students recopied their questions onto lined oaktag cards, filed them, and printed the book title and date next to their names on a wall chart. The chart let future readers of those books know who had prepared questions for their small-group discussion. An example of questions prepared for one popular book is shown in the figure on the next page.

When the first conferences took place and I saw pairs of students off in corners of the room talking together, I was excited. That day I wrote in my log, "I know something is coming out of all this talk about books. Kids make their own meaning by deciding what they want the conference to focus on. I think readers are extending their thinking by hearing other views." Listening to the tapes of the students' talk, however, showed me how wrong my assessment was. The children weren't having conversations, they were re-creating the quizzes that followed the stories in the basal readers I had discarded: one student was asking all the questions, and the other was answering!

After discussing the problem with my students, we decided that question writers should give their own opinions about each question and that the talk should bounce back and forth between the readers. Unfortunately, my tapes indicated that the talk still didn't sound quite right. As I noted this problem in my research log, its cause became clearer: "Of course! It's all those questions coming from one reader. It's not natural. When my friends and I talk about books, all of us raise questions. And not simply questions, but points and issues, too."

That realization led me to discuss the book conference procedure once again with my students. Together we agreed that all readers of a book—not just the first—would determine questions and issues for discussions. On each question card below the questions written by the first reader, I typed the following directions:

To all who read this book:

1. Choose four questions from the above that you want to discuss.

2. On the back of this card write three things or questions that you think should be included in the conference.

3. Remember that all readers should respond to each question or idea.

A Fifth Grade Question Card

Book title: <u>Anastasia on Her Own</u>
Author: Lois Lowry

What do you think Anastasia's house looked like?

In the beginning, did you think the house schedule was going to work? Why or why not?

What do you think Annie was like in the beginning of the book?

How did Annie change by the end of the book?

What was your favorite part? Why?

If you were Anastasia, would you throw Annie out? How come?

I wonder if Mrs. Krupnik would've let Annie come over for dinner if she was there. What do you think she would have done?

How do you think the story might have ended if Anastasia didn't call her mother and tried to clean the house herself?

If you had to rate this book on a scale of 1 to 10, how would you rate it and why?

Did you read any of the other books in the series? How does this book compare with the ones you read?

Once all participants were involved in the discussion's agenda, the talk sounded real. Looking back, I realize that my research activities of writing in my research log and listening to tapes helped me come up with insights that I might otherwise have missed.

To study the nature of the students' collaboration, I sat in on several peer conferences. I observed students coaching and reminding one another of events, encouraging and agreeing with one another sometimes and offering contrasting views at other times, contributing information to build a larger meaning, completing one another's thoughts, and asking questions to elicit more information. Next I began to pay more attention to the responses themselves. What sense could I make out of what I was hearing? Although it was easy to recognize thoughtful conversations, designing a framework for analyzing and categorizing responses proved difficult until I discovered a study conducted by Purves and Rippere (1968). After studying the written responses of adults and high school students to a literary work, these researchers identified four main categories of response: engagement-involvement, perception, interpretation, and evaluation. With some adjustments to their subcategories, I was able to use this framework to analyze my students' responses. Following is my framework with examples of students' comments, most of which were prompted by other students' questions:

• Engagement-Involvement
Talking about how they would change a book's title:
> "I'd call it [*Cat Walk*] *Names of a Barn Cat*. Because he started out as a cat without any name, then he got Tootsie Wootsie, Snowshoe, and then Mistletoe and then Mac."

Reacting to events in the story as if they were not fictional:
> "I felt sad when Leslie died. I would have probably screamed, yelled, and locked myself in my room."

Reacting morally to the characters or incidents:
> "I didn't like Viola Swamp because she's every child's nightmare and not the nicest substitute. She wasn't really nice to the children."

Going beyond the story:
> "I think Sam will get some other friends when they find out if he's nice or not. He's alone because they think that he's dumb, but he's not...."

Making connections to their own lives:
> "The author says how fat Elsie was. I once knew this girl who was really fat. At first I thought that she was really ucky, but then when I got to be friends with her, I didn't think she was like that anymore."

Making literal statements:
> "The people Taran met helped him learn things that would help him in his life. The claymaker gave him a lesson that some things are gifts...a gift you can't make; it's born with you."

• Perception
Perceiving events in the story by quoting, paraphrasing, or summarizing:
> "Attean was picking up words from Robinson Crusoe, and then he'd start saying 'So rain come soon, by golly.'"

Identifying and describing characters by telling who they are:
> "Sam was a whiz in math so he caught on easily to that, but he really didn't catch on easily with reading. Alicia is like the brain; she acts like the teacher."

Perceiving setting:
> "I thought the cabin was pretty big, but it says in the book that it was

small, and there was one window by the bed, and there were some hooks on top of the door, like on top of where the gun was."

• **Interpretation**

Relating parts of the story to their own knowledge of the world:

"I think some kids have dyslexia and spell backwards. Sam might have spelled 'pot' as 'top'."

Using the vernacular to describe and interpret characters:

"Fudge is a pain-in-the-butt, a little brat."

Drawing inferences about the meaning of an event:

"I think he knew that Attean was very proud, and that's why he didn't want him to hear that the native in the story was a slave to Robinson Crusoe."

• **Evaluation**

Appraising the book subjectively:

"This should win the Newbery Award because it's the funniest book I've read."

Relating or comparing a book to other books:

"This book had too many facts about immigration. I liked *Year of the Boar* better because it had more of a story."

Listening to my students talk demonstrated to me the importance of organization in bringing readers together to share ideas. Collaborative groups helped these fifth graders think for themselves as they stimulated, focused, and expanded their classmates' thinking about literature; the response conference became integral to my reading workshop.

Adaptations and new directions were necessary each year because of changes in grade level assignments and in the makeup of each class. My continuing research was guided by my classroom experiences, the theories I developed through earlier research, and by new knowledge in the field of literacy development acquired from professional books, articles, conferences, and workshops.

Grade Three

The first year I taught third grade I quickly encountered two new problems on which to focus my research. First, the format of the response conference which had worked so well in fifth grade needed to be simplified. Most eight-year-olds were not yet able to formulate the kinds of questions the fifth graders had written to guide their talk, nor were they able to conduct discussions without me. The second problem became apparent when children asked if they could read a book with friends. This may have been a carryover from the shared and paired reading experiences the students had had in first grade or perhaps from their basal reading groups in second grade. The problem was that the reading groups they chose were based on friendships and therefore reflected a wide range of abilities. I did want to preserve the heterogeneous grouping that had worked so well for my fifth graders, but the books these children selected were too difficult for some and just right for others. My challenge, then, was to establish predictable, uncomplicated means for children to talk in small groups after completing a book independently and to come up with some way that children in mixed ability groups could read and think about a book together. As in the past, I planned to tape-record the children's talk and to keep notes for myself in a research log.

An idea for revising the response conference came from Harste and Short (1988). Exploratory thinking, they say, occurs when students must deal with anomalies—puzzling or surprising situations that have no easy solutions. Our first opportunity for a response conference arose after four boys who loved hearing John R. Gardiner's *Stone Fox* read aloud decided to read it on their own. I asked the children to come up with two questions about "things" in the book that they didn't understand, that puzzled them, or that made them wonder. This was not difficult for them because the themes of the story—loss, loyalty, and heroic deeds—are fairly complex for young readers. Stephen, for example, could not understand why Grandfather had lost the will to live. "If Grandfather liked Willie and the potato farm so much," he said, "why did he want to die?" Kevin wondered why Stone Fox was "mean enough to hit Little Willie" when he discovered the boy in his barn.

I helped the four readers write their questions on oaktag cards, and our first conference was ready to begin. Stephen asked his question first; "I dunno," was the response from the others. My students needed some gentle nudging to risk responding. "Why not begin with 'maybe,'" I suggested as a way of letting the children know that there was no single right answer. Then Robbie volunteered, "Maybe Grandfather would lose his farm if he could not pay the taxes." And Kevin wondered, "How could a person get $500 out of nowhere?"

The notion that the loss of his farm would make Grandfather want to die so perplexed the boys that they tried to determine why the farm was so important to Grandfather. George responded pragmatically: "He got money from the farm. Every harvest got money. And if he didn't have the farm, he wouldn't get money." Kevin took a different perspective. He pointed out the significance of Grandfather's feelings about his work on the farm:

Kevin:	He had fun doing that.
My prompt:	So the farm was more than just a way to make money. It was...
Stephen:	his home.
Kevin:	And he had fun working there.
Robbie:	Yeah, he liked it, waking up early, making breakfast for his grandson. He liked doing all that. Like when he said to Little Willie, "I'll put your food in the chicken house" and he really did!
Stephen:	He would laugh. He would laugh. He just sort of joked.
My prompt:	So the farm meant a lot to him?
George:	Because he was proud of his work.
Stephen:	And if they got rid of the farm, Grandfather would die for sure.

Later in the discussion, Kevin's question about why Stone Fox hit Little Willie brought out the fact that Stone Fox always carried a gun. As the boys tried to understand Stone Fox's motives, they developed a logical and sympathetic explanation for his anger toward the farm community:

Stephen:	He needed to carry a gun around because the white man would always come around and...
Robbie:	make fun.
Stephen:	Yeah!

Robbie: Because he had no home. And they made fun of him because they took all his land away.

Kevin: They took all his land.

Robbie: They took all his acres, over a hundred acres.

George: They took away all his people's land, not just a little.

Robbie: So he was just buying it back. He was very smart.

From my students' discussion of *Stone Fox,* which continued for almost 30 minutes, I learned three significant things about the way membership in a group promotes critical thinking. First, children of diverse abilities serve as resources for one another. The thinking of any one individual enlarges the collective thinking of the group, and listening to multiple perspectives expands the thinking of each individual. Second, in conversation, students move back and forth from inference to reference. The questions they raise lead them to refer to specific information in the text to justify their reasoning, as Robbie did when he quoted Grandfather and described daily routines. Finally, talking about a book with friends is a social event that stimulates and energizes the group. These readers were still eager to pursue ambiguities and search for solutions when our reading workshop ended.

In response to children's requests to read a book together, I needed to develop some way of bridging the gap of group members' abilities. Borrowing from Palincsar and Brown's (1985) reciprocal teaching strategies, I planned a four-step procedure: summarizing, questioning, clarifying, and predicting. This procedure would follow a group's silent reading of a portion of text.

Stephen, Kevin, and George discovered copies of Armstrong Sperry's *Call It Courage* hidden away on a high shelf in our library and announced that they planned to take turns reading aloud from the book. I was dumbfounded. Not only was the text of this survival tale far too difficult for Kevin and George, but "round robin" reading was the last thing I expected to see in our reading workshop. Hoping that the boys would realize they had made a poor choice and would select a different book, I agreed. Together we decided that each reader would "assign" himself a portion of the text to read. The length of each read-aloud could range from less than one page (I had George in mind) to three pages, and any member of the group could join in or assist a reader.

I explained to the group that readers use certain strategies to help them understand challenging stories. On a card I printed the following directions:

1. Talk about what you learned from the part that was read aloud.

2. Ask questions about things that surprised you or that you didn't understand.

3. Try to answer the questions. Make guesses.

4. Predict what you think might happen next.

During the group's second meeting, I heard Kevin read aloud two pages with some support from Stephen. The boys began their discussion by summarizing what happened in those pages:

Stephen: Now Mafatu's on the island.

Kevin: Safe from the Sea God.

Stephen: But not safe from the cannibals.

Kevin: Well, there might be cannibals there and there might not.

Stephen: Well, he's afraid of it right now.

Kevin: Yeah, but he doesn't seem to be very afraid right now. He's just lucky to be alive on the island and he's real glad to be away from Moana, the Sea God. [Laughter.]

George: I would be really glad.

Stephen: Imagine that. Being out for a week on a thing, fighting the sea to live. I could never survive that. No food, no water.

George: No food! [Laughter.] I mean I would...I would, really....

Stephen: Yeah, I know.

George: It's so, so weird.

Stephen: [Laughter.] I mean I would never do that.

George: I wouldn't either. That really explained mostly everything to us.

The dialogue ended and the laughter showed me that I need not have feared that the group would mimic the round-robin style of a basal reading group. As the readers pictured themselves in Mafatu's situation, it was clear to me that Stephen and Kevin had helped George go beyond what he could have comprehended on his own.

When it was time to ask questions, Kevin wondered about the dangers that Mafatu would face. Kevin's questions inspired thinking and talking:

Kevin: But we still don't know if there's going to be cannibals and if he'll have to run away.

George: Yeah, I think so because I just turned to this page and it says "drums," so there might be cannibals coming.

Kevin: Maybe.

Stephen: Maybe he'll hear drums. I predict that he'll hear drums.... Maybe in the next chapter, he's gonna be sitting there...

Kevin: and then he hears drums late at night and the cannibals come or something.

Stephen: Maybe he explores.

George: [Excited.] Anything, anything can happen!

Stephen: Once I read this book, *Robinson Crusoe*. And it was about the same thing. He got shipwrecked and then he came to this island and there were cannibals.

Stephen's description of an episode in *Robinson Crusoe* set off another round of predictions: Mafatu might find bones to make into weapons or wood to build a shelter. Eager to discover whether their predictions were right, the boys read on until they completed the story. Yes, George did stumble over words when he read, but Stephen was always there, ready to help. A dictionary also helped the readers when they debated the meaning of words during their discussions.

Collaborative learning in this reading group was a form of apprenticeship, I realized. George, like any apprentice, was immediately plunged into a difficult but meaningful task. At first, with the support of competent helpers, George just managed to get by without having to bear the full load of the text. By listening to Stephen and Kevin read and by participating in discussions about the unfolding events, George gradually understood the meaning of the exciting adventure. By the end of the book, George was reading more fluently and, by the end of the year, he became a competent helper for another apprentice.

My third graders taught me several important things about grouping and thinking. I learned that when children determine membership of reading groups, those groups tackle reading as if it were a social event. Literature discussions become pleasurable, as Stephen describes in the excerpt from his literature log shown in the figure. Reading and talking require risk-taking, but these children were not afraid to take guesses, make inferences, or stumble over words while reading because they were surround-

Excerpt from Stephen's Log

When your Reading with a friend it's like a whole nother recess. you get to be with your freind and discuss the Book and if you have a partener and you Don't understand something you can alwa?s ask your Partener. and if your reading a hard Book you might want to read with somebody on a Higher Level in reading. I myself am a very good reader.

ed by friends. Listening to their talk, I was reminded of the ways my fifth graders responded to literature. These third graders also became personally involved with characters and events in books, drew on their knowledge and experiences, made sense of characters' motives, and evaluated a book's worth.

I also learned that a variety of groupings is necessary to accommodate students' preferences. Some simply like to sit next to a friend who is reading the same book and talk only after completing several chapters. For example, Kristin's literature log tells how she reads with Joy: "When we are in a good interesting chapter we don't want to stop because it is too interesting. But at the end of it we do to find out what she leard [learned] and what I learnd to see what her prodict [prediction] was and what my prodict was."

Then there are able readers like Rachel who prefer to read the entire book with an option to stop and talk only if the need arises: "My philosophy is to read the whole book then have a big long conference. On the other hand...if you don't understand a word or part, you can ask your partner. Like when I didn't understand woebegone little figure but Cathy and I decided it meant sad pathetic little figure."

Finally, I learned several significant things about my own role. Reflecting back on my silent classrooms of the past, I see that my teaching and my classroom have changed. As I attempted to encourage my students to become thoughtful, independent, and collaborative readers, I gave them a substantial voice in determining what and how they would learn. By encouraging the social nature of children's literacy activities, I let my students know that they can learn from one another as well as from me.

Observing, listening, and reflecting in my classroom over the years have been my main sources of learning, wonderment, and surprise. While research has at times highlighted my errors and faulty expectations, it also has removed the blinders that shut out new teaching possibilities. For me, research has become a way of knowing and finding out that has no end.

References

Atwell, N. (1984). Writing and reading from the inside out. *Language Arts, 61,* 240-252.

Christenbury, L., & Kelly, P. (1983). *Questioning: A path to critical thinking.* Urbana, IL: National Council of Teachers of English.

Harste, J., & Short, K. (1988). *Creating classrooms for authors.* Portsmouth, NH: Heinemann.

Palincsar, A.S., & Brown, A.L. (1985). *Reciprocal teaching of comprehension strategies: A natural history of one program for enhancing learning* (Rep. No. 334). Urbana, IL: Center for the Study of Reading.

Purves, A.C., & Rippere, V. (1968). *Elements of writing about a literary work.* Urbana, IL: National Council of Teachers of English.

Chapter 9

Sow a Thought, Reap an Action

Jan Hancock

Hancock has been a teacher, district language advisor, and lecturer in education at the University of Wollongong. She now works at the University of Western Sydney, Macarthur, New South Wales, Australia, where she continues her research on the notion of responsive evaluation.

When I returned to classroom teaching after having spent some years as a district language advisor, I was eager to practice what I had been preaching to other teachers. I support the whole language philosophy of learning and feel that its teaching practices best foster learning; I had been advocating its application in classrooms across my district. I discovered that implementing whole language was not going to be too difficult, except in one area—assessment. The school I returned to was using traditional testing methods—that is, formal, summative, and in some cases standardized measures. However, I wanted an approach that sat comfortably with my teaching philosophy, that complemented rather than contradicted it. And so I began to experiment with assessment procedures that I felt were in harmony with my instructional practice. As my experiments progressed, I recognized the scope of the challenge I had created for myself. I decided to formalize my research process and began to track my experiences and report them. This chapter reflects that formal entry into teacher research.

The inquiry began in an Australian grade five class in January and concluded in December when school ended for summer recess. My research journey is described here through excerpts from my journal, student reflections (written and oral), and comments from colleagues who served as observers. These reflections track the gathering and interpretation of data I collected to try and understand the process of evaluating the language learning of my 27 students.

What I call "level 1" data focused on the day-to-day goings on in my classroom. I hoped this data would reveal the underlying beliefs that were driving my instructional practices. This was achieved by reflecting on my students' and colleagues' interpretations of these practices and my own responses to their interpretations. These multiple interpretations were sought to avoid problems of solitary self-reflection that can arise when a teacher researcher carries out discourse of (in Plato's words) "the soul with itself." As Habermas (1974) states, "The self-reflection of a lone subject...requires a paradoxical achievment: one part of the self must be split off from the other part in such a manner that the subject can be in a position to render aid to itself.... In the act of self-reflection the subject can deceive itself" (p. 29).

My level 2 data attempted to discover what was happening when I used particular procedures to assist in the assessment of student learning. With this data I was trying to address the heart of my dilemma about assessing language growth and development: on one side of the dilemma was the issue of the traditional assessment practices already in place that I believed were decontextualized and unrelated to the learning experiences of my classroom; on the other

was my belief that I could evaluate my students' literacy learning in a whole language context on the basis of responses that I received from them. I was aware that I carried around in my head notions about students' abilities, their progress, and particular things that I thought might assist this progress. It was "tacit" or "personal" knowledge and was therefore intangible; I had no way of showing that this knowledge really existed. I realized that the beliefs I had always drawn on needed to become more concrete and "provable" if they were to challenge seriously the accepted means of assessment in my school. I therefore needed to transform my "informed intuitions" into "hard" evidence.

I spent considerable time trying to identify what it was that caused me to develop beliefs about my students. I came to think that I responded unconsciously to a set of indicators—which I call "cues"—that signaled student development. My level 2 data would therefore be aimed at uncovering these cues as my students responded to experiences in the classroom. The resulting "responsive evaluation" data consisted of students' responses to surveys, examples of work from their portfolios, my own field notes, parents' comments, and the like. At the outset I didn't realize that the feedback I gave my students on their material was, like my instructional practice, drawn from the very beliefs I was trying to identify and explain. I needed to articulate my personal theory of teaching, and my own thoughtful reflection was all I could rely on.

This brief overview will, I hope, give the impression that my research path was not a linear one. This is the nature of teacher and action research. They are types of inquiry in which theory and practice intermingle constantly. As Carr and Kemmis (1983) explain, "Action research does not follow a straight line from problem to solution. Through the process of reflection upon both theory and practice, reciprocal links are created whereby each informs and influences the other" (p. 172). In what follows I will explain in more detail the steps I took and the understanding I gained from my research journey.

Level 1:
Reflection on Classroom Practices

Data at this level were aimed at answering the following questions:

- What are my teaching practices in language arts period?
- Do participants in this research have the same view of these practices?
- What beliefs underlie my use of these practices?

By reflecting on my students' and colleagues' interpretations and my own responses to these interpretations, I recognized that I organized the two-hour language arts period into a progressive flow of events each day. These events I determined to be "core episodes" that supported and built on one another. During each episode, teaching and learning focused on one of the four language modes—reading, writing, listening, or speaking. This did not bring about fragmentation of language learning because the episodes were interrelated, interdependent, and—above all—relevant to the learners and their experiences. The episodes operated much like a restaurant menu: appetizer, main course, and dessert categories all have their own selections yet together constitute a whole meal.

The following sections present excerpts from my data and show how the episodes were perceived by students and teacher.

Core Episode 1: Shared Reading

Student reflections (from interviews).

Brandt: First Miss reads us a book. The books are usually different [from one another]. If it's a real long chapter we only read half or if there's a real short one we read two chapters.

Davie: After the chapter, we have a discussion and predict what's going to happen in the book and then we see whether our predictions are right.

Jessica: We make comments about the story and what we think about the characters.

My reflections (in discussion with colleague). By reflecting on books they've already read, students can draw out similarities and differences in characters, thereby deepening their understanding of the book I've just shared. Discussion is intended to foster understanding of character development and the author's intentions. I encourage the children to see that the author is outside the text—that we can make meanings outside the actual words used—and that fiction follows patterns. The better we are at recognizing those patterns, the deeper our understanding. I use the term "prediction" frequently in conjunction with shared reading. It involves confirmation and is based on informed opinion; it is not a guess.

Core Episode 2: Silent Reading

Student reflections (from interviews).

Liza: Then she gets us quiet so we won't be restless when we do silent reading.

Jessica: Miss makes the point that we read every day.

Davie: We pick our books to read. In silent reading time Miss comes around and she asks us what we are reading and how much we've read. She keeps a record.

Greg: We have our own reading cards for the date we start and the date we finish it.

Kylie: She comes around and lets you read to her. We have silent reading for about 20 minutes. Then sometimes we have sharing and tell the other people what your book's about.

My reflections (from journal notes). I believe I will have more success in helping children develop literacy if I have close at hand those texts that I constantly speak of, read from, and use as references. Therefore I establish a class library with many books, fiction and nonfiction, that suit the experience of the readers. I display them attractively to create a positive atmosphere for books and reading. Asking children questions while they read helps me keep in touch and provides an opportunity to see how the children are enjoying particular books. I ask questions such as "Have you finished that already? Did you find that book boring? Is that why you stopped?" I believe that children sense that what they read is important to me. This matters!

Core Episode 3: Writing

Student reflections (from interviews).

Steven: After that we write in our writing folders.

Greg: In writing some people write research and nonfiction or fiction stories.

Alan: Sometimes we have editing sessions with each other. When someone edits it they put a line underneath the wrong words and then you look in the dictionary and when you find the word you put it in your word study book.

Jessica: When we do the editing we give them ideas for their stories if we know about the thing they're writing about.

My reflections (from journal notes). Through regular writing I believe children come to know that they get better the more they do it. By giving them real purposes for writing, I believe they realize that it is a tool for the expression of their ideas, knowledge, questions, and feelings. I believe in establishing the conditions for a balanced diet of writing. Sometimes I let children choose their own topics; other times I assign topics related to the focus of content area study. All writing undergoes drafting, editing, and revising. I maintain a high profile for spelling and vocabulary through the use of word study books.

Core Episode 4: Sharing Writing

Student reflections (from interviews).

Romina: Miss picks people to share on the carpet and they sit on the chair and they take control of the class as they read their piece.

Alister: When a person has finished reading, we make some comments to see if they can fix the story up, make it longer, or make it a bit better.

My reflections (from journal notes). Sharing is, I believe, one part of the process of editing and refining writing in preparation for going public. At the outset I demonstrate sharing to show children that written pieces must conform to certain conventions before publication and that they must communicate some meaning to an audience.

Reflection on Data from Videotapes

One of the most useful sources of data for my research was the videotapes I made of a few language arts periods. My procedure was to view each tape two or three times and then write about what I had seen. I found that my reflections became a mixture of description and thought that helped deepen my understanding of what I was doing in the classroom, why I was doing it, and how I might improve my practice. This process also helped me understand the learning strategies some of my students were using. The following excerpt from my log of "video reflections" shows what I mean:

> The retelling/recall discussion centered on the characters. I noticed in particular the sitting arrangements. Steven, Liza, Alan, Brandt, and Bernie chose to sit on the periphery. Whether this was because they felt less inclined to participate or that they found the book boring remained to be seen. Regan, Joelle, Arno, and Terri chose to sit close to me; Philip sat there because I requested it, due to his habit of talking and distracting his neighbors. Jessica, Sasha, Martin, Liza, Joelle, Regan, Greg, Alister, May, and Boyd were well engaged during the session.
>
> At the conclusion of the chapter reading I asked the children if they had anything to say about the story

and suggested they might comment on the characters and the characters' feelings. Hands went up and Joelle and Kylie gave responses and made predictions. At this point I tried to return the discussion to characters and recap a few incidents where the characters' behavior demonstrated a growing relationship. I even used the word "relationship" and asked if they understood it. Most said they did. Brandt's hand went up when I asked for someone to tell me about other incidents where we saw a relationship between characters developing. His response was yet another prediction. I didn't criticize his comment or point out that he had not commented on the relationship.

I also accepted Joelle's and Kylie's responses even though they were unrelated to the direction I had suggested. Kylie followed her first prediction with a second one. Adrian was quick to pick up that this second prediction contradicted her first. Perhaps this is what he does silently—i.e., makes an inflexible prediction to the storylines he encounters? He must often be surprised and confused when they aren't confirmed with further reading. Could this be part of the barrier he has to overcome in his growth toward more independence in reading? I took this opportunity to suggest to the children that a reader can make a number of different predictions that don't necessarily have to be along the same line.

Then I initiated another discussion: "Have any of you ever been fishing?" Children talked among themselves and I realized they were eager to share. I allowed this to go on for what seemed a long time. I then called their attention to another question related to the fishing trip in the chapter under discussion. The children agreed that this was the young boy's first successful trip. I asked, "What gives you this impression?" Davie answered, "Because he was really excited when he brought the fish in." I continued this line of thought: "There's a reason why they were so successful with their fishing. Do you know why?" Boyd suggested that it was because they had a net. I agreed that that certainly helped. Then Adrian suggested the fact that the man was an Aborigine could be the reason for their success. At first Adrian spoke softly and obviously was not confident. I loudly agreed with his suggestion and probed him for clarification: "What difference does that make?" Davie whispered to Adrian, "Aborigines know how to fish," which brought about Adrian's more detailed response, "Because Aborigines know how to fish better than white men." I'm very pleased with Adrian's replies; they demonstrated his thinking and his growing ability to infer meanings. I'm also pleased with the collaboration that was evident in Davie's assistance—he usually takes the glory for himself, but this time he didn't.

I felt that this brought us back to the initial purpose for the discussion—the characters and their relationship. I expressed my opinion that the characters had shared exciting incidents throughout the chapter and that in this way they had come to know each other much better. I asked what one character thought and felt about the other. Many replies were given; some related responses were off the mark. Joelle gave the suggestion that the young boy admired the Aborigine's knowledge about how to live. I realize that I didn't encourage her to elaborate on her suggestion. Instead I replied with an evaluation that implied that that was exactly what I thought, too.

I then directed discussion toward the setting.

What I began to understand from reflection on the data was that it was indeed possible to draw out my beliefs about teaching and the activities I consequently valued in relation to each core episode in my literacy class. By "beliefs" I mean the things I hold as personal axioms, the abstract knowledge about teaching my research was intended to pin down. "Activities I valued" in this context has a broad meaning—that is, the behaviors, attitudes, and understanding upon which I place a high degree of importance corresponding to and emerging from my beliefs.

The beliefs and values I became aware of through reflection appear in what follows, classified within episodes.

Core Episode 1: Shared Reading

I believe...

- personal reading processes are enhanced by responding to shared texts.

I value...

- giving time for response and interaction related to meanings constructed from text;
- participation through contributions that draw out inferred meanings and predictions;
- recognition of similarities and differences among texts;
- relating texts to personal experiences.

Core Episode 2: Silent Reading

I believe...

- sustained silent reading widens the experiential base on which readers can draw to understand the texts they are reading;
- reading is encouraged when texts are chosen by the readers;
- comprehension is enhanced by discussion and retelling of texts.

I value...

- regular time for sustained silent reading in an environment that provides a wide array of texts from which to choose;
- children's free choice of their own reading matter and their decision to abandon a particular choice if it does not sustain their interest;
- frequent opportunities to discuss books;
- asking and answering questions about text meaning, characters, plots, and settings.

Core Episode 3: Writing

I believe...

- abilities in writing can develop by broadening the experiential base on which writers draw;
- writing is enhanced by knowledge of the purpose of and audience for writing;
- writing is enhanced by the use of techniques that can be drawn upon as models;
- writing involves recursive processes;
- writing conveys meaning most effectively when it conforms to certain writing conventions.

I value...

- regular periods for sustained writing in an environment that provides meaningful purposes for writing matched to the experiences and interests of the writer;
- the ability to fulfill the purpose of and direct the writing to a particular audience;
- drawing on the techniques of other writers to provide models for personal writing;

- a progression through the processes of editing, redrafting, sharing, and publishing;
- persistence in efforts to make final written products conform to certain conventions.

Core Episode 4: Sharing Writing

I believe...

- the meaning of writing can be clarified by sharing that writing with others.

I value...

- regular opportunities to share and discuss writing;
- willingness to share personal writing and to comment on others' writing;
- the ability to clarify meanings and to recognize and correct errors in conventions in own and others' writing.

Reflections on level 1 data confirmed that each core episode supported my beliefs about literacy learning. Each episode had a central focus on one of the four modes of language, and I was reassured that my program provided immersion in, demonstration of, and practice with each mode. I also felt that I was valuing each learner by giving the children the responsibility to control much of their learning and by accepting their representations and approximations. These conditions reflect a whole language philosophy (Cambourne, 1988).

While I was happy with the informal and incidental feedback I was providing, I felt the need to be more formal and consistent in assessment. It was time to move on to my level 2 data.

Level 2: Deeper into Responsive Evaluation

In order to provide credible information to the students, myself, parents, and the school administration about my students' progress in their development of literacy, I felt I needed to monitor the students' engagement in learning and the knowledge, skills, and understanding they brought to their use of each of the four modes of language. The questions that remained to be answered were these:

- What assessment procedures can I use to monitor students' engagement in the core episodes?
- What clues will emerge from these procedures and how can I use them to measure engagement?

I needed various assessment tools that could provide for consistent monitoring of student development. Responsive evaluation procedures such as "kid watching"—that is, observation, interaction, and analysis (Goodman, Goodman, & Hood, 1989)—seemed most appropriate. I anticipated that the clues these procedures would reveal would alert me to the need for direct intervention to support the learning of some students. This intervention would be aimed at promoting engagement in and subsequent development of those students' language learning.

I employed a number of responsive evaluation procedures, including students' reflections on the core episodes as indicated by their responses in interviews, writing portfolios, reading logs, and their answers to specific questions on reading and writing surveys. I also sought parents' input on how they saw their children responding to language learning. Finally, I relied on my own journal notes and observations.

In what follows I describe the information gleaned from a few of these data sources.

My Journal Notes

The records in my teaching journal proved to be an excellent source of information. This was really a diary, with a dated entry for each day of the week. Instead of keeping anecdotal records for each child's activities in particular language sessions, I decided to use the diary and record those incidents that I thought highlighted engagement and nonengagement. I hoped these notes would monitor responses and alert me to the need for some form of intervention to ensure better engagement. When children who were generally well engaged in any core episode made significant gains in their development of literacy abilities, this was also recorded. Following is an example of records extracted from my journal that trace the engagement and nonengagement of one student in silent reading over two weeks. This form of tracing became a tool for assessing students' progress; it also directed my teaching.

> *Monday, Week 7*: Davie is chopping and changing—said he finished but I'll have to check his comprehension by listening to him read and monitoring miscues. I'll have him retell some of the story tomorrow. Late in the core episode he chose a joke book and settled.
>
> *Wednesday, Week 7*: He's still changing every day—reading poetry and nonfiction. Changes text a few times during one session.
>
> *Thursday, Week 7*: Chose a picture book. I decided to hear him read it aloud. Discovered that in the main he reads for meaning and employs some good strategies. However, he allows phrases he doesn't understand to go by in order "to get on with it." We both enjoyed reading together and I realized some of his strengths. He needs to read more.
>
> *Tuesday, Week 8*: Seemed uninterested in the story he was reading. I was

disappointed and showed my surprise that he should be bored with "Cow Dung Custard." He was halfway through yesterday and had shown so much interest. I sat with him and read him the next few episodes of the story (he followed along) just to whet his appetite again. This worked to some extent—he got back into it.

Wednesday, Week 8: Davie finished "Cow Dung Custard" and shared it with the class although the retelling was somewhat confused toward the end. May is reading "The Killer Tadpole." Davie asked her, "What's it like?"; seemed to ask in a manner that meant "I might read that next." I sense his growing interest in reading—a breakthrough—but I realize that he might revert to his old pattern at times. Change seems to be more likely now, though.

Student Reflections

Complementing my journal notes were the children's own reflections on their learning in each core episode. I asked the children to record their thoughts in part to raise their awareness of the processes involved in, attitudes toward, and outcome of their reading and writing activities. I asked them to reflect on how they thought they were doing and what they enjoyed or didn't enjoy in the language episodes. These reflections were recorded three times in the first term. The final reflection was edited by a peer, redrafted, and taken home to parents as a form of self-evaluation. Here are two children's reflections, the first unedited and the second a final draft:

Joel
24th Feb.

In these past two weeks a lot of things have happened. Our teacher has finished reading "Midnite" and started a new book called "Hating Alison Ashley" by Robin Klen and it

is about a girl who starts school and she is very elegant and her name is "Alison Ashely" and her school is not so elegant as she is. I like it and weh're our class is doing a cross word in our writing folder and where typing it in our computer we got not so long ago and I was reading a book called Every child's anser book but I got bored of it because it was only ansers to questions that I could figure out myself.

Davie
3rd March

I like the Books that the teacher is reads to us. I thing that I am geting beder at writing an speling and I like word study and I like in every morning the Excitement of the eggs stile to hach. and I liked research. and the character wheel ant the book Hating Alison Ashley and I liked the future story I like reading I am not a fast reader I take my time I like both kinds.

The student reflections in some cases confirmed my tentatively formed opinions on student attitudes to the language episodes. Davie showed awareness of his own reading difficulties. He also showed increased engagement in activities from the core episodes.

Other insights gained from student responses and reflection on my own responses resulted in adjustments to the way I orchestrated the learning environment. For example, Joel's reflections of March 24 stated, "The one thing that bothers me is the shelf. There's not many good novels on the shelf like 'Charlotte's Web'." This response was expressed by other students in different ways, such as "I never know what to choose" or "I haven't found anything yet that I really like." I reflected on these comments and concluded that I needed to provide more diverse books with a variety of text and concept complexity, and that I should further promote the books that were already on the shelves. I also needed to talk about choosing books. Romina's comment in an interview undertaken a few weeks later indicates how I shifted my practice:

> Last year I didn't really like reading because I couldn't find any interesting books and this year I've found a lot of interesting books.... You shouldn't just judge by the cover because the cover might be boring but the book might be interesting. I used to always read the first page and if I didn't like it I just put it back. Miss said not to do that because you've got to give a book a chance and now I've been doing that I've been liking a lot more books.

Collaborative evaluation form. Another responsive evaluation procedure I used was to ask students periodically to complete an evaluation form on the silent reading and the writing episodes. (What I will share here relates only to reading.) This "collaborative evaluation form" (described in more detail in Hancock, 1992) was central to my process of evaluating students' reading. The students used their own records (reading logs, etc.) to obtain information to complete their sections of the form. Two examples of completed forms appear in the figure.

The purpose of counting titles under certain categories was simply to reveal to the reader his or her preferred type of book. I explained to students that total number of books read was not important since books differed in length and in content. Each reader reads at a different rate, some readers like to take books home, and others read only in silent reading time. Therefore it was not important how many texts were read but what particular types were read and how often texts of different types were not completed. I stressed my interest in seeing each child's patterns in choosing books. After I read the information they gave me, I told them I would be able to make suggestions about their reading and comment on the information they provided.

The gathering of information for the collaborative evaluation form involved the children in reflecting on their own reading. This process reinforced the need for accurate record-keeping on their part in order to record and reflect on what they had achieved. I overheard many comments that showed children's surprise at their reading achievements as they revisited and reconsidered their silent reading records.

Evidence of Engagement

My analysis of all the data collected from the various responsive evaluation procedures began to reveal cues to engagement and nonengagement that prior to my inquiry I had recognized only subconsciously. The set of cues that emerged are shown in the material that follows. Cues were evident in each of the core episodes of sharing reading, silent reading, writing, and sharing writing. Note that the wording that describes each cue represents the extreme end of a continuum. In reality, student responses ranged along the continuum and could vary from day to day. My role as facilitator of learning involved recognizing the cues, interpreting them, and determining the support each learner needed in order to move forward.

Core Episode 1: Shared Reading

Cues of nonengagement.
- Rarely contributes to discussion following reading session.
- Is confused when retelling events from the previous day's reading.
- Rarely volunteers predictions about upcoming events, characters' actions, or outcome of text being read.

Completed Collaborative Evaluation Forms

Name: Joel

1. Number of books I've read completely: 14

2. Types—
    Fiction: 2
    Nonfiction: 5
    Picture books: 3
    Poetry: 4

3. Number of books started but not finished: 2

4. Favorite book read: Sister Madge's Book of Nuns
    Author: Doug Macleod

5. Why I enjoyed this book: I liked it because of the comedy, the action, and the rhymes.

6. How I'm coming along in reading: I think my reading progress in kind of good

7. My teacher's comments on my reading: Joseph, I'm really pleased with your reading, too. How about trying some fiction? You might like Deezle Boy.

Name: Davie

1. Number of books I've read completely: 17

2. Types—
    Fiction: 2
    Nonfiction: 5
    Picture books: 6
    Poetry: 4

3. Number of books started but not finished: 14

4. Favorite book read: Tailypo
    Author: Joanne Galdone

5. Why I enjoyed this book: I like it because I took it home and read it to my brother

6. How I'm coming along in reading: My reading is o.k. but there is not many good books.

7. My teacher's comments on my reading: I like reading Tailypo with you. You should try harder to find books that suit you, though. What about Hank Pank in Love?

- Consistently makes inaccurate predictions about and draws mistaken inferences from text.

Cues of engagement.

- Contributes to discussion following reading session.
- Gives an accurate retelling of events from the previous day's reading.
- Makes predictions about upcoming events, characters' actions, or outcome of text being read.
- Makes predictions and draws inferences that are closely related to the text.

Core Episode 2: Silent Reading

Cues of nonengagement.

- Has trouble choosing a text to read and finishing it.
- Often asks for teacher's assistance in choosing a text.
- Always asks for others' opinions on particular texts before deciding to read them.
- Type size and book thickness always influence choice of text.
- Reads one type of text repeatedly.
- Takes a long time to select text and to settle down to reading; often returns initial selections and makes other choices during reading period.
- Keeps a book for three or four sessions before deciding it is not interesting.
- Stops reading when an unknown word is encountered.
- Is reluctant to read aloud to the teacher.
- Has difficulty remembering earlier reading.
- Doesn't share exciting or interesting parts of text with peers.

- Doesn't make predictions or analyze characters or events during reading.

Cues of engagement.

- Makes reading selections easily and finishes most selections.
- Rarely asks for teacher's assistance in choosing a text.
- Uses the opinions of others along with own opinion based on jacket blurb, etc., before deciding to read particular texts.
- Type size and book thickness do not influence choice of text.
- Reads a variety of text types.
- Selects text and settles down to reading quickly; is not easily distracted.
- Decides quickly if a book is not interesting.
- Reads on past an unknown word and uses context clues to determine meaning.
- Willingly reads aloud to the teacher.
- Remembers earlier reading.
- Shares exciting or interesting parts of text with peers.
- Makes predictions and analyzes events during reading.

Core Episode 3: Writing

Cues of nonengagement.

- Has trouble thinking of writing topics.
- Doesn't think of writing topics or ways to improve current writing outside of writing time.
- Asks for help with ideas for writing.
- Writing proceeds slowly; projects are often abandoned.
- Worries excessively about spelling and other mechanics in early drafts.
- Writes only during writing time.
- Writes in the same genre repeatedly.

- Takes a long time to begin research for expository writing projects; has difficulty taking notes from reference texts.
- Has difficulty recommencing with a writing project from day to day; often forgets ideas for writing in progress and abandons the project.
- Resists having others edit personal writing.
- Resists editing others' work.
- Reluctant to revise.

Cues of engagement.

- Can usually choose a writing topic.
- Thinks about writing topics and ways to improve current writing outside of writing time.
- Rarely asks for help with ideas for writing.
- Writing comes easily; projects are usually completed.
- Does not worry about spelling and other mechanics in early drafts.
- Chooses to write at times other than writing time; writes at home.
- Writes different genres of text.
- Is resourceful in research for expository writing projects; takes good notes from reference texts.
- Recommences writing easily from day to day.
- Accepts others' editing of personal writing.
- Enjoys editing others' work and does so effectively.
- Revises effectively.

Core Episode 4: Sharing Writing

Cues of nonengagement.

- Listens to others' comments and editing but does not change writing as a result.

- Is reluctant to share writing and is embarrassed to ask questions about difficulties with writing.
- Does not make suggestions to help others with their writing.
- Does not participate in whole-class discussions of writing.

Cues of engagement.

- Listens to others' comments and editing and changes writing as a result.
- Overcomes embarrassment to share writing with others.
- Makes frequent suggestions to help others with their writing.
- Participates in whole-class discussions of writing.

Using the Data

Data such as that gained from the collaborative evaluation forms, along with data from my other procedures, provided information that enabled me to review students' patterns of reading over the year and report this accurately to parents and the school administration. What had become clearly evident with Joel, for example, was his preference for nonfiction and the subject matter of these texts. However, according to my criteria of deep engagement in text, Joel's reading patterns did not reflect this level of involvement. When he chose fiction it seemed to take an unusually long time to complete. My interventions, intended to foster deeper engagement in fiction, consisted of comments in his log book, suggestions of books he might try, and encouragement to dip into a variety of text types. Finally Joel was alerted to interesting fiction books through retellings by peers. His book selections beginning in the third term reflected a more settled and engaged pattern of reading.

When Joel was asked by an interviewer, "Do you know more about reading than you did at the beginning of the year? What things have you learned, and how did you learn them?" he replied as follows:

> At the beginning of the year I used to ask Miss something, what was this and other things. I really wanted to figure out what did it mean, if you put the whole sentence together. Later in the year, I started looking things over and over again and then I skipped that bit and read it, and then when I keep on reading about it, or flipped back, I figured out what the thing meant. I thought that to keep on reading would make me more confused, but it made me understand it a bit more. She has helped us a bit, 'cept it's me that done it. I've done most of it, the figuring out. Up to now I haven't had much troubles about reading. I don't really have to ask Miss now; I just figure it out myself.

My data on Davie, on the other hand, led me to conclude that although engagement was present at times, it was not maintained. Davie still had difficulty in choosing books that matched his interests and in using the graphophonemic, semantic, and syntactic cueing systems of the reading process. I concluded that more sustained reading would help him develop these abilities, and that with increased assistance from me, his peers, and others he would be able to make better book selections. At the end of the year, Davie still required this support but he had made significant progress.

Davie was asked during an interview, "Do you know more about reading than you did at the beginning of the year? What things have you learned, and how did you learn them?" His reply was as follows:

> When I used to sit next to May I improved a lot, 'cause May helped me in choosing a book. It's hard to choose 'cause I read a lot of books. I like looking at the books but I really like adventures and that. When Miss comes around and helps me...when you've read good she encourages you. She gives up her own time to help you and I've improved a lot. Even my writing has improved.

Action–Reflection–Action...

Prior to my inquiry many of my perceptions about my students' achievements were intangible. Over the course of the inquiry these perceptions became more concrete as I reflected on the descriptions, analysis, and evaluation of my practices. I found that my own perceptions of my students' learning were further enhanced by the learners' own views and reflections on their learning.

What seemed to be occurring for everyone in the classroom was a reciprocity of thought and action—that is, reflection affected action, and action itself was constantly reflected upon. And that is the essence of action research for teachers: honest reflection results in understanding that enhances the teacher's ability to act in respect to the events or phenomena that have been the subjects of reflection. The major understanding I gained from my research is that I now know that action in concert with reflection by both teacher and learners is a powerful tool for finding out about and assessing my students' paths of growth and development in language learning. The pleasing result of my research is that I am now much more confident in both my reflections and actions and feel that my assessment practices are in line with the rest of my philosophy of teaching.

References

Cambourne, B. (1988). *The whole story.* Gosford, NSW, Australia: Ashton Scholastic.

Carr, W., & Kemmis, S. (1983). *Becoming critical: Knowing through action research.*

Victoria, Australia: Deakin University Press.

Goodman, K., Goodman, Y., & Hood, W. (Eds.). (1989). *The whole language evaluation book*. Portsmouth, NH: Heinemann.

Habermas, J. (1974). *Theory and practice* (translated by J. Viertel). London: Heinemann.

Hancock, J. (1992). In C. Bouffler (Ed.), *Literacy evaluation: Issues and practicalities*. Canberra, NSW, Australia: Primary English Teachers Association.

Chapter 10

A Look at the Process

Mary Ann Nocerino

Nocerino works in the Fairfax County Public Schools' Office of Research and Policy Analysis in Falls Church, Virginia, where she assists teams of teacher researchers in district schools. She also works as a consultant and assistant director of the Northern Virginia Writing Project and teaches a research seminar at George Mason University.

I became interested in teacher research through my work as a reading resource teacher in an elementary school. I conducted research on the relationship between reading and writing, focusing on what happened when children read their own writing aloud. Later I became a special projects teacher based in my district's Office of Research and Policy Analysis, where I made extensive use of research on school-based planning and assessment and conducted research for program evaluation. A primary purpose of that office, where I continue to work, is to support schools in their efforts to make use of research for instructional decision-making. Because teacher researchers conduct their own research to inform their teaching, the office supports such school-based projects.

The Langston Hughes Intermediate School Collaborative Research Project provided me with the opportunity to work with and support teacher researchers. The project involved research related to underachievers, with an emphasis on underachieving minority students. At the time, the research-group project at Langston Hughes was unique. In my school district, a few teacher researchers conducted research on their own, and some were enrolled in a graduate seminar on teacher research at a local university. There was, however, no group of teacher researchers working together in the same school, provided with ongoing support by the school system. In fact, we were aware of no other school system in the United States where this kind of project existed.

The support provided by central office included funding for two planning days in the spring, four days of summer seminars, and one day a month for group meetings. At the all-day meetings teacher researchers shared and discussed their data, talked about other research related to their topics, and explored research methods. Central office also made available two staff members (besides myself) who were interested in learning about teacher research and ways to support the process and an expert teacher researcher from the language arts instruction office to serve as resource people. We supported the project in several ways. Sometimes we facilitated sessions, provided articles, reviewed teachers' data, and brought other teacher researchers to the meetings. We helped the group in its contact with the principal and the rest of the staff. We were readers and editors for the research papers, which central office published as a collection.

In addition to supporting teacher research activities, central office staff conducted research of its own. One staff member researched the group process and the other researched the effects the teacher-researcher group had on the rest of the school. My own research focused on the research process and concentrated on two teachers in the group. I collected data by keeping field notes on the meetings and conversations I had with the two teachers, conducting formal in-terviews, and reviewing some of the teachers' data. Other group members added to my data by sharing their field notes and thoughts with me. Both teachers reviewed drafts of my research paper for accuracy.

We were a research group of 12. Sometimes we met in small groups during the all-day monthly sessions; other times we met after school. Early in the school year when I explained my research topic to a group of three teacher researchers, Sherry volunteered to be one of my case studies. I then asked Rita, who was not in my small group, if she would participate. I appreciated both teachers' willingness to participate. Throughout the study, they were generous in sharing their time and thoughts with me.

Sherry

Sherry was a physical education teacher who had been asked by the principal to take the place in the research group of a participant who had transferred to another school. The principal felt Sherry would provide a different perspective on the study of underachievers and underachieving minority students. The previous year she had decided to begin work on a master's degree at a local university. Sherry was also enrolled in the Teacher Expectations and Student Achievement (TESA) training program.

Already feeling over-committed, Sherry was reluctant to take on one more project, especially a collaborative teacher-research project that sounded as though it would entail a great deal of work. Sherry claimed she had managed to keep a low profile in the schools where she had taught over her 12-year career. She felt teachers with high profiles always managed to get asked to serve on one more committee. However, she indicated it was difficult to turn down a popular and respected principal, and, as she said, "I thought it would be good for me to partici- pate." Throughout the year, Sherry was pulled by the conflicting feelings of wanting but not wanting to be involved in the proj- ect.

At our spring planning meetings, Sherry thought about researching the topic of learning styles. After spending several months thinking about her research ques- tion, she decided on something different: What happens when underachieving stu- dents are placed in leadership positions in the P.E. class? Her question was formulated during a faculty meeting when a guest speaker was addressing an unrelated topic. Sherry was thinking about her performance- evaluation objectives, which were due to her principal shortly, when suddenly things seemed to click. Her work with minority students, her involvement with TESA center- ing on high expectations for underachievers, and her master's degree in middle school ed- ucation all came together. Her research question was a natural outgrowth of her teaching and provided a way to link all her projects together.

In essence, Sherry's research became part of her daily teaching and lesson plan- ning. Although defining the research ques- tion took place relatively early in the pro- ject—in October—and created a framework for some of her efforts, Sherry felt that "defining the question was probably the most difficult part of this task." Part of the difficulty was that the process of defining the research question triggered so many other questions: Is my research question worthwhile? What will my colleagues think of my question? Will I figure out an answer?

Once the question was established, however, Sherry moved ahead systematical- ly. She selected four underachieving stu- dents for her study; she identified specific activities and provided leadership positions for these youngsters; she collected data and examined the students' responses to leader- ship opportunities.

Because her students did not have many written assignments, Sherry's data consisted primarily of her observations of student behavior in the gym and her inter- views or conversations with the students. The log she kept of these conversations and observations became a critical source of data. She also interviewed other P.E. teach- ers about the four students, who moved into different gym classes during alternating quarters. In addition, Sherry talked with the learning disabilities teacher and anoth- er teacher researcher who taught one of the targeted students. She also reviewed the contents of her students' cumulative record folders.

In December, during a small-group meeting with three other project partici- pants, Sherry expressed concern about her research log. She was uncertain she was col- lecting her data correctly. Since the topic for discussion at the large-group meeting the following week was data analysis, her small group encouraged her to bring her log. Sherry agreed to consult the group about in- terpretation of her data and to seek advice about how to collect additional data. Sherry was self-conscious about sharing the writing in her log because she felt it was rough and messy, but, reluctant as she may have been, she agreed to take a risk. She also knew that by bringing her log to the group she might get closer to making sense of it.

At the large group meeting, Sherry dis- tributed sections of her log that described one student's behavior: "First day of foot- ball. Jimmy's response to my comment that we must learn the skills before we play was '[Expletive.] I already know how to play.' Jimmy has very negative comments to make about everything we do. I think that Jimmy is a good candidate for my leadership idea."

The group responded to three pages of Sherry's log by asking for clarification, posing questions, and providing suggestions—as well as humor and understanding. They talked about the implications of leadership for students and about self-confidence and achievement. Sherry's sharing her data also offered an opportunity for the other teachers to reflect on their practices and assumptions about teaching and learning. Sherry left the meeting feeling relieved that she was on track and with some further ideas for data collection.

One concern of any researcher is whether the data will shed light on the research. In March Sherry reported, "I'm really pressured about data analysis. I'm not sure I know what I have, if I have anything." On the first day of spring vacation, Sherry decided to formalize her analysis and prepare a report. She began by reading through her log several times. She had been thinking a great deal about her study and, prior to this day, she had come to some tentative conclusions. She began to write by telling what happened. She reread her narrative and then reworked and rewrote where she felt she needed to. In sketchy places, she went back to her data to verify and clarify her thoughts. As she crafted her paragraphs she returned to her data and used them to support her ideas and conclusions. She went through an entire legal pad of paper.

Sherry drew several conclusions in her final paper. She noted that the performance level and behavior of her four students improved. While all four of her targeted students benefited, she wrote that "for long-term benefits, providing leadership opportunities must be an ongoing process. A few random opportunities have little or no bene-

fit for the student. When I stopped reinforcing Kathleen, she lapsed into her old habits." Based on interviews with the other physical education teachers, the subsequent performance levels and behavior of all four students were not maintained after they left Sherry's class.

Rita

Rita taught math and science. She had 13 years of teaching experience and a master's degree, had been active in exploring computer applications to math, and had worked with the National Energy Education Day project. She joined the research project after the initial spring meetings: when one original member of the group was promoted to a position outside the school, other members put a note in Rita's mailbox asking her to talk with them about the research group. Rita told me: "I am always looking for something new. I bore easily." She had intended to seek a transfer to a school where she could teach more science classes. After attending the first project seminar day in June, she made a commitment and decided she would not transfer because she did not want to interrupt the project or pull out of the group.

Initially, Rita's research topic centered on using games to make science fun. However, early in the project—during the August seminar days—she changed her topic to "exploring what happens when students use writing to learn science." The use of writing to learn in science class was new for Rita and was not widespread in the school system. Rita decided to try a different teaching strategy and examine what happened.

Two people contributed to Rita's topic selection. She admired another teacher researcher, Barbara, who taught English and was a consultant to the Northern Virginia

Writing Project. The previous year, they had sometimes talked about writing instruction. Marian, a central office staff expert in teacher research and writing instruction, had distributed to the group two articles about teacher research and using writing to learn. During one of the seminar days in August, Rita found herself seated between Barbara and Marian and became involved in a conversation about writing in the content areas.

Rita's choice of topic was further influenced by her school's growing emphasis on writing in the content areas. Every teacher was required to assign a minimum of one piece of writing a quarter. Rita felt that although she met the requirement, writing was not really integrated into her teaching. That bothered her.

In comparison to the rest of the group, Rita defined her research topic early in the process, and this meant she was able to move quickly into establishing her data sources. First she had her own research log. She designed writing assignments for her students and had them use logs to write about what they were learning in science. She also gave her students simple surveys. In addition, she had the data sources available to most content teachers: assignments, tests, and grades.

At one point Rita counted more than 20 writing activities she had designed for her science classes. She targeted some of her underachieving students and began to look at their writing for their use of content vocabulary. As she looked at her data, she further refined her research question. The research topic began to reflect her interest in the vocabulary of science.

Rita quickly collected boxes of data and, like other teacher researchers, began to ask "What does all this tell me?" At the suggestion of one of the central office staff members, she began to analyze by making a schematic web of her research project. This web provided structure for her to organize her research and draw some tentative conclusions. On a snowy day in February when schools were closed, she created an outline and turned to her data to document her findings.

Rita's research gave her another way to look at her students—through their writing. She found a new way to learn about their interests and to determine what they were learning. From her students' logs and the surveys, she learned that they were eager to share their writing and they felt that writing helped them learn. The data also showed that when writing replaced the worksheets-after-the-film routine, students' interest and comprehension were increased.

Rita's research influenced various aspects of her teaching. Her research report states that she no longer uses worksheets, she now gives essay tests instead of short-answer tests, and, most important, she gives her students time to write.

Reflections and Implications

My own research indicated that the teachers had a number of questions that recurred throughout the duration of the research project. The following questions were raised and answered only to be raised and answered again with further understanding and depth:

- What is my research question?
- What constitutes data?
- What am I learning?
- Are my conclusions valid?
- How do I report my research?

Sherry and Rita certainly asked themselves these questions, but they approached the research process in different ways and experienced the project differently. Rita was quicker to focus her research question. Sherry decided to expand on something she was doing in a limited way, while Rita decided to explore an approach to teaching that was new for her. Because of the nature of their classrooms and teaching assignments, they collected data in different ways. One used a research log to record observations and interviews, while the other used student learning logs, class assignments, tests, and surveys as well as a research log. Sherry selected four students for her research, while Rita collected data from the entire class. Rita used a schematic web and outline to begin the analysis, while Sherry began by crafting paragraphs after thinking about her conclusions. Rita's report started to take shape in February, while Sherry's began in April.

The different approaches to answering common recurring questions suggest the variety of processes that can be used by teacher researchers. These differences underscore the importance to teacher researchers of flexibility in defining what they want to learn and deciding how to go about learning it. It is flexibility that permits questions to be answered with understanding and depth; it is flexibility that encourages the exploration, development, and refinement of meaningful research.

My new knowledge about the recurring questions in teacher research will be important in my future work with teacher researchers, particularly those new to research. I feel that my findings could also be useful to teacher researchers. My experience with the project and the two teachers has led me to believe that, above all, teachers need time to meet in a group. In this project, the group became a research community in which the sharing of data helped to verify, change, or clarify an individual's direction. The group also became a vehicle for important discussions of teaching and student learning.

Part Three

Middle and High School Teachers Are Researchers

Chapter 11

Renewing Inspiration through Research

Carol Minnick Santa

In addition to serving as editor of Part Three of this volume, Santa is a former member of IRA's Board of Directors and past chair of the Teacher as Researcher Committee. She is a curriculum and staff development consultant and language arts coordinator in School District #5, Kalispell, Montana.

In my first years of teaching, I did everything I was supposed to do: I had my three reading groups, worked hard to create meaningful seat work, and did my best to follow the advice offered in my basal manual. Yet something was wrong—I was going through the motions of teaching, but I didn't feel like a teacher. My work seemed superficial. What was wrong? Why weren't my third graders excited about learning how to read and write? Why didn't I feel fulfilled?

My discomfort continued to grow. Perhaps I just didn't know enough, I thought. I enrolled in graduate school and began working with struggling readers at the university reading clinic. I taught only one or two children at a time and had many opportunities to talk with my professors and other graduate students about what I was learning about my students. My confidence and satisfaction as a teacher began to grow.

In looking back on those years, I now understand why I began to feel differently about teaching. My clinical work provided me with my first experience as a teacher researcher. No one called it teacher research in those days, but that is exactly what it was. My lessons did not come from a prescribed curriculum, but were geared to the strengths and needs of my students. I observed carefully and took copious notes on each student's reading and writing abilities. Students chose their own books to read and wrote about what they were reading. My lesson plans developed as we went along. If my students had difficulty pronouncing or writing words that followed specific patterns, those patterns became topics for brief lessons. I taught when needs arose. My students and I were the experts. Our curriculum became a group effort.

It seems to me that I have believed in teacher research throughout my career, even if that belief was unconscious in my first years in the profession. Teacher research values the practices that I discovered during my clinical experiences; it moves the philosophy of clinicians into classroom situations. What worked for me in my teaching was not etched in a curriculum manual, but emerged from observing, talking, and writing about my students. I learned about teaching and made instructional decisions by taking time to think and talk with colleagues about what I was learning. I based instructional decisions on my own research. I was a learning professional.

The articles in this section provide clear examples of both teachers' and students' exploration of learning. They are different in terms of methodology and topic, but they share a common scholarship and emphasize the voices of students. Each of the authors is, in effect, a classroom clinician.

Two chapters are case studies of individual writers. Phyllis Whitin, a seventh grade language arts teacher, tells about Cynthia's remarkable change from an insecure, powerless writer to a self-confident author. Whitin documents Cynthia's growth through observations, conferences, and

Cynthia's papers and journal entries. We can learn from this piece ways to support and inspire student writers. In the next case study, Katie Wood captures the essence of Jo's struggle to become a writer. She tells a powerful story that will stay with you. This piece also provides a model for evaluation. Wood explores Jo's difficulties from every avenue and then takes a clinician's stance as she reflects on her discoveries. The lessons learned from Jo and the procedures Wood used for gathering data have broad diagnostic and instructional implications.

In the next chapter, Dawn Cline discusses her "purist" application of Atwell's (1987) workshop model in her seventh and eighth grade language arts classes. She describes how she organizes and manages her classroom, her strategies for evaluating students, and her methods for evaluating her own teaching. This practical how-to chapter is packed with ideas applicable to a variety of middle school teaching situations.

Next, Kathleen Jongsma takes us into her junior high classroom to show us first hand how she uses portfolio assessment as a tool for students to examine themselves as readers and writers. Not only does this chapter provide practical suggestions for using portfolios, but it gives us insights into the value of portfolios for students. Jongsma also provides a methodology all teachers can use for examining the effectiveness of portfolios.

The first chapter oriented toward high school teachers is an investigation of prereading strategies. In it, Lee Patton demonstrates how a teacher-research project can make broad changes in a curriculum. After discovering how important prereading strategies were to his own literature classes, he proceeded to convince other teachers in his district to begin their own investigations. Soon other language arts, science, and history teachers followed suit. Their methodologies and insights created a research momentum that went far beyond one classroom and led to broader curriculum change. Even more exciting, Patton provides us with strategies for change that could be useful in our own districts. We all can watch research spread from classroom to classroom when teachers have opportunities to support one another.

Jeannine Hirtle's chapter demonstrates how to apply key principles from Atwell's workshop model to a literature curriculum. Her ideas are particularly relevant to classrooms where students read assigned books. She describes how her high school students use discussion and journal entries to link their personal reading to assigned classics. We also see how she facilitates discussion groups and leads her students toward writing successful analytic papers. She concludes that students can respond to and analyze difficult classic works in the same way they do their personal reading.

Sometimes our research produces surprising results. This is exactly what happened in a study conducted by Mari McLean and Christine Gibson. They investigated the effectiveness of using computers in a high school writing class with students who had previously failed a composition course. They examined students' attitudes toward writing with paper and pencil as opposed to writing with a word-processing program. The authors predicted that students would find computers beneficial. However, interviews indicated different results. While the teacher felt computers had a positive effect on at-risk students' writing process and products, the students' positive attitudes about class seemed more a function of an excellent teacher than the computer. Thankfully, the human element seems more important than the machine.

In the end, these chapters tell stories of success. They exemplify how teacher research has led to a clearer understanding of teaching and learning. They are stories of children and teachers working together; they are stories of teachers exploding with renewed confidence and energy. Teacher researchers have a zest for their profession that infiltrates classrooms and schools. On these next pages you enter their classrooms. Enjoy your tour—I guarantee you will return renewed.

Reference

Atwell, N. (1987). *In the middle: Writing, reading, and learning with adolescents*. Upper Montclair, NJ: Boynton/Cook.

Chapter 12

Finding a Voice: One Girl's Journey

Phyllis E. Whitin

Whitin teaches seventh grade language arts at Irmo Middle School in Columbia, South Carolina. As part of her doctoral studies, she is researching the potential of responding to literature through visual representation.

I had not planned to do a case study that fall, but as I wrote about Cynthia in my journal, I sensed her story would be a powerful one. I realized that she could help me investigate a question that I had been pondering for some time: In what ways can I encourage and promote self-confidence in an adolescent who has not felt successful as a writer? I decided to keep careful notes about conversations, conferences, and group discussions in which Cynthia participated. Second, I wrote my reflections about each incident in my journal. Finally, I photocopied most of her drafts of written work over the course of the year. I reread my notes and reviewed her drafts frequently in order to make decisions about a curriculum that would support her growth.

Forging a Path

Cynthia looked uncomfortable as the seventh grade class debated possible topics for writing one day early in the school year. Her eyes studied me, but I couldn't read her feelings. I predicted that she wouldn't want to write, but I didn't know why she would feel that way. I knew that in the elementary grades she had had little opportunity to choose her own topics for writing. I guessed that inexperience might be the problem, but I soon found out there was more to her reluctance.

At lunch a colleague who also taught Cynthia came into my classroom. "What did you say the kids had to write about?" she asked. Her glance caught the list on the board: pets, sports, trips, hobbies, family.... Her puzzled look told me the list didn't have the answer she was looking for. "Cynthia seemed awfully upset third period," she continued. "She said she couldn't possibly write about any of the topics you assigned."

I thought hard before Cynthia's class period the next day about what my colleague had told me. Cynthia had looked more troubled than angry. Why was she reluctant to write? Did she have a topic in mind but was afraid to investigate it through writing? That day I was surprised to find Cynthia writing when I stopped by her desk. She looked up and asked me how long her piece had to be. I replied that it could be as long as she liked. Cynthia said her friends had told her that hers wasn't long enough. She handed me her draft. It read, "On June 13, 1989 my grandmother died. She died of cancer. Her last words to me were I love you, Cynthia, be good and don't get into too much trouble. I loved my grandmother so much I can't even express my true feelings."

I understood what had happened. A few days earlier I had shown the students a series of drafts from an earlier year. One author had written about his grandmother, who had died. I realized that this draft had so affected Cynthia that she had not taken in any of the other possible topics for writing. Cynthia was burdened by the story she had to tell. I looked up and told her that I

was sorry about her grandmother and that I knew she had loved her very much. I didn't know what else to say. After a heavy pause, Cynthia admitted that shortly after her grandmother died, she had been disciplined severely at school for bad behavior. In her eyes, she had betrayed her grandmother's dying wish. To fail a grandmother who had loved her so much was more than Cynthia could bear. Small wonder she didn't want to write.

I told Cynthia that she didn't have to write about her grandmother. I explained that she could tuck the idea away and write about it another time, that some topics are too painful and must wait. Second, her writing could be private and not shared with anyone—including me. Third, she could leave the piece the way it was or revise it. We talked a little about her feelings of guilt and about how her grandmother had made Cynthia feel special and loved. In the end, Cynthia told me she thought she'd rewrite the piece.

That night I wrote Cynthia a note. I told her that good people make mistakes. That she had been "bad" in sixth grade didn't mean that she was a bad person or that she was always going to get into trouble. I knew her grandmother would love her today for the person she was.

Over the next few days Cynthia rewrote the draft several times. Some of the drafts were secret; some were shown to other teachers. As our first writing celebration approached, Cynthia spent more time with me elaborating on and editing her text. One day she asked if she could type her final story on the computer and leave room for a photo of her grandmother. On the celebration day Cynthia was the first to raise her hand to ask for a turn to share her writing. The final version went like this:

On June 13, 1989, my grandmother died. Her last words to me were I love you, be good, and don't get into too much trouble. She was the kind of person that always had a smile on her face. If you messed up she always said "that's OK".

When I was four she taught me how to crochet, as well as other things. At some point I feel as if I let her down but I know I'm going to make her proud of me. Even though she's not here with me today, she's in heaven with the other angels. Now she's not suffering anymore.

Cynthia gave her finished work to her mother.

After nine weeks, Cynthia completed a questionnaire asking for her reflections on her writing, and we met for a conference. She then wrote a letter to her parents explaining what she had learned and the goals she had set for herself for the second quarter. She ended her letter with "In order to be a good writer I must have a positive attitude about what I am going to write. That is what I have done this nine weeks. I have also learned uncountable new things."

What happened to Cynthia, the child who felt she couldn't write about anything? I thought several factors played a part in her growing confidence as a writer. Cynthia needed to know that her writing was for her, not for me. She told me later that she had written her grandmother's story "to remember her by." Cynthia had taken control of what she chose to write, how she wrote it, and what she did with it. She had decided to elaborate on the piece she eventually titled "The Greatest Woman in the World" and how to format her final product.

I learned that I needed to listen and provide opportunities and then step aside as Cynthia wrote, reflected, and took risks. Finally, I needed to show Cynthia that I cared about her, not just her writing.

Calkins (1990) quotes the advice to teachers of Avi, the noted author of young adult fiction, about what to do if a child won't write: "First you have to love them" (p. 11).

Recognizing the Responsibility

Early in November I stopped beside Cynthia's desk, where she sat busily writing. I asked how it was going, and she snapped, "I'm just writing. I want to get credit for the day." Part of the grade I must assign for the course is based on "active participation" during class. Students are supposed to be writing, reflecting on their writing, discussing their writing, or in some way demonstrating that their energy is going into writing. Cynthia was abiding by the rules, but I could see at a glance she was frustrated. "It's not all that easy to write," she told me. "You must expect us to dream about writing." I smiled and said that maybe that would be a good idea. I admitted that writing is hard, then walked away.

At the end of the period Cynthia handed me the following draft:

> All about Second Period
>
> In second period, our teacher exspects [sic] us to write like writing out of style. She exspects us to go to bed dreaming about what we are going to write the next day in grammar/composition. But she doesn't understand that writing is complicated. The class is not really boaring [sic], but the poetry is not my favorite thing in the world. We have read poetry about termites, dreams, dogs, and summer. So as you can see grammar/composition is not easy.

Later in the day Cynthia came to apologize for being rude. I replied, "Well, Cynthia, actually you wrote the truth. Writing is hard, and I do expect a lot. But it's worth it, and I have confidence in you." Over the next few days Cynthia wrote pieces about her other classes, which were more complimentary than the piece about mine. She made copies for other teachers and inspired classmates to write essays of praise for my colleagues. I thought Cynthia was trying to rebel while staying within the class rules.

The following Monday was a day of complete surprise. Cynthia was again writing and writing. I asked her what she was writing. The words were barely out of my mouth when I realized I'd asked the wrong question. She shrugged me off with "I don't know." I waited a while and she explained that she had been "trying and trying" to write over the weekend. Her mother had recommended a magazine article to her and she had felt moved to write about the topic—epilepsy. Cynthia explained that she had had a seizure at age four but that she seemed to have grown out of whatever had caused it; another relative had died from complications from epilepsy. I guessed that Cynthia's fascination for the topic was partly driven by fear of the disease.

Cynthia then handed me the paper, saying, "As far as I'm concerned, it's finished." Her tone of challenge made me think that Cynthia was anticipating that I would require a set order of steps for writing, including revision. Instead, I realized that Cynthia had sorted through and revised her piece in her head all weekend. I nodded and skimmed the story, which opened with "Oh God, my baby's dying" and went on to explain that although epilepsy looks frightening, those who live with the disease "are humans just like you." Cynthia asked if I would read the paper to the class.

I was determined to read that piece with all the fear Cynthia's mother probably felt when Cynthia had had her seizure. I rehearsed it in my head and faced the class. When I finished, the students seemed stunned. They told Cynthia that they admired her for her courage. They asked her questions, and Cynthia answered with medical terminology from the magazine article. Spurred by their interest, Cynthia reread the magazine article that night and answered her classmates' questions in an expanded version of her piece. She later typed it and gave a copy to the science teacher.

During the next few weeks the class was involved in studying family history. Cynthia tried to interview her mother a number of times, but her mother kept saying that nothing interesting had happened in her life. Finally Cynthia came to class with a hilarious childhood tale. When I asked how her mother had come to tell her the story, Cynthia said that she had given her a deadline. I had to smile to myself. Cynthia had realized that writing is hard, that it requires discipline, but that we all have a story to tell. Now she had taught the same lesson to her mother.

Cynthia had recognized both her responsibility for writing and its potential. Cynthia was used to school being a place where students followed instructions and teachers helped when things got hard. Becoming a writer didn't fit into her notion of school. When she realized that she was the author of her own learning about writing, she felt overwhelmed. In fact, she tried to force me to assume her view of the teacher's role. She challenged me to make negative comments about her writing, in part, I think, so she could transfer the responsibility for decision-making to me; she also tried to make me change by criticizing my class and praising other classes. Cynthia taught me a great lesson in listening, as well as a lesson in when to walk away and not listen anymore.

Over time, as Cynthia thought hard about her writing, she realized that to be an author one must view the world with writing in mind. As she took charge of her writing, she relied on the classroom's structure to provide her with time and a supportive environment to write. She had "tried and tried" to write her epilepsy story at home, but when she got to class she was able to put it together. The extended periods of time for writing in my class encouraged Cynthia to plan for her writing. She began to be more comfortable in expressing herself and to discover her talent and feelings. As she became a risk-taker, she found for herself that language is a powerful tool.

Personalizing the Process

As Cynthia took more responsibility for her writing, she began to develop a personal style. In the evaluation conference following the second nine-week unit, she said that to be good writers, people must "think hard beforehand on what they are going to write." Thinking beforehand became an important strategy for Cynthia. She "wrote" a lot in her head before she committed anything to paper and stopped to mull over possible directions when she was not happy with a draft. She remarked to me that her mother "didn't understand" her writing process. When I asked Cynthia to elaborate, she said that at home she walked around repeating sentences and combining them in different ways and that sometimes she thought aloud to help her over rough places in writing. Cynthia clearly had constructed her own flexible writing process.

Cynthia did not see a "final" draft as the end of a writing cycle. When I looked through her writing folder, I found an extra copy of her September grandmother piece. She had scratched out the sentence "Now she's not suffering anymore" and in its place had written, "In a way I'm happy that she's there and not here because she's not suffering anymore. As long as she is happy I'm happy." No one else ever saw that revision, but Cynthia did revise the piece again for the class magazine we put together in January. When she showed me her typed copy, I saw that the ending now read, "Even though she is not here in my presence, she remains in my heart. Even though she is not in my presence she is in heaven with the other angels." I asked Cynthia about the changes. She said that she had pulled the piece up on the computer, reread it, and decided to rewrite the closing to make it "sound better." I agreed with Cynthia. The new ending had a musical, soothing tone.

When I reflected on Cynthia's creative process, I found my views about revision broadening. When Cynthia went to the computer lab, she was usually not typing a first or second draft since her early drafts and revisions had occurred in her head. On the other hand, Cynthia was a flexible thinker about final drafts. As she remarked in a written reflection in April, she finished all the writing projects she undertook. However, if she returned to a piece of writing after some time had passed, she was not afraid to rework it. Writing was fluid to Cynthia; it grew with her.

Cynthia's perception of herself had changed as she recognized that she could take charge of her own learning. Through her writing and sharing, her views of the potential for her future writing enlarged. She wrote for different purposes, brought more pieces in progress to class sharing times, and she began to look for an audience outside of the classroom.

Reaching beyond the Classroom

Another surprise came on the day after Christmas break. As I burst ahead with back-to-school enthusiasm, Cynthia raised her hand. "Are we going to share today? I need a title for my piece."

"Which piece is this?" I asked incredulously.

"I wrote it last night. My dad is leaving for Saudi Arabia today, and I couldn't sleep."

I thought to myself, "So what does Cynthia do when she can't sleep? She writes. I know she wouldn't have chosen that alternative four months ago!" Aloud I said, "Well, what if you read it to us?"

Cynthia began, "My opinion of the Persian Gulf problem." Students sat in awed silence as she listed several carefully documented reasons why a military solution did not seem like the best choice to her. She also engaged in name calling, aimed at both Saddam Hussein and George Bush. The piece brimmed with emotion, and after a period of quiet pondering, the class began to talk. "Cynthia," I said, "if this piece were a bit more formal, it could be a letter to the president." I spoke of the right we have to express our opinions to our elected officials, no matter what our position may be. Her classmates gave Cynthia suggestions of ways to maintain the strength of her argument while making its tone more respectful and courteous. Our discussion lasted the entire period.

Over the next few days Cynthia worked in the computer lab to develop her essay into a letter while preserving the power of her voice. The essay and letter enabled Cynthia to use writing to explore her personal stance on an issue and to attempt to persuade others to take action.

On several occasions over the next few months, Cynthia wrote about her opinions on different issues. In February the class composed speeches. Cynthia chose to prepare hers on child abuse since she had recently read a series of newspaper articles about the subject. She researched her topic further by visiting the guidance office and interviewing her mother, who had known children who had been abused. Cynthia's speech, like her essay about the Gulf War, was persuasive and emotional. Her classmates' positive reactions gave her the courage to volunteer to deliver her speech to a larger audience. Several students asked to work in an author's circle with Cynthia to help her revise her speech.

Toward the end of the period, I stopped by and discovered that the students' agenda had changed. They were engaged in a passionate discussion of the horrors of child abuse. They pleaded with me to allow them to research the support services of our city. They wanted to find ways in which they could help. Soon the students had contacted several social service agencies and formed plans. They designed posters to put in classrooms asking for donations of food and childcare supplies for a local shelter. Cynthia and a few classmates wrote a letter to the shelter asking for more information, and a representative came to speak with interested students. Cynthia and what had become a committee under her direction presented the shelter representative with the collected goods. The project culminated with the presentation by the committee of certificates of participation to all those who had contributed.

The entire project had grown out of Cynthia's use of writing to move others to action. She had begun to see that her voice was powerful and would be heard. She had brought pieces of writing home as gifts and her mother had shared them with friends. Cynthia had generated discussion, both oral and written, about international relations, current events, and social welfare. She now saw herself in a new way and decided to write about it:

Who Is the Real Cynthia

Some people think of her as a mean person, she is not mean that's just her on the outside. On the inside she is a real nice person, she likes most animals, including her older sister. She likes little kids. She loves to help the less fortunate. By now you have guessed this person is Cynthia. Cynthia may seem mean on the outside, but on the inside she is a sweet person. Cynthia is considerate of other people's feelings. If she's mean to you it's her way of saying she likes you. But, after you get to know her better you'll find that she's very sensitive to other people's feelings, as well as her own. Cynthia doesn't like to see people abused (especially children). One thing you should know about Cynthia is that she's not as mean as she seems to be. Never judge a book by its cover.

At her evaluation conference in March, I urged Cynthia to try reaching a larger audience by submitting a piece of writing to an outside publisher before the year's end. I pointed out that increasing numbers of people at school were being affected by her writing. She held strong convictions and communicated them effectively. Toward the end of the school year, she wrote a piece entitled "A Prejudiced World" and sent it to a magazine with a carefully written business letter. During summer vacation, I received the following letter from Cynthia:

> Dear Ms. Whitin,
> It gives me great pleasure to tell you I received a letter from [magazine's name]. They ask that I give them permission to publish my paper in their other magazine....

My eyes filled with tears. The tears came because Cynthia had found her voice—not the teacher's, not the curriculum guide's, but her own voice. She knew she could adjust her style to her purpose. She had obviously accessed the formal structure of the letter she had received to notify me of her own success. I found myself traveling back to September, when Cynthia had been defensive and burdened by guilt. Her grandmother had died on June 13 two years ago. Her last words to Cynthia were to be good, that she loved her. Now it was June 13 again. I knew that Cynthia's grandmother would be proud to see her now.

Cynthia had traveled a remarkable path. At some points, such as when I wrote her the note in which I distinguished between being a bad person and simply making a mistake, I felt as if I were Cynthia's counselor. At other times, such as the day she led the class through her political essay, I felt as if I were running to catch up with her. Cynthia forced me to take a hard look at my teaching, and I had fresh insight into the concept of a negotiated curriculum (Harste, Short, & Burke, 1988). I realized that Cynthia's path was praiseworthy because it was her own. We may be inspired by it and learn from it, but no one else will follow it. Cynthia had her own purposes as well as her own process of writing. She discovered *her* voice and in so doing she discovered herself. She, in turn, helped me discover new parts of myself. As I watched her moving forward, I wondered what unseen paths might be followed by future students.

Implications for My Teaching

The research I conducted through my case study of Cynthia taught me several invaluable lessons. First, I gained a broader understanding of a negotiated curriculum. I did not follow a predetermined guide nor did Cynthia and I create a long-range plan together at the beginning of the year. Instead our curriculum developed over time as various experiences generated new opportunities; we grew in understanding of each other as we and the class became a community of learners. Now I see more clearly that a negotiated curriculum implies the influence of the learner's reading and writing within a social context over time.

Second, my work with Cynthia taught me that writing can have many effects on a learner's life: overcoming fear, developing self-discipline, expanding personal relationships, and generating insights about oneself. The work of different learners reflects their different needs and talents. I feel I now value more deeply the individual's growth through reading and writing and will continue to celebrate the diversity of learning in my classroom.

Third, Cynthia demonstrated clearly that there is no fixed sequence of steps in writing. She constructed her own process of writing and adapted her strategies for different purposes. As I noticed her flexibility, I reflected more closely on my own writing strategies. I began to value more fully the extent to which authors envision, shape, and reconsider ideas and images before putting any words on paper. I must support learners as they discover personal literacy strategies.

Finally, Cynthia taught me to be a better listener. Although I would like to be able to say that I always intended to listen, I found that many of my silences when talking with Cynthia occurred by chance. I often was at a loss for words, and I feared that I might alienate Cynthia by saying something wrong. I discovered that a cushion of silence allowed Cynthia time to reflect and develop her own insights. In turn, her thoughtful comments enabled me to make decisions about my role as a facilitator and supporter of students' work. Observing Cynthia interact with her peers also contributed to my understanding of her growth.

As I became involved with Cynthia's personal struggles and her attempts to resolve them through her reading and writing, I was challenged to observe more closely the other individuals in my classroom. I look forward to applying what I have learned from my research with Cynthia with future students, both those who are reluctant writers *and* those who write with enthusiasm.

References

Calkins, L. (1990). *Living between the lines.* Portsmouth, NH: Heinemann.

Harste, J., Short, K., & Burke, C. (1988). *Creating classrooms for authors.* Portsmouth, NH: Heinemann.

Chapter 13

A Case Study of a Writer

Katie Wood

Wood has been a seventh grade teacher and an instructor at the University of South Carolina. She now works at the Teachers College Writing Project of Columbia University in New York, New York.

When I needed to study student writing for a university course I was taking, a colleague recommended that I undertake a case study of her student Jo, whom she had difficulty "figuring out." Jo was in the eighth grade, in average classes making average or above-average grades. But Jo couldn't write. It really was that simple. Her writing looked like that of a third grader, and often it made her feel just that small. On the surface, Jo acted as if her difficulty with writing didn't bother her, but when she was put under a bright light something very different, very disturbing, was evident.

Jo was an exceptionally insecure teenager, made that way in part by years of failing every time she put pencil to paper. She dreamed of going to college, but I feared that a dream was all it would ever be. Through a series of interviews, Jo and I together captured the essence of her struggle to write. For the first time, Jo articulated her frustrations and her beliefs about her shortcomings as a writer. Because her responses were so thought provoking and have a voice of their own, I am including excerpts from the interviews in this report of my study.

After each response, I have included my perceptions, developed after many moments of reflection.

I hope the progression through our interviews will help readers of this chapter feel a sense of something evolving and revealing itself. If the chapter disturbs you, then I have achieved some of my purpose in sharing this case study; if it inspires you, I will consider it a success. My teaching practice will never be the same after my work with Jo. Here is our story.

Starting Out Together

When Jo walked into Room 114 at the appointed time, she looked around at everything, except at my eyes waiting to greet her. I finally decided to go for her ears instead. I introduced myself and told Jo a little about what I was doing. I asked her if there was anything she would like to tell me about herself, but she just showed me how well she could shrug. Since the informal chat stage was going nowhere, I decided to move on to the more formal interview about her writing.

One of the first questions I asked Jo was how she felt when she knew she had to do a writing assignment. She replied, "I know I won't pass it, so I don't usually waste a lot of time on it." That was all I got. She said it and her look challenged me to accept her answer and move on to the next question. I knew she was sincere, but at that early stage in our association I couldn't help but wonder if she wasn't just a little lazy as a writer—my "typical teacher" response. Later in the interview, she admitted that she did want to do better. I had seen some samples of her writing, and my feeling was that I'd be lucky to get her to write a complete sentence. Then I realized that maybe I was like her—I was giving up before I started. At least we had some common ground.

Next, I asked Jo if she had tried to get anyone to help her. "Not really," she replied. "Anybody who does gets just as frustrated as I do. I just can't write. It's no big deal." I was quickly learning how determined and stubborn Jo could be. She obviously had a great deal of experience with defeat since she was so hard on herself, yet, in a strange sort of way, her challenges to me indicated some self-confidence. I wondered at this point if she came from a family in which reading and writing were encouraged. If not, she probably had difficulty getting help even when she sought it. I remembered that she had agreed eagerly to working with me. I interpreted this as her either seeking help or wanting attention—and maybe both. I decided to put the issue of confidence on hold and move in a less threatening direction.

I asked Jo what she was interested in and might enjoy writing about. She replied, "Not much. I play sports some. And I like to go to the movies." I couldn't seem to get Jo to elaborate on anything in conversation and I began to understand what it must have been like for her when she was asked to do so on paper. She didn't really seem shy, she just didn't have much to say—or else she couldn't express it very well. I thought that maybe she was trying to convince me she was a "loser," both as a writer and as a person. I already knew this wasn't the case, though, because I had seen her quite animated with other students in certain situations. I decided to explore this.

I asked Jo if she wrote letters or notes to friends or if she wrote anything that wasn't required for school. I should have anticipated her response: "I talk on the phone a lot so I don't have to write notes. I don't write anything I don't have to." This, to me, was progress: I had found out that she did like to talk with people. Now I just had to get her to converse with me. Maybe she would when she was a little more comfortable with me, I thought to myself, or maybe I should just telephone her! I saw then that I had to stick to things she knew something about or was interested in. She used a shrug as a standard response. I thought her apparent disinterest might be covering some real feelings of inadequacy.

Knowing that students love to talk—and sometimes complain—about what they did in other teachers' classes, I asked Jo if her English teacher wanted students to use any particular method or process when they wrote. She replied, "Yeah, she has one. But the only thing I seem to always do is put it off until the last minute. I hate to write rough drafts. When she makes us do them, I usually just copy over the one I have. I do the best I can to start with, and I can't find my mistakes very well." I admit that I was amused by this statement, but also saddened. Jo's looking for mistakes in her papers was almost equivalent to searching for the proverbial needle in a haystack: there were so many problems, she couldn't possibly know where or how to start. Her procrastination about writing was consistent with everything else she had told me. She believed she would not be successful, so she figured there was no point in wasting her time. Her teachers told me she always did the assignments and handed them in on time, but they were simply unsatisfactory. This told me that Jo was fairly mature and responsible, and I suspected it really did bother her that her writing was deficient by most standards. Calkins (1986) says that people have a need to do good work and that we all want to succeed. I didn't think Jo was any different.

At the end of our first interview I decided to see if Jo was making a connection between reading and writing. I asked her if she felt she was a good reader and whether she liked to read. She said, "I like to read if it's interesting. I go to the library and check books out. I think I'm a pretty good reader. I can usually pronounce big words even if I don't know what they mean." I was thrilled at this first overt sign of confidence, although I was a little surprised that she showed such an interest in reading. My experience had been that people who liked to read usually wrote fairly well. I wondered about her definition of "reading." Did she see it as being able to recognize "big words"? This was an area I decided to explore in some later meeting.

After the first interview I was not sure how to proceed. I still did not know what really interested Jo. I wrestled with the idea that she was simply avoiding the issue and didn't realize how critical it was that she work to improve her writing. I saw avoidance in a lot of what she said. Was she unwilling to do what it would take, or was she convinced that there was nothing she could do? I decided to leave writing out of our next meeting. I felt an almost nosy desire to know what Jo was really like and what might be feeding her sense of inadequacy.

Making Progress

In subsequent interviews, I asked Jo how her parents reacted when she did poorly at school. What did they say about her not passing the state basic skills test?

> I usually get grounded for bad grades. They try to make me study more, but I don't think that's the problem. My mom gets a lot madder than my dad and she's the one that always goes in to talk to the teachers. She's got this thing about wanting me to go to college.... Every time I make a bad grade she acts like I just threw all my chances for college away.

I was excited when Jo said, "I don't think that's the problem." Did this mean that she might know what the problem was? I hoped so. There was obviously pressure at home for Jo to succeed, but I wondered how much help and support were available. I believe there is a fine distinction between pressure that motivates and pressure that only raises unrealistic expectations. Jo seemed to be suffering under the latter type of pressure, although I was aware that she might be distorting the situation to cover her own feelings and wishes.

I tried to steer the conversation away from whatever hostility Jo felt for her mother at that moment. I asked if her father ever talked about wanting her to go to college. She replied, "He just agrees with my mom. He cares about me, but I don't think he worries about my future. I guess he thinks I'll be okay because I don't get into trouble." That last line said a lot. I wondered if Jo also thought she would "be okay" as long as she stayed out of trouble.

Her tone of voice in this last response showed a real tenderness toward her father. It seemed from Jo's description that her home environment was essentially positive, although it was not a place where literacy was particularly valued for its own sake. I also thought that Jo's struggles with her mother might be having a negative impact on her attitude toward school. I asked her to go back to her parents' reactions when she failed the writing portion of the basic skills test. "Do they realize you must pass this to graduate and you must be able to write to go to college?" I asked. She answered as follows:

> When I first got my scores, my mom wasn't really sure what they meant. But then she had a meeting at school and they explained it to her.... She said I wasn't trying hard enough and

that she was going to make me work on my writing for an hour every night. We did it for about two weeks and then we just stopped. I guess she got tired of it and gave up. Anyway, I think she thought the problem was my handwriting.

For the first time I began to see that Jo had a good grip on the problem—maybe even a better understanding than her parents and teachers. I was disappointed to hear that her mother had given up on the hour-a-night work on writing—although it was probably an unrealistic undertaking to start with—because I expected that Jo saw it as another failure related to her writing. With a little direction, Jo and her mother might have set up something that worked; now, I thought, they will probably never try again.

Jo began to open up to me this way during our second interview. At this point, I was no longer worried about her *ability* to express herself, but rather about her lack of confidence in doing so. I felt that this could possibly be overcome by our establishing mutual trust, and that this might eventually be the key to helping her with her writing.

My next interview was with Jo's language arts teacher from the previous year. I wanted to get some insights about Jo as a writer from someone who had been in a position to evaluate her work. I started by asking her to give me some adjectives that described Jo as a writer. She responded this way: "Underachieving, underconfident, sometimes lazy and unwilling, below grade level, generally unreceptive.... On the other hand, she was often creative and emotional. The negatives do outweigh the positives and they do come to mind first." This response distressed me. I couldn't help but wonder how many of Jo's teachers had shared similar feelings about her, feelings that in all likelihood they had had difficulty in concealing completely at all times.

I asked Jo's former teacher to talk about her in more general terms. This is what she said:

> One of the things that frustrates me so about Jo is that she is such a likeable student. She's a lazy writer, but she is responsible in that she always has her work done and has tried to prepare for class.... She is very honest, always ready to admit she hasn't fixed anything on her paper because she can't find any mistakes. She is an average reader and, believe it or not, she did well on grammar exercises and tests. Even her spelling work was passable. She just couldn't apply any of it.... Nothing she learned outside of writing labs was applied within them. When we began to write, she closed the doors.

She spoke those last few lines with an emotion-filled voice. She seemed so frustrated by her difficulty in understanding what was "wrong" with Jo.

This lack of understanding was echoed by Jo's teacher of that year, the colleague who had recommended that I undertake a case study of her. I thought she was on to something when she said to me one day, "Jo closes the doors." If there were doors, there must be something behind them. How could we open the doors? I asked Jo's teacher if there was any writing that Jo did successfully, any time she felt Jo was really making progress. She thought for a minute, and then replied as follows:

> I picked up on Jo's creativity and imagination in her journal writing and poetry writing. Both of these types of writing have an "anything goes" appeal to students. The journal was a terror to read, but it had some *good* stuff in it. Jo is very sensitive. I had some limited success with working journal entries into themes, but even then I had to direct her in every step. Jo has little or no editing capabilities with her own work. She enjoyed writing poems, especially in standard forms where you just fill in the information.

I couldn't wait to see what Jo had to say about journals and poetry. Her apparent enthusiasm for poetry was particularly interesting to me because the "gifted" students I worked with usually hated writing poetry. I began to wonder if Jo's problems were simply with structure and mechanics. Maybe her inability to structure her writing properly was inhibiting her ideas and creativity. When she did not have to concentrate her attention on structure, grammar, and mechanics, she was an expressive and even emotional writer. But, as Jo's teacher said, the result "was a terror to read." That didn't mean it had no value, but Jo herself often *felt* it had no value because it was difficult for others to follow and, more important, did not accurately reflect her thinking.

I pursued the topic of editing with Jo's teacher by asking if Jo could edit other students' papers with more success. She replied, "In fact, she can do an adequate job of editing other students' papers. She wasn't the best editor I had, but she was often better at editing others' work than her own. This reminds me: other students hated helping Jo edit her papers. They just didn't know where to start." I asked if she thought Jo knew that her papers were avoided, and she said, "Oh, most definitely."

At this point I really felt sorry for Jo. I had to keep my sympathy in check because I knew it wouldn't help her, but I did wonder if it was sympathy that had promoted her through eight grades. I consciously redirected my speculations to try and determine why Jo couldn't see mistakes in her own papers. Maybe she was like the other students who didn't want to edit her work—that is, she was giving up before she even started. I wondered if she was editing as she wrote.

I was now trying to isolate *how* her writing managed to come out so badly. I asked Jo's teacher to comment on my theory that Jo's inferiority complex was blocking her writing. Here are her thoughts:

> Jo has an inferiority complex for sure, but I don't see it as part of the problem; I see it as a result of the problem. For years teachers have been trying to help Jo, show her the way, and she rejects it. I'm afraid there is a lot more stubbornness involved than some psychological problem. Jo is a bright girl with a problem she hasn't taken a mind to solving yet.

I agreed that at least some of the problem was in Jo's seeming unwillingness to take steps to improve, but I also believed there was some more deeply rooted difficulty. Her inferiority complex about writing was born out of unsuccessful writing experiences. I wasn't sure she was or ever had been an inferior thinker; the negative feelings she had about herself were simply reinforced each time she endeavored to express those thoughts in writing.

Jo did realize the magnitude of the problem. I thought she understood it more than anyone else and that it was overwhelming her. She was the one carrying the weight around, and after so much failure she saw improving her writing as almost equivalent to changing the world. I knew she would never get the help she needed in an "average" English class, which was exactly where she was headed for the next year.

Reaching a Conclusion

My original purpose for our final interview was to find out what Jo saw as successful in past writing experiences. Over the course of the interview, however, I found out a great deal more. I began by asking Jo if she could remember a writing assignment that she really liked or felt she did well on. She didn't have to think long. "When I was in sixth grade," she said, "we got in little groups and had to write these scenes, like little plays. We had to come up with all the parts for everyone to say. I always came up with the best lines. Some of them were really funny. I didn't have to actually write, though; one of the other kids was like a secretary who wrote everything down." Jo was very animated in her description of this experience, although her tone suggested, probably correctly, that if she had been forced to write the lines, she wouldn't have been so enthusiastic. I wished I could just help her find some way to capture the creative spark on paper without losing all its meaning. There was so much fear of the structure and mechanics of writing in Jo.

I asked what her success as a playwright told her about herself as a writer. She said with a grin, "I guess it tells me I've got as good ideas as anyone else as long as I don't have to write them down." For the first time, I sensed in Jo's tone a spark of hope that I tried to reinforce. It was hard to decide what to ask next because I didn't want to destroy what I thought we were on the brink of achieving—a feeling of confidence in Jo. I asked if those same good ideas were in her head when she did have to write. She answered this way:

> They are most of the time if it's something I like, like plays. But I've got all these ideas in my head and when I try to write them, they don't come out the way I mean for them to. What's on my paper is a lot different from what's in my head. I know I have a lot of problems with spelling and sentences and stuff, but that's not really it.

Jo was finally discussing the problem in terms other than "there's nothing I can do about it." She identified a part of the problem no one else knew about—her conscious awareness that her writing was not expressing what she really felt. She was so lost in a fear of structure that she couldn't make her writing speak for her. How many essay questions on tests had she failed when she actually knew the answers?

I wished I had an easy solution for her, but instead I wanted to know at what point Jo realized she wasn't saying what she meant to say. This was harder for her to answer, and she thought for several seconds before saying, "Whenever I hear my papers read aloud or my teacher writes notes that show she doesn't know what I was talking about. When I read what I write it makes sense to me, but I guess that's because I know what it's supposed to say." Then she chuckled and said, "Even when *I* hear it read aloud by someone else, sometimes I don't know what I meant to say. It's embarrassing sometimes." I realized that sometimes I had felt this way about my own writing, but I got the impression this was an everyday occurrence for Jo. I hated to hear her voice her embarrassment, but at least I finally felt like we were getting somewhere.

I was still afraid to suggest what she might do, however, because we were making too much progress to risk getting sidetracked. Now I asked Jo to be more specific about readers' misinterpretations of her writing. Did they occur in relation to details or to the overall meaning? She thought that both were a problem, and then she elaborated as follows:

> I have a lot of trouble with times. Do you know what I mean? Like I mean to say something happened at this time and it comes out sounding like some other time.... And when other

people read my stuff they don't read it like it is supposed to sound. I mean for something to be funny, and it ends up being sad or even way out. I guess that's because it's so hard to read.

I assumed that what she meant by her "trouble with times" had to do with establishing chronological order. I didn't pursue this because I didn't want to dwell on negatives that day. It could, however, be the same problem with assimilation of information that caused her to have difficulty with structure. I was also interested in her view that her writing lost its meaning because it was hard to read. Jo seemed to be figuring out so much on her own all of a sudden. I wondered if she had actually been thinking about these issues quite seriously—everything she said was so insightful.

Next I asked Jo about poetry and journal writing, an area in which I knew she had had some success. Here's what she said:

> I had a teacher who would give us the first parts of lines of a poem and we just had to fill in the end. I could really do that. Sometimes we did have to do poems by ourselves, and I did okay on them. I really don't think they were that good, though. They were just a bunch of words I threw together. I guess that's what a poem is.... I guess I did like those journals, too. I liked it better when she would tell us to write our feelings about a certain thing than when we had to write about just anything. I never knew what "anything" was supposed to be, really.

I knew what she meant. Asking a child with so many fears to write about "anything" was unreasonable. She was already afraid of having to write about "something"; she couldn't even comprehend "anything." This made me recall her teacher's comment that Jo was more successful at writing on assigned topics than at free writing. She had said that Jo would produce a sentence or two every ten minutes of free-writing time.

I was now convinced that Jo was quite accurate in her assessment of her writing. There had to be some way to capitalize on her insights. All of a sudden Jo came out with this unsolicited piece of information:

> When I first started school we had to trace our letters out of this book. I always could do them about the best in the class. The teacher would hang mine up all the time. But then later we had to do them without looking or even tracing and I couldn't do that. I never had good handwriting since we quit tracing.

Even this story of *hand*writing had an unhappy ending. I was beginning to think that Jo had *never* had a positive writing experience. I longed to go back and talk with Jo's former teachers and find just one success story. There was so much to learn from Jo and her past experiences because there are so many students like her.

We ended this interview with a look to the future. I asked Jo if she thought that with a lot of work she could become a good writer. She shrugged and waited for me to say something else, but I didn't give in. Finally she said, "I guess so, with a lot of work. But sometimes I wonder if there's just something wrong. It seems like if I was going to get it, I would have by now." How could she help but feel that way? She was of average intelligence, going into the ninth grade, and she wrote like a third grader. I no longer saw Jo's unwillingness as stubbornness or laziness; I thought she was realistic in her assessment of the situation. If there was one thing I had learned, it was that Jo was a bright child. I suddenly had a wonderful image of her writing a textbook on working with disabled writers. I'd be the first one to purchase that book.

Learning from Jo

After our interviews ceased, Jo continued to visit me almost every day. I helped her whenever I could with whatever I could. We had become friends, and sometimes I felt as if we were peers because I had learned so much from her. Indeed, my practices in the classroom have changed as a direct result of my experiences with Jo. Here are some things I have learned.

First, Jo taught me about the worthlessness of the second draft to the reluctant writer. This student completely closes the door on the idea of a second draft because the first one is filled with so many obstacles. I have taken the pressure of redrafting off the students in my writing classes. Instead, we write in pencil and skip every other line. Students make corrections and additions in the lines as needed. Sometimes after revisions are made, they choose to copy their work over to make the pieces look better, but this is not required. This simple change has done wonders for my students' attitudes about writing. Before, these reluctant writers saw a second draft as a whole new assignment.

Second, Jo taught me that reluctant writers need specific strategies for getting started in their writing. They have good ideas, but getting them together, separating the good from the bad, and coming up with that first line can be almost impossible for them. I now sometimes go against everything written about "letting students find their voices" and give students a first line for something they want to write about. In a sense, I see this as modeling, though certainly some students become dependent on my leads. Still, when they need help getting started, I give it to them.

From Jo's descriptions of her home, I realized that many students do not live in an environment where they are expected to write or read. Many of them have no one they can ask for help, and finding a quiet spot can be nearly impossible for some. I have stopped requiring students in my classes to work on writing outside of school. Instead, I have created the most supportive environment for writing I can in my classroom. Positive comments—something I wish Jo had had more experience of—are essential, and these students practically beg for them. I have one boy who wants me to come over and read every new sentence he writes. And you know what? I try to do just that. These reluctant writers just want me to laugh or be properly disgusted (they love gore), and my reactions seem to give them the incentive they need to write the next line.

I learned from Jo that many reluctant writers know a lot about the nature of their problems in writing. Jo could pinpoint the very things that were troubling her writing; the problem was that the solution was too tough. For reluctant writers, this is usually because there seem to be too many problems to fix. Now I ask my students explicitly to tell me what their biggest composition problems are. Most of them make accurate diagnoses. My theory is that the first step—a major one—is identifying the problem. I am still working on how best to motivate my students to search for solutions.

From the interview with Jo's teacher, I "learned" something I think I already knew but had not come to terms with. The skill-and-drill, part-to-whole method of teaching the mechanics of writing does not work. Jo could complete all the worksheets correctly, but not one thing transferred to her writing. I wish I could tell you that I have given away the textbooks that cluttered up my classroom, but I admit that it's taking me some time to work through this one. I can tell you, however, that the grammar books have made it to the shelf in the corner.

Finally, Jo taught me how important it is to celebrate small victories. Reluctant writers need a climate in which they can be successful over and over again. Sometimes this means letting a student simply tell a story instead of writing it on paper; sometimes it means suggesting they dictate into a tape recorder and then transcribe on paper; often it means displaying work and chastising my fifth-period "honors" students when they snicker at it.

Thanks to Jo, I am a new kind of writing teacher. I'm in no hurry. I keep quiet, so I can listen a lot. And I've learned that it's not the end of the world if a subject and verb does not agree. See! The world is still okay, and so am I. I hope that my students will see that they're okay, too.

Reference
Calkins, L.M. (1986). *The art of teaching writing*. Portsmouth, NH: Heinemann.

Chapter 14

A Year with Reading Workshop

Dawn M. Cline

Cline teaches seventh and eighth grade reading improvement classes in the Humble (Texas) Independent School District. (The research described in this chapter was conducted when she taught in Spring, Texas.) Her particular research interest is in the area of comprehension growth in reading improvement students.

For seven years, I used basal readers with my seventh and eighth grade students but I wasn't very comfortable with this approach. I felt that part of my job was to instill a love of reading in my students, but I didn't think I was succeeding. After reading Atwell's (1987) *In the Middle* early in one summer vacation, I felt sure I had found a solution. In Atwell's literature-based approach, students select novels to read. Her students improved in literacy and fluency, and they enjoyed reading; I wanted this for my students also. I decided to find out if my students would show marked progress in reading and increased enjoyment of it if I adopted Atwell's methods. To measure students' progress, I would examine their writing, their performance on the Gates-MacGinitie Reading Test, and the number of books they read.

My classes consisted of students from multiethnic, low- to middle-class socioeconomic backgrounds. I was confident a reading workshop approach would work in my seventh grade on-level/below-level and above-level classes, and it seemed perfect for my eighth grade reading elective class. However, I was hesitant about trying a reading workshop with the eighth graders in my reading improvement class. For these students, books were something to be avoided at all costs. If I *could* get them started in reading workshop, I wondered if they would choose good literature to read. Would I constantly have to hound them to continue reading? What kind of anguish would I put myself through when I tried to get them to write their reactions to what they had read? Would they ever become deeply involved with books or would they just get bored? Although I was apprehensive, I eventually decided to go ahead and try reading workshop in all my classes.

Getting Started

I spent the next month preparing grade sheets, reading logs, letters to parents, minilesson topics—and for anything that could possibly go wrong. I concentrated particularly on how to introduce reading workshop. Since it would be so radically different from what the students were used to, I was concerned that I not create a state of panic when it was first implemented.

I began at the end of the first week of school. That day I explained reading workshop in general terms to all my classes, passed out an introductory letter, and discussed the management plan. I told my students they would be selecting the book they would like to read the next day, and if they were reading something at home, they were welcome to bring it. Next, I asked them to complete a reading survey that I had adapted from Atwell's book. Finally, I spent about 10 minutes reading a book aloud, and then I asked the students to react to what I had read and make predictions about what might come next. This was intended to ease them into writing.

The second day we began by discussing their responses on their reading survey.

This led to a broader conversation about what I hoped to accomplish in the reading workshop. I told my students that I was concerned that many of them had read fewer than five books the previous year, and I suggested some things that I thought they would learn with this new approach. (I will admit that they were visibly skeptical at this point.) I let them know that I wanted everyone to respond freely in reading workshop because we could learn from others' opinions. Finally, I talked about procedures for selecting and checking out books, and then gave the students time to make their choices. I assisted when necessary and made suggestions when asked. At the end of class, I read aloud, and then we discussed the selection. During the second week, I administered the Gates-MacGinitie Reading Test and began introducing details of the reading workshop, such as dialogue journals and the grade sheet. My teaching followed a routine of minilesson, silent reading, and read-aloud followed by discussion.

At this early stage my students were still a bit confused about what was expected of them. At the beginning of the second week, one student asked, "Mrs. Cline, do we get to read today?" (I was at least happy to hear "get to" instead of "have to"!) When I replied, "Yes, every day you will get to read books you have chosen," I was met with stares of disbelief. I knew my students were wondering when the inevitable onslaught of comprehension questions would come. By the end of that week, though, they were more comfortable. Stu, an eighth grade reading improvement student, hung back a few moments after the bell rang on Friday and quietly asked if he could read his book over the weekend. I wanted to hug the boy! The enthusiasm of many of my students reassured me that this was the way to teach reading.

By the beginning of the third week, most students were doing a good job of responding to the books I read aloud, so I began teaching them a few ways to react to books in writing. To help them get started I had prepared a handout based on a list in Atwell's book.

This sheet listed 20 ideas of how to respond to reading, as follows:

1. What were your feelings after you read the opening chapter? After you read half the book? After you finished the book?

2. Did this book make you laugh? Cry? Cringe? Smile? Cheer? Explode? Record some of your reactions.

3. Are there connections between the book and your own life?

4. What character from this book would you most like to be? Why?

5. Would you like to acquire a personality trait of any particular character? Describe the trait and explain why you like it.

6. Would you have used a different name for any character or place? What name and why?

7. What makes you wonder in this book?

8. What confuses you in this book?

9. Is there an idea that makes you stop and think or prompts questions? Identify the idea and explain your responses.

10. What are your favorite lines?

11. What questions would you like to ask the author of this book?

12. How have you changed after reading this book?

13. What do you know now that you didn't know before?

14. What questions about this book would you like answered?

15. Who else should read this book? Why?

16. Who shouldn't read this book? Why?

17. Would you like to read more books by this author? Why?

18. If you could see inside a certain character's heart, what would it look like? His or her soul? His or her brain?

19. What do you think will happen next in the story? Why?

20. What do you predict the characters will be doing 10 years after the story ends?

Following a suggestion from Atwell (1987), I asked my students to write their reactions to books in the form of letters to their friends, their parents, or me. I gave a minilesson about the conventions of letter writing and then let the students get started. Letter writing quickly became an important part of reading workshop.

Settling into a Routine

By the fourth week of school I had established a pattern for reading workshop in all my classes. I began most classes with a 10- to 15-minute minilesson on a focused topic. At first I conducted four or five minilessons a week, but I quickly realized this provided too much information for students to digest. After experimenting a bit, I decided that two or three minilessons a week with quick reviews in between were most effective.

I was used to following a curriculum guide, so I was initially apprehensive about Atwell's advice that minilessons should evolve from the students' needs. By the end of the second six-week unit, however, I found it was getting easier to detect those needs. For example, some students had acquired a favorite author. At that point, I did a lesson on the more formal requirements of writing a letter to an author that could actually be mailed to him or her. Some students asked me why there were sometimes blank lines between paragraphs, and this led to a minilesson on breaks to indicate scene changes. I found that these lessons seemed to take the edge off and make more palatable the drier skill lessons I continued to teach to cover certain aspects of my district's required curriculum.

On Tuesdays and Fridays, I checked on students' progress. Students told me the title and author of the book they were reading and what page they were beginning on that day, and I shared with them the same information about my own reading. The Tuesday check helped me see if students were reading over the weekend; the Friday check helped me track their progress during the week. This was a public process. I felt that discussing reading progress this way would provide some letter-writing ideas for students who had read the same book.

The heart of our reading workshop was the time when we selected new books, read quietly, or shared thoughts about books with others through discussion or writing. This time lasted about 30 minutes in most of my classes, although more time was needed early in the year for the letter-writing portion. In fact, it was at least three months before I began to see consistently well-written letters from most of the students.

In order to monitor how students were responding to books, I decided at an early stage to have them alternate their writing: one week they would write to me, the next week to a classmate. In my responses to their letters, I prodded students to make predictions, think about characters' decisions, tell how the story affected them, and explain what they had learned from the story. Slowly, I began to see less plot summary and more personal response. Sometimes I asked them to address a specific topic such as point of view, setting, or identification of conflict, and I always encouraged them to try and teach something with their responses. As students became more involved in their reading, they discovered it took a page or more to reflect thoroughly on what they had read. For students who found writing difficult, I suggested they write a little each day or write at home. I also reassured them frequently that I considered this "first draft" writing. I did not correct mistakes, but modeled corrections in my responses. Student-teacher conferences or minilessons remedied consistent or common errors.

This is not to imply that reading workshop involved no evaluation. For each six-week period, students worked toward a page-requirement grade, a participation grade, and grades on their writing in reading logs, notes from minilessons, letters to me, and letters to classmates. For the page-requirement grade, I simply assigned a letter grade equivalent for number of pages read: 250 to 300 was an A, 200 to 249 was a B, and so on, with bonuses awarded for pages read above 300. I started the page requirement at a low level to build students' confidence and raised them after the first and third six-week units. I was delighted to find that most students read more than required. In assigning participation grades I took into account involvement in discussions, engagement with books, behavior, and the like. Readings logs were simply lists of books read; grades for these and for minilesson notes were assigned based on completeness and accuracy. Letters were graded for completeness, although here I also took into account the depth of students' responses to the books they were describing. Finally, at the end of each six-week unit, I gave a test on material covered in minilessons, separate skills instruction, or vocabulary lessons. The grade on this test combined with the other grades to produce an evaluation of each student's achievement in six weeks of reading workshop.

I felt that this system of evaluation offered students many opportunities for success. Students knew what was expected of them and were responsible for their own performance. In addition, I encouraged students to improve their overall grade by setting and meeting goals for extra work. This could involve reading 100 additional pages, writing more letters than required, writing to an author, or comparing and contrasting books by the same author. I was pleased that many of my students tackled these projects with enthusiasm.

Research Results

Throughout the year I returned to my research question: was reading workshop having a positive effect on my students' achievement in and enjoyment of reading? I examined students' letters, test results, and number of books read to try and find out; I also asked for students' reactions to reading workshop. All my data demonstrated that the answer to my research question was a resounding yes.

The differences among students' letters written at the beginning of the year and those written later in the year when the workshop was well established are perhaps the most dramatic indicator of change. Following are a few (unedited) samples. Although the later letters were written to me and therefore it would not be surprising if the students had expended more effort on them, the increased level of detail and per-

sonal connections they display is nevertheless remarkable.

On September 15, Kitty, a seventh grader, wrote as follows:

> Dear Cindy,
> This book is very good. I've read alot. Mine's kinda sad cause this girl is in a wheelchair.
>
> Love 4 life,
> Kitty

This is the letter Kitty wrote on January 9:

> Dear Mrs. Cline,
> Hello. I'm reading a book called *Alexandra* by Scott O'Dell. It's a sad book. You know like that book called *A Time to Love, A Time to Mourn*. Well Alexandra's father died and I started to cry. It's so sad. I hate sad books like that because all they do is bring you down. I am always thinking about what I would do man. I couldn't live without my dad or my mom. I almost start crying just thinking about it. In this book I'm reading Alexandra and her family are divers and her grandpa lives with them too. Well that's how her dad died was from diving and her grandpa is crippled. It's very sad. Have you read it? What are you reading?
>
> Love, Kitty

Tony, an eighth grade reading improvement student, wrote the following letter to a classmate on September 21:

> Dear Maria
> My book is really boring but it has a few good part in it. How is your book. My book is named "Corky and the Brothers Cool" P.J. Petersen. Its a really stupid name.
>
> Love
> Tony

By February Tony had shown remarkable improvement. He was beginning to attend to aspects of the author's craft and to show his appreciation for a specific genre:

Dear Mrs. Cline,
I just finished A Killing Freeze by Lynn Hall. It had a really good ending I thought. I never would of thought it was Bernie that killed Mr. Moline. As soon as they said something about the icicle I knew that could have happened. I don't know why she just didn't stay in the police office instead of running off.
I want to read more Jackrabbit books. Can you give me the names of some good ones since you've read all of them? I thought that book was really good. Well I got to go. Bye.

Tony

One of the most poignant letters came from Sofia, an eighth grader who came to school with little or no knowledge of English. After only one week in reading workshop she was trying to make personal connections to books. This is what she wrote after reading *The Giving Tree* by Shel Silverstein:

I fill, this story is very sad, because the people who meet the tree take all it parts, but they never think about the tree fills. Only one person give it company.

Although the letters provided me with invaluable data about how my students were developing as readers, I was also pleased with how well they did on the Gates-MacGinitie test. On average, my seventh grade on-level students increased their scores by 6 percent, and the eighth grade elective students showed a 3-percent improvement. But these students had begun the year with high scores, so it was the gains made my reading improvement students that pleased me most: between Sept-

ember and May their scores increased by an average of 33 percent.

Students also far exceeded my expectations of the number of books they would read during the year. In previous years my students had read an average of five books; this year, my seventh grade on-level students averaged 20 books, seventh grade above-level students averaged 45, eighth grade reading improvement students read an average of 25, and eighth grade elective students read an average of 65.

At the end of the year I asked my students what they thought of reading workshop; I also asked them what they had learned about reading. Their responses to both questions confirmed my own evaluation of the overwhelming success of this approach to reading instruction.

In retrospect I feel that my anxieties about starting reading workshop were understandable, but I am glad that they subsided quickly. While my data provided concrete evidence of success, my most valuable insights came from the enthusiasm of my students. They continually commented on how much they liked reading workshop; most began to say that they liked to read. At times I had to re-energize a few reading improvement students, but I never had a student refuse to read. Students were thrilled by the number of books they had read and by how much they knew about young adult literature and authors. They quickly became critical readers who sought out high-quality books and debated the merits of authors such as Lois Duncan, Gary Paulsen, Richard Peck, and Norma Fox Mazer.

Reading workshop provided the logical solution to two problems that I think are common to most reading classes. It solves the problem of finding books suitable to a range of reading levels because rather than assigning a common text, students choose books that they can read. It also solves the problem that arises when some students have already read a book being taught as a whole-class novel. More important, though, is the personal stake students have in books they choose to read themselves. These are the books they learn from, and with such books, they build their own reading skills.

In the future, I would like to expand my students' interests into nonfiction, poetry, and other genres; I would like to broaden modes of response beyond letter writing. Ultimately, I would like my role to decrease, so that my students' ownership of and control over their own learning can increase. One of my main goals is to implement reading workshop electives in upper grades where reading is not a required subject.

From my viewpoint, reading workshop has many benefits. Nothing is routine; the workshop is always changing and challenging. It builds students' confidence about reading, particularly for students who experience difficulty. Wide reading of trade books results in learning on a variety of subjects including literacy. It is an approach that is adaptable to any set of curricular demands. Most important, reading workshop builds fluency and helps instill a love of reading even in the most reluctant readers. After seven years of using basals with middle school students, I now feel that I am finally teaching reading.

Reference

Atwell, N. (1987). *In the middle: Writing, reading, and learning with adolescents*. Upper Montclair, NJ: Boynton/Cook.

Chapter 15

What Students' Written Reflections Reveal about Literacy

Kathleen Stumpf Jongsma

When this chapter was written, Jongsma was teaching at Pat M. Neff Middle School in the Northside Independent School District, San Antonio, Texas. She now supervises that district's K-12 reading program, conducts staff-development programs, and continues research in alternative assessment, reading/writing connections, and literature-based reading programs.

My seventh and eighth graders are becoming good monitors of their own growth in reading and writing. Most can describe what genres they like, the characteristic styles of their favorite authors, the kinds of reading and writing they do best, and what reading and writing goals they still want to accomplish. Through discussion with me, their peers, and their parents or guardians, they have learned to reflect on their literacy processes.

When I began the research described here, I didn't know that my students could handle the above processes so adroitly. I was concerned that many of my students did not seem to be involved in self-assessment or in monitoring their own learning. As a teacher, I was constantly looking for ways to help my students evaluate themselves more critically. I wondered if keeping portfolios of their work and reflecting on portfolio contents would help students look at their reading and writing processes more carefully. I wanted to know if they could then use information from their portfolios to establish goals and to plan future strategies. In this chapter, I share what I learned from my study and how the use of portfolios helped my students reflect on their own literacy and progress as learners.

First I need to tell you a bit about my students and our classes. We follow a reading workshop format where most of the reading is from materials we select ourselves and most of our writing is in response to what we read. I read and write along with my students. Minilessons are used for purposes of skill development, for extending awareness of literary conventions, and for introducing genres and authors. In class, we write to each other, to parents, to administrators, and to published authors about what we are reading and how we are growing in reading, writing, and thinking about books. We share things from books we have enjoyed and urge others to read what we have read so we can have good discussions.

I teach one class of advanced readers enrolled in a one-semester elective. These students are highly motivated and responsive in their writing. The majority of my students, however, are enrolled in year-long reading improvement courses. They are less motivated and less responsive; many dislike reading and writing intensely when they enter the class in August, and many have unhappy memories associated with their literacy difficulties. My school is in Texas, where state law requires seventh and eighth grade students who score below the 40th percentile on the most recently administered standardized test to enroll in reading support services. Many of my students have attended such support programs since second or third grade. At the beginning of the year in which I first started experimenting with portfolios, my reading improvement students' scores ranged from the 2nd to the 39th percentile on the district's selected standardized tests. These students, although all to some extent struggling with literacy, were diverse in their abilities, in

their attitudes toward teachers and learning, and in their feelings about themselves as learners.

My advanced and my reading improvement students keep their own "literacy portfolios," Manila folders stored alphabetically in large, accessible plastic crates. Most of my students pick up their portfolios as they enter the room and keep them at their desks for our 45-minute reading period; others pull their portfolios as needed. They personalize their portfolios with drawings, photographs, clippings from their favorite magazines, and messages to future portfolio readers; they fill them with materials of their own choosing as well as with writing I suggest they include. Portfolios include such things as reading response notebooks, poems, artwork, summary cinquains, story pyramids, character and topic maps, story maps, notes to one another, and tapes of our reading; materials can be work in progress or finished pieces.

Students arrange their portfolios to their own liking. Many place materials in chronological order, others arrange by genre of material, and still others organize thematically. Some students organize around a specific topic—putting all the items on one book together, for example. Once I worked with some younger students who organized their papers into two categories: things they liked and things they didn't like. I have yet to see this scheme used by my older students, but it is a sensible way of organizing and certainly fits my instructions to students that they should choose their own way of organizing materials. Without some organization, however, portfolios tend to become unmanageable, and conferences about contents and goals become difficult. Organizing is a crucial step for the reflection that is enunciated in conference discussions and in written pieces.

It is the aspect of reflection about reading and writing that is the focus of this chapter. As students add to their portfolios over time, they are able to monitor their own progress and they discuss their progress with me and with others. At a minimum, my students write down their reflections on their progress in literacy every three to six weeks. Many students, however, do this more frequently, inserting written comments into their portfolios whenever they feel the need.

Many readers of this chapter will be familiar with the student-to-student comments discussed in Atwell's *In the Middle* (1987). Since she does such a good job of describing how students share reflections with one another through reading response notebooks, I will concentrate my comments on reflections shared with different audiences—parents and the teacher. The many statements from students and parents I've included are reproduced without editing. I find when I read reflections such as these that I am particularly impressed by how students home in on their own problem areas and gain insights on their own literacy.

Reflections to the Teacher

> I like reading but I hate writing. Sometimes I read when I am supposed to be writing. Reading is one of my best qualities but when I write I usually have trouble getting started. I think the reason that I have trouble getting started is because I'm not sure what people would think about my writing. But I am getting over that. I have always liked reading. When I was in second grade I was reading 100-200 page books. Whenever I have extra time I either play basketball or read. I hope to improve my writing and continue reading like I do.

A seventh grade student in our school's gifted and talented program wrote this note to me toward the end of our semester-long advanced reading course. It is an apt picture of his progress in our class. He was an avid reader but an extremely reluctant writer. In this piece, he opened up and gave me insights into why his writing wasn't keeping pace with his reading: his concern over how his work would be received by others inhibited his progress. As he gains more confidence—or "gets over that," as he says—writing should come more easily for him.

Another student in the same class has a different perception of herself as a reader and writer. Toward the end of the course, she wrote as follows:

> I looked over my reading and writing skills, and figured out my reading skills are very accurate. My reading is at a medium speed. When I write I think about what the book and what the author is trying to say! I like to read and write, but sometimes the reading just doesn't go with the writing. I've read books that I feel shouldn't be written, and I've read books I've felt should be a #1 seller. Reading is fun and writing is tiring.

A classmate reflected this way in March:

> I think I am getting better as a reader because I'm reading more and making up more ideas about the characters in a book. Also I'm reading slower and not trying to speed read. Since I've taken this class, I think I'm a better reader.

In May he was more explicit:

> As I am looking back in my portfolio I see that I've improved my writing, for instance I didn't elaborate a lot at the beginning of the 6 weeks but now I see that I have elaborated much more. I also see that I have improved

on my spelling and punctuation. I think that since I took this class I have sharpened my reading skills. For instance first of all I liked to read but not a lot, but now I've taken this class and now I love to read. I feel sorry for the people who can't read because they're missing out on some good stuff! I found that I really like mysteries. Because I love actions and suspense. A perfect book that I really enjoyed—The Hardy Boys *In Self Defense*. It is a perfect example.

Early in the semester, another student in the same class talked about his reading and writing this way:

I believe I'm doing better than I was last year meaning I'm reading more books. I'm also writing very much more, and the funny thing is I like it. I'd also like to do more story pyramids.

Later in the semester, he expanded on his ideas about reading and writing:

I have been reading and writing more this year than I have in many years. This portfolio contains most of my writing for this semester. I like the reading more than the writing, but the writing is ok. All the stuff in my portfolio is part of every book I've read this semester. The book I'm reading now is *A Wizard of Earthsea*. It's probably the best book I've read this year. I like the author's style and the way she describes and develops all the characters.

These four students from my advanced reading class clearly show a deeper involvement in literacy over the course of the year. The greatest growth, however, usually comes in the reading improvement students. Their written reflections show their developing maturity and their increasing awareness of what gets in the way of their progress in literacy. For example, at the end of

one six-week period, one girl wrote the following:

Last 6 weeks I failed my classes because I'd rather go out with my friends then do my work. The way I plan to improve is by going home after school and spending less time with my friends.

Later in the year, she saw herself quite differently:

As I look at my reading and writing, I see that I've grown to read more and enjoy it. My writing is nitter [neater]. I write more, and I have more Imangiantean [imagination]. I've learned that Reading can be fun, and it helps you with all your other classes. That also Reading is something that you will use all your life.

A student diagnosed as severely learning disabled wrote this in October:

I'm going to try to get a 95 or higher this six weeks. I will try harder and listen to instructions. I with study and read more and more. And turn in all of my assignments.

In November, this student showed his growing awareness of his literacy processes:

In reading I have grown in a lot of different ways. One, I've learned how to read faster, and to understand more. I have learned how to listen more and how to skim faster. I've liked the crosswords and word searches a lot. I like the letter writing to each other and the progress reports because none of mine are bad. The only thing I don't like about this class is the homework assignments but I have enough time in the week so I was able to turn them in. My goals for the next six weeks will be trying to get stuff done faster and keep my pace. I can try to keep track of my stuff and keep my mouth closed when the teacher is talking or when we have work to do. I will try to act better and cooperate in class more often.

Another reading improvement student wrote this near the beginning of the year:

I feel that I have grew in a lot of different ways. I feel my vocabulary has got better. I feel my spelling is getting better and wirking with other people is easier. My reading is getting better. My writing I feel is getting better. I feel that this class has help me a lot.

In April this student wrote as follows:

My portfolio is a neat thing to have, to see the work you done from the first six weeks. My grades have been pretty good and my conduct is good. I am going to try to read or write every night and work on my writing more.

Later in the same month he wrote this:

During the year in reading, my writing abelate [ability] has improve alot. Also by looking in my portfolio my Vocabulary has improved a lot. Sense the beginning of the year my vocabulary has been improving, one thing I need to work on is my writing. I also need to improve on my spelling. I am not a very good speller so that one thing I need to improve on for the rest of the year.

In these pieces, students described growth over time. Many were justly proud of their accomplishments; others were honest in admitting they hadn't worked hard enough to see much growth. Almost all, however, agreed that portfolios were "neat" things to keep and to share with others, including their parents. From the entries I could see growth on many different levels. Obvious areas of change included more elaborate syntax and vocabulary and better understanding and appreciation of audience as they wrote to me, their peers, their parents, and others. From their reflections I could

see increasing understanding of the texts they were reading and better processing of various literary devices we had discussed. Most of all, however, I could see growing self-confidence in reading and writing abilities. As they reflected on their literacy, these students were growing in their ability to monitor their current learning; they were also growing in their ability to project areas where they still wanted to improve.

Insights I gleaned from reading their portfolio entries, as well as specific goals they stated, led to subsequent individual and class discussions, minilessons, and cooperative activities. As a researcher, I was finding that my research questions were being answered affirmatively; as a classroom teacher, I was using the data collected to make daily instructional adjustments based on student need.

Reflections to Parents

Another strategy my students use to communicate growth in reading and writing is to write letters home to parents or guardians at the end of every six-week grading period. In these letters, students tell about what they have read, how they feel they are progressing, and what they like about learning. Usually, parents write back. These letters are wonderful links to the home; they spur parents and children on to talking about books, and they provide an opportunity for parents to see their children's growth in literacy through their writing. Because I attach these letters to individual progress reports that contain all the student's grades, parents receive a good overall picture of how their children are maturing in reading and writing. Examples of students' letters and their parents' responses follow.

This letter from one reading improvement student sums up a novel very well:

Dear Mom:

In reading, I've been reading, *Dear Lovey Hart: I'm Desperate*. At first I thought it was boring, but now it's getting pretty good. It's about this ninth grade girl named Carrie. Carrie is a real quiet girl. She gets picked to be Lovey Hart for her school paper. Of course, she says yes. The thing is she can't tell anyone. It gets real hard. She helps a lot of people and even saved a girl's life that was on drugs. She can only tell this guy named Chip who already knows she's Lovey Hart. Now she's starting to fall in love with him, but her best-friends already in love with him. Now she's the one who needs helpful advice. It's a great book. The other book is or I mean looks pretty good, too, but I haven't got that far in it.

The student's mother wrote back as follows:

Your book sounds interesting; I would like to read it! I know how one can help so many people out then realize that once in awhile you need help too. I wonder who Chip really likes? Thank you for sharing about the book you are reading.

Love, Mom

Later in the year, I received a follow-up letter from the student's mother. It said, in part, "I have enjoyed going over my daughter's books and sharing with her on what she brings home to read."

A written exchange between a second reading improvement student and her mother went this way:

Mom,

Hi! How are you? Well I'm supposed to tell you what I have read. Well this book is called *The Pigman's Legacy*. This book is about a little boy named John. And John tells an adventure about him and a girl named Lorraine. There is another book called *Why So Blue*? Its about a little girl who is always sad. I really don't know that much about this book cause I just started reading it. Well I'll write you back later.

Love, your daughter

Her mother wrote back this way:

Thank you for telling me about the books you are reading. Books can take you to different places. If you read about different topics, you will enjoy your assignments. Let me know how you are doing, or if you need help. Your grade is great—I'm very proud of you! I love you. Mom

In a letter to his mother, a severely learning disabled student had this to say about his reading, writing, and learning:

My three books I read are: *White Fang, Superman*, and *Don't Care High*. *White Fang* is about a white wolf that's in a race during the winter, in Alaska. My reaction on this book was ok. *Superman* is a good book on a man with superpowers. *Don't Care High* is about two kids that are friends. Paul and Jerry are the two boys. Jerry makes it so Paul who is running for student body President gets elected. Paul changes the whole school around. My reaction—exciting.

In reading I have grown in a lot of different ways. One, I've learned how to read faster, and to understand more. I have learned how to listen more. We have read articles on how people dress at other schools, and we have used comparison and contrast with the dress code of their school and our school's dress code. We compared different things like characters and people we know. We have been helped with assignments. Reading is a pretty fun class because it helps me, and because Mrs. J. is a nice teacher.

His mother was clearly pleased with his progress:

It's always nice to hear what is going on in your life outside of home. Furthermore, it is even nicer to hear about your classes in school. I like to know what you do in those eight hours away from me. Thank you for sharing your reading class. Keep up the good work. I'm very proud of you.

Perhaps the best discussion of books occurred between one particular mother and her daughter, an advanced reading student. From this exchange, I learned a great deal about parents and their children as well as a considerable amount about some young adult books. The exchange began with this excellent letter from my student:

Dear Mom,
     During this six weeks I have done a lot of reading! We also did plenty of writing. I would like to share some of the things that I have read with you.
     At the very beginning of the year we read short stories. My favorite one was "Zoo," a science fiction story, by Hoch.
     A little later in the year we were reading a novel assigned to each of us. The novel that I was assigned was *Up a Road Slowly* by Irene Hunt. It was about the troubles of the world, seen through the eyes of a young girl.
     Just recently Mrs. Jongsma started reading *Wolf Rider*, a book by Avi, to us. *Wolf Rider* starts with a prank phone call. The person on the phone said that he killed someone. I am curious about what is going to happen.
     We also read some Young Adult Choices books. The Young Adult Choices book that was my favorite was *Balyet*, by Patricia Wrightson. An aboriginal legend is the reason for all the commotion in this story. But the question is: will the legend repeat itself?
     I hope that during the next six weeks I can read even more than what I read this six weeks.

The mother responded with these words:

I like when we share stories; that way I learn about more books than if I relied only on the ones I read. Science fiction is not one of my favorites although I enjoyed *Future Shock*. Maybe if I read more science fiction I would get to enjoy it.
     My imagination equates *The Zoo* with urban politics. I think I would have liked *Up a Road Slowly*. Seeing the world's troubles through the eyes of a young girl might suggest some novel solutions.
     Reading a story like *Wolf Rider* in segments surely builds up one's curiosity and interest. It reminds me of a "to be continued" episode on television, but better since you can always read the portion you miss for yourself.
     I particularly like stories that are about Australia's original residents. The Aborigines have such interesting legends. What does Balyet mean?
     I, too, have read a fair amount this past six weeks. Much of what I read was technical and focused on my classes. I did read some short stories and one book which I would like to share with you. The title of the book was *The Chosen* by Chaim Potok. The major characters are two fathers and their two sons. Each father has his reasons for the way he chooses to raise his son. The twist comes when the two boys decide what they plan to study and do in life.
     The book is somewhat traditional in its focus—fathers and sons. Yet, it is nontraditional in that at least one father is openly loving and caring throughout the book while the tenderness in the other father finally surfaces near the end of the story. I enjoyed the book, but it made me think how an author might treat such a story which had mothers and daughters for the central characters.

A Positive Experience

Engaging in this piece of classroom research was a positive experience. I learned a great deal from my careful reading of my students' reflective portfolio pieces. I knew so much more about each individual's literacy processes and interests than I had known in previous years. My original research questions were answered—and more. Yes, I learned that students were able to monitor their own literacy, to reflect on their literate activities, and to project their literacy goals. Over the course of the year, dated pieces showed growth in these important areas. If I had any doubt that lower level students could engage in reflective activities, those doubts were erased by actually looking at student papers. I am now firmly convinced of the viability of portfolios as places for student metacognition and reflection, and I've become a strong portfolio advocate. I believe that portfolios work well for students of all ability levels.

For the parents of my students, participating with their children in these literacy reflections was also a positive experience. In their letters to their children and in subsequent conversations with me, parents described the pleasure of corresponding about books and class activities. They commented on how their children's understanding grew. They wrote or spoke about how much they learned about their children's literacy by reading what their children had written. Based on these experiences, I would certainly include reflection to parents as part of future literacy portfolio activities. Writing for parents seems to be a highly motivating activity that encourages strong student reflection and expression.

For students who have experienced difficulties as well as for those who find learning easy, keeping literacy portfolios and reflecting on reading and writing growth appear rewarding. The examples in this chapter, a small sample of the range of student reflections gathered during the year, suggest a growing awareness by students of their competence in literacy and a growing satisfaction at accomplishing literacy goals.

Reference

Atwell, N. (1987). *In the middle: Writing, reading, and learning with adolescents*. Upper Montclair, NJ: Boynton/Cook.

Chapter 16

Into the Woods: The Impact of Prereading Activities

Lee Patton

In addition to teaching English at Douglas County High School in Castle Rock, Colorado, Patton is a writer whose work includes fiction, plays, and poetry. This chapter was written when he served as a resource teacher and mentor in his district.

As I observed a second-year English teacher distribute novels to her eighth graders, I recalled my own practices—or lack of them—in introducing readings to my students over the course of several years of teaching. Like the teacher standing in front of this class, I supplied only a few remarks on the content, a teaser about the plot, favorable reviews from former students, a word about the author and social context, and a schedule for quizzes and chapter discussions.

"I didn't think of any prereading activities or questions," the eighth grade teacher remarked after class. "Should I have?" That's my question, too. Nothing in my training as a literature teacher or in my observations and consultations with colleagues led me to ask it, let alone attempt to answer it. Although reading teachers have used prereading strategies for decades, literature teachers are taught to focus on what happens *after* reading, to be adept at follow-up and agile with close analysis of an already finished reading experience. This is, to us, perfectly logical, of course: of what relevance is a reader's readiness, motivation, and thoughtfulness in the prelude to the prelude? What do these things possibly have to do with the heart of our matter—the interpretation and understanding of a text?

The Bear, the Mole, and Genetics

As a classroom teacher released from teaching to work alongside our district's first- and second-year teachers, I have had a unique chance to explore these questions in a variety of classrooms, primarily with middle and high school English teachers but also with science and social studies teachers. I began with a hunch, formed because of a handful of incidents, that prereading strategies might be far more important than I had previously supposed, and, indeed, might even be crucial.

My first experiment with prereading strategies began with William Faulkner's "The Bear" in an American literature class. This story is widely anthologized because it is one of Faulkner's few self-contained, shorter pieces. And even though the version I traditionally taught was edited (some would say butchered) for student consumption, the majority of my third- and fourth-year high school students still had difficulty with it. My original approach was to sermonize briefly on Faulkner's significance and (daunting) style, give my students the gist of the story's structure, and leave them struggling alone in its Mississippi wilderness of subordinate clauses.

One year I tried something different. I began class by asking, "Have any of you had experiences hunting in the woods?" When several hands, male and female, shot up, I invited each student to comment briefly. This soon evolved into a debate on the moral propriety of killing defenseless animals which, however predictable, was deeply felt and passionate on all sides. After pro and con defined their positions, the central question arose naturally: Beyond the technical

skills involved, is there anything of importance to be learned from a hunting experience? This inspired the most interesting recollections—and reflections. Young men and women spoke spontaneously of tests and perceptions and courage, confidence gained and lost, of moral repulsion and moral victory, and, most of all, of relationships with fathers, elders, and mentors that were enriched—or estranged—by the challenges of hunting.

We spent most of the period in what I've come to call the "emotional activation of prior knowledge," although this kind of discussion is obviously intellectual as well. But had this been nothing more than a time-consuming, random rap session? I had only had a few minutes to comment on the story, pointing out its leaps in time and asking students to think about how Ike, the boy in the story, would answer their own central question. As my students left class with the reading homework, I sat back and realized that we'd just discussed several of the story's key issues with more depth and passion than previous students had done after *finishing* the story. But how, I wondered, would our discussion affect their subsequent comprehension and analysis?

The next day I unconsciously began my research by having the students complete the same quiz as I had given to previous classes. Even though this group had generally performed below the average for the course, their scores were far above their own prior achievement and that of other, brighter groups that had read the story without "emotional activation." So, this approach seems to help in the literal level of understanding, I thought. But how will they perform at higher levels of analysis?

The follow-up discussion was distinctly improved as well. The question about Ike's "learnings" seemed to organize the story into palatable, coherent units for most students, so that they could easily infer how his understanding deepened from age 7 to 11 to 14. Most important, Ike seemed to be one of them, another teenager who had much to learn in the woods, alive behind the exertions and exaltations of Faulkner's prose. Unlike previous students who typically resented Faulkner for the difficulty of his prose, this group accepted his style as part of the challenge. Example by example, question by question, from puzzlement to speculation, most students reexamined the story with a compulsion to understand that was not so different from Ike's own urge to discover.

With this I stumbled on something that would guide my research: Ike's progress in the story provides a metaphor for a more discovery-based, thoughtful approach to teaching and mentoring that I would try to grasp and define. Ike comes to discover that the object of the hunt is not to kill the bear but to appreciate its existence and power in the wild. None of his mentors, who guide Ike's forays into the woods from a watchful distance, tells him this. In the end, Ike's father helps him clarify the possible meanings of his communion with the wild, but always indirectly, with poetry and questions, by thinking aloud with his son.

Exactly what aspect of the wilderness metaphor resonated for my research into prereading? Maybe I was questioning ever more urgently (yet at a "watchful distance") the usefulness of my role as "high priest" charged with interpreting sacred texts. Maybe Ike's long and deliberate opportunity to discover his own meanings served as an imaginative model by raising a crucial question: How did his mentors provide the opportunity so well and completely? Perhaps, I thought, that as a teacher and mentor, I should be more a guide than a high priest,

more a framer of opportunities than an oracle.

I made another discovery when I visited a chemistry class. The teacher had asked me to help her determine the source of some tension she'd sensed: why did the students seem so frustrated by the problems following the assigned chapter on the unit of measurement called the "mole"? Because the students had studied the chapter the previous week, I was surprised when the teacher spent the entire period teaching the assigned chapter as if it were new learning. The students were full of questions as they worked to solve the problems scattered through the reading. Confused by their confusion, I began to question students when they moved into study groups. No student I spoke with had actually "read" the chapter; the standard technique was instead to "jump ahead to the problems at the end of the chapter, then go back to the sample problems in the chapter if there are any we can't solve." Every student regarded as irrelevant the thicket of prose that I had myself spent two hours hacking through; yet I, a slower study in the sciences than most of them, understood the mole, its evolution, purpose, and significance, and had found the class discussion simply redundant.

I asked the students what strategies they had applied to "get ready" for "reading" the chapter. "Strategies? What strategies?" one A student answered, while tearing her incorrect solutions into tiny, angry fragments. "Dude, this is chemistry."

I explained how I'd scanned the chapter for context, skimmed the boldface headings, studied the charts, read the sidebars, and read the chapter summary before reading the chapter itself. The student looked at me as if I were crazy. "The main thing is," she explained, "to concentrate your energy on the problems. And if you can't solve them, that's what she's here for." She pointed to the teacher, who was busy tutoring another frustrated study group.

The teacher's lamentations after class echoed my own: if only the students had some strategies for tackling the dense prose of the chapter, then each one could walk into the problem-solving session prepared for higher level challenges rather than having to puzzle over the basics explained in the reading itself. How many history and biology teachers spend the bulk of class time explaining information already "covered" in chapters no one—student or teacher—seems to expect anyone to "know," even though everyone expects the chapter to have been "read"?

An alternative approach—a possible link between prereading strategies and intrinsic motivation—had been provided by the same teacher in her biology class a few weeks before. With 20 minutes left at the end of the period, she spontaneously introduced the next unit—genetics—by throwing the students questions about the odds their own children might be born with a disability or illness. The students came alive with responses, a controlled and happy chaos of questions, remarks, anecdotes, and puzzling case histories. In the midst of a controversy about genetic propensities, two second-year students at my table thumbed through the next chapter, scanned the boldface headings, captions, photos, and sidebars, and shot up their hands, saying, "The answer's right here, you guys."

Prereading Strategies and the Flow Experience

This prereading session in a biology class and my own students' discussion of "The Bear" are examples of what Csikszentmihalyi (1990) defines as "the flow experience," an animated engagement that "distinguishes enjoyment from the rest of life" (p. 115). By hitting on issues of vital importance in an open, speculative atmosphere, the tenor of the discussion was changed from listless compliance to animated engagement. Csikszentmihalyi indicates that this intrinsically rewarding involvement can make scaling a treacherous cliff, swimming in polar seas, or even reading Faulkner a personal compulsion. With the cooperation of several Douglas County teachers, I set out to trace the impact of prereading strategies, "flow experiences," and activation of prior knowledge on student achievement.

Curious as to whether she could find "hard evidence" of prereading activities' impact on comprehension, Marisue Swindle, a reading teacher at Cresthill Middle School, conducted an experiment with two similar seventh grade reading classes. The first group was asked to read a science chapter on disease and was provided with "during reading" and "after reading" strategies but received no "before reading" activities; the second group was asked to use all three strategies. The results on the same reading comprehension quiz indicated a significant difference in achievement. The second group, which had applied prereading strategies, averaged 5 fewer wrong answers (out of 14 questions) than the first group.

Steve Johnson began his first year at Highlands Ranch High School teaching European history. He quickly discovered that students do not necessarily understand or retain the facts they read in textbooks, synthesize and evaluate what they comprehend, or have a burning desire to read the chapters. Just as quickly, Steve set an ambitious goal for his teaching: he wanted to encourage open, critical thinking about and beyond the "facts" of history.

He became curious about the impact of prereading during the second semester, as the class approached the chapter on the French Revolution. He decided to introduce the unit by using a structured inquiry model in which students formulated questions about a discrepant event—in this case, an absolute monarch's sudden and absolute loss of power. Steve's students spent the period forming ever more focused questions that required them to listen carefully to each other, reevaluate, and reconceptualize as they drew on any shared prior knowledge that was related to French history. Because the period ended before the answer was revealed, several students threatened to find it in the textbook. Some of them actually hung around for a few moments begging for a peek at the chapter. Steve and I heard and overheard positive comments from students on the period's events—comments offered from both extremes of the achievement spectrum.

Results on the unit exam indicated that students' increased motivation improved scores: first semester students, who had read the chapter "cold," scored an average of 75 percent; second semester students scored an average of 82 percent. "But the numbers weren't as important to me," Steve reflected, "as was the change in the atmosphere for learning." Consistent with the idea of the flow experience, Steve's students, having been challenged from the beginning to think creatively, made a more personal connection to the facts of the Revolution. One day I visited the class and found students clamorously debating whether the introduction of the metric system of measurement in August 1793 had had any impact on the chronology of post-revolutionary events. Most striking was Steve's observation that students had an improved "mind-set for thinking and speculation" throughout the

unit, along with his own increased tendency to continue activating this mind-set when he introduced new historical situations and moral dilemmas. In essence, the students were asked to speculate—and sometimes to take a moral stand—at each turn of history, not only learning the facts as they proceeded but internalizing them and their ongoing, dynamic meanings.

Tom Ward, who was teaching Jack London's *The Call of the Wild* at Castle Rock Junior High, wanted to see if writing could both guide analysis while reading and serve as preparation for more focused writing to follow the reading. Tom translated five or six of the novel's major thematic motifs into general topics for students to respond to in personal writings—observations on the impact of greed, for example, the relationship between man and animal, or the survival instinct. Tom felt that these writings and the discussion that ensued led to greater awareness of the themes as they developed in the novel. Because he planned to teach higher level thinking overtly, he had each student trace one particular theme. He found close correspondence between the prewriting, the "envisioning" during reading, and the better-supported thematic analyses his students wrote after they had finished the novel. In the end, Tom concluded that the prewriting activity helped focus his students' exploration of themes.

Gretchen Simons investigated the impact of speculative questions—one concrete, one abstract—prior to introducing her grade 10 students at Ponderosa High School to J.D. Salinger's *Catcher in the Rye*. In open discussion, the students charted their responses to the first question: What has stayed the same since the 1950s and what has changed? Then they were asked to keep in mind the second question—Is it possible to remain sincere in a world that seems to be full of phonies?—as they progressed through the novel. Gretchen felt that the specific responses, while energetic, weren't as important as the tone the questioning process established. In her class, journals were "the way in" to each student's meaning making and, like Tom, Gretchen felt that prereading activities helped focus and enrich written responses. The discussion, for example, echoed through students' journals as they found specific instances of the surprising lack of change in adolescents' concerns over two generations. The second question had larger ramifications. Students wrestled with the paradox of Holden's constant complaints about phoniness and his own "phony" and dishonest behavior, leading several straight to the theme of self-delusion. Most significantly, the students tenaciously traced the theme to the book's end, linking Holden's surrender of the role of "catcher in the rye" to the theme of sincerity. "I think they took the opening question as permission to go on questioning all the way through," Gretchen concluded.

Ann Kitchin, an experienced English teacher at Cresthill Middle School, decided to conduct the most elaborate of the investigations of prereading that I observed. In collaboration with a team of eighth grade teachers, Ann decided to teach the play version of Anne Frank's *The Diary of a Young Girl*. She wanted the students to think about the social and historical implications of antisemitism and prejudice. Since most of her white, suburban students had had little or no direct personal experience of the brutality of discrimination, Ann and a colleague who taught social studies devised a role-playing activity based on the film *Eye of the Storm*. The eighth graders were herded into a room on a pretext, and there came under the direction of a teacher who treated the blue-eyed students to games and snacks while the rest completed worksheets and endured numerous reprimands. Afterward, the students discussed—with considerable passion—the emotions aroused by the unequal treatment. In class a few days later, Ann led a discussion of discrimination as a social phenomenon but drew no overt connections between the eye-color activity and the play prior to the reading.

After the students had finished reading and discussing the play, I distributed a survey to determine whether their reading and understanding of *The Diary* had been affected by the eye-color activity. In response to the question "Did you make any connections to the eye-color activity as you read the play?", 56 students responded in the affirmative and 28 claimed to have made no connection. I say "claimed" because the majority of these 28 students answered later questions in a way that indicated the activity was very much on their minds. Most students affirmed that the eye-color activity helped motivate them to read the play—despite the teacher's having made no explicit connection between the two—including most of those who claimed to have made no connection at all. Most important, 59 of the 84 respondents were able to state how the eye-color activity helped them understand the play's "main ideas and concepts" in personal and emotional terms like these:

- "When we talked about anger and hatred, I remembered the anger most people felt the first day."
- "[The eye-color activity] did help me see the racism on TV and even in my own neighborhood with my black neighbors."
- "Every time [while reading the play] I thought about how people could be so cruel and heartless, I wanted to do something about it."

The student's responses didn't surprise Ann, who concluded that the activity helped "the entire unit go better." Even though she characterized these students as less academically inclined than some of her other students, their achievement on all indicators—especially the unit final exam—was high and the "comfort level" for sharing thoughts and questions was much improved. But the greatest indicator of improvement was the quality of the discussion of the play's themes. "The students were more specific," Ann said, "and their challenges to each other were much more emotion-packed and thoughtful." Questions were more in-depth, written responses more sophisticated. "This year's were so much better," Ann concluded, "that I threw last year's 'best' examples out."

Three Resulting Themes

In my observations of these intensely self-challenging teachers, I saw three recurring themes, each of which connected effective prereading activities to the notion of the flow experience's intense and intrinsically motivating nature. First, questions led to more questions: the activities themselves provided students with a model of a thoughtful, questioning demeanor with which to proceed into reading. The fact that this was confirmed through greater student achievement in classroom after classroom around the district reminded me of how each reader rewrites and renews a text and that the text, in turn, "rewrites" the reader. By engaging students' prior knowledge and encouraging their thinking, we send the message that good reading equals active thinking.

Second, I could not help noticing the number of times I used the word *emotional* when discussing my research, or the number of times I searched for adjectives to describe students' emotions during the discussions I observed. Is a personal, emotional connection a precondition for critical reading? My observation, the students' reactions and achievement, and the teachers' reflections suggest that the answer is yes.

Finally, in several cases the teacher's approach seemed to become more innovative as the reading or unit study proceeded. It was as if the prereading strategy kept on activating new ideas for teaching particular segments. For example, a reading log assignment evolved into a prereading activity for the next scene or chapter; a single prereading question evolved into an inquiry about the historical aftermath of the events described in a particular chapter.

I am going back to teaching literature next year, and as I plan my courses I will begin with these conclusions. Before my students take off downriver with Huck Finn and well before Huck himself lights off for the territories, we will be reflecting on abusive parents, puritanical relatives, the possibility of friendship across age, caste, and race, and any crises of conscience we've wrestled with. Passing out the book will not be the way we start with a novel, it will be one of the ways we continue to proceed.

Reference
Csikszentmihalyi, M. (1990, Spring). Literacy and intrinsic motivation. *Daedalus*, 115.

Chapter 17

Connecting to the Classics

Jeannine S. Hirtle

Hirtle teaches grade 11 at McCullough High School in The Woodlands, Texas, and works as a trainer for the New Jersey Writing Project in Texas. In her teaching she emphasizes the process approach to writing and collaboration in order to establish a rich learning environment.

After years of watching disheartened as my students' eyes glazed over in English class, I decided I needed to do something dramatic to bring classic American literature to life for them. These young adults could not easily relate to Hester Prynne and Arthur Dimmesdale's guilt in *The Scarlet Letter*; they could not identify with Edwards' methods of persuasion in "Sinners in the Hands of an Angry God"; and *The Autobiography of Benjamin Franklin* seemed to them self-serving and meaningless for today's high-tech, fast-paced world. How could I bridge the gap of time and culture? How could I help my students realize that some of the problems these writers tackle are universal and timeless? How could I help them see that literature and the history it reflects are cyclic and that the solutions to the problems we face today may be available to us in the literature of our ancestors?

At the same time I was puzzling over this problem, I discovered Atwell's *In the Middle* (1987b). Atwell's book opened up for me the idea of student ownership of exploration and learning. Her simple system of providing books, choices, time, and opportunities for response made it possible for her students to become personally involved in literature. I began to mull over how to take her ideas and combine them with the essentials of my district's American literature curriculum. Nothing came into focus for me, but I became convinced that I could not go back to directing study questions and handing down assignments. I was miserable with that approach.

Then I read Fulwiler's *The Journal Book* (1987), and something clicked. Through journals or response logs, my students could track their journeys through literature. I went to our school library to search out contemporary novels that matched by genre or theme the classics in the district's curriculum. The students could choose from among these novels and, I hoped, they would make connections between them and the assigned texts. Personal responses could be made in journals or discussions.

The next item on my agenda was to organize how I would bring students together to discuss, question, and argue about the issues raised in both the contemporary and the classic works. Again Atwell offered a suggestion. In "Building a Dining Room Table"(Atwell, 1987a), she describes how she, her husband, and a few friends gather around her dining room table to discuss books. How could I create a similar atmosphere in my classroom? How could I get students to discuss, care, and become involved?

Class discussions in the past had often been dominated by one or two people who had actually done their homework and were outgoing enough—or who felt sorry enough for me—to risk speaking up. I knew this needed to change. A colleague shared with me *Using Discussion to Promote Reading Comprehension* (Alvermann, Dillon, & O'Brien, 1987). The authors define *discus-sion* as differing from simple recitation in three significant ways: (1) participants in a discussion must present multiple points of view and be willing to change their minds; (2) they must interact with one another; and (3) discussions must be more substantive than the typical two- or three-word recitation. I decided to bring discussion into my classroom in the form of a "reading round table." At the outset, to keep discussion alive and interesting, I would give points for questioning, answering, defending, and extending.

I took all these elements—student choice of contemporary literature, assigned classics of American literature, response journals, and seminar-type discussion—and combined them into a program that I hoped would help students connect with literature in a personal way and would lead to an increased level of analytic thinking. Two research questions evolved: (1) How can I facilitate students' engagement in literature and their development of critical thinking? and (2) How does students' writing reflect their engagement and critical thinking?

Methodology

As my research progressed, I decided to organize my description of it around two case studies. This chapter is the result. Bissex (1990) defines *case study* as "a reflective story of the unfolding, over time, of a series of events involving particular individuals.... The researcher includes...intentions and meanings in the meaning she makes of the story and, as interpreter if not also actor, is herself a character in it"(p. 20). That is what I have tried to communicate through these case studies.

The first case study, which focuses on my first research question, describes my own interactions with 120 students in grade 11 in a large suburban high school through one unit of study during the 1989-90 school year. The data sources were my students' responses journals and essays, and my evaluations of them at the close of each instructional unit. The student journals included comments from me, which I wrote regularly—sometimes daily, but most often weekly. I also kept records of my observations, particularly observations of students' participation in discussions.

The second case study attempts to address my second research question by presenting Erin's responses over the course of the year. Because I analyzed her response journals during the summer after school was over for the year, Schon (1983) would call this case study "reflection on action," a sort of reflection after the fact. In this analysis, I tried to discover the developmental changes in her levels of thinking from the beginning of the year to the end. I chose Erin because she was typical of the student who did not personally connect with literature at first. When she began to do so, she made startling progress in critical thinking.

At the beginning and end of the study, I talked with a colleague at a nearby university. Those sessions served to focus my questions and to provide a structure for this report.

What Can I Do?: Case Study #1

I was eager to see how my decision to adopt new instructional methods in my classroom would affect students' response to literature. The instructional cycle, which was repeated in each unit throughout the year, included these elements: an assigned text; choice of a contemporary novel connected to the assigned text; response logs with teacher comments; book talks; seminars; critical analysis papers; and evaluation. I hoped that with these elements I would find at least part of the solution to my first research question: How can I help my students become involved in literature and think critically about what they read? The description that follows is based on what happened during one unit that year and shows what I felt was a successful outcome to my research question.

To help them connect with Nathaniel Hawthorne's classic *The Scarlet Letter*, I had my students select a related novel from a list of contemporary fiction. As they read, they were asked to write their reactions to the novel in their response logs. I gave the students what they thought were minimal and far too general instructions:

> Each time you finish reading a section, jot down your reactions. What you write will be determined by how you respond. Did you especially like or dislike a section? Why? Do you sympathize with a character? Why? Did a section confuse you or impress you? Why? What would you especially like to remember? Do you see a theme emerging? Does anything seem particularly symbolic? Note any words you don't know and look up the definitions. Write any questions you'd like answered.

I was immediately greeted with a barrage of questions: Do you want all of this for each chapter? How many vocabulary words do we have to have? How many pages does each entry have to be? Does spelling count? What about punctuation? How are you going to grade? I was concerned about words such as "do you want," "have to," and "must be," so I again explained that this was a personal process and that each individual would be in the driver's seat when it came to deciding amount, content, and number of vocabulary words. Spelling and punctuation would not count; those skills would be checked only in papers that had been edited and submitted for evaluation. Grades for the journals themselves would be based on effort. Most of my students were suspicious. Some resented the lack of specific guidelines; others were looking for a trick; a few were delighted because they thought the amount of work would be minimal. I urged them to trust me and told them that they were beginning what I hoped would be an exciting journey toward connecting to *The Scarlet Letter*.

The next day I began reading and responding to what the students were writing in their logs. I was dismayed to discover that almost no one responded in a personal or critical way. What I read were pages and pages of summaries. Instead of repeating the instructions to the whole class, I responded by writing questions in the logs. To one student's summary of the episode in which Louie Banks quits the football team in Chris Crutcher's *Running Loose*, I wrote, "Have you ever heard of anyone being intentionally injured in football? What would you do if you were in Louie's position?" That sparked a dialogue, and it opened the door for this student to write more personal comments in his journal.

Not all the students had problems becoming personally involved with their novels. Alisha found many points of connection in Richard Peck's *Close Enough to Touch*. She first related to the theme of loneliness:

> In the book *Close Enough to Touch*, the main character is very close to his girlfriend Dory. They do a lot of things together and they are in love. Then Matt is left alone because of Dory's tragic death. I have never had anybody close to me die, but I can easily relate to Matt. In grade nine I got really close to a boy and I fell in love. Then that summer he moved away. This was really hard for me because we were like best friends. I felt so alone and sad.

She then mentioned an episode from a television show that related to the guilt Matt was experiencing.

During the time Alisha was reading this book and responding to it in her log, a student at our school committed suicide. Alisha's response to this tragedy was played out in her log:

> Matt tells Linda, "Dory's beginning to fade for me. I can't remember her face. Not missing her is about as bad a feeling as missing her. I'm somewhere between grief and guilt."
>
> I can somewhat relate to Matt's guilty feeling, although my situation is much different. When Stan died I sort of felt guilty for not knowing him. I felt guilty for being so happy while he must have been so very unhappy.

Writing these sorts of journal entries about contemporary novels and personal events seemed to help Alisha have a more personal response to the *The Scarlet Letter*. She began to write descriptively about the book in her log and to give her own opinions about Puritan society:

> The people outside the door start saying Hester Prynne should be put to death. The people watch her come out of the prison with a baby. She holds the baby close to her, to hide the letter "A" sewn on her dress. I get the impression that decorations on clothing are not socially accepted. She is wearing the red "A" so that everyone will know what she has done.
>
> Hester is very beautiful and delicate, but she must feel very bad inside. She will be alienated from everyone else because of the scarlet letter. "It had the effect of a spell, taking her out of the ordinary relations with humanity, and enclosing her in a sphere by herself."
>
> Hester had to show herself and the baby to the people. "The unhappy culprit sustained herself as best a

woman might under the heavy weight of unrelenting eyes, all fastened upon her and concentrated on her bosom." Hester must have felt very alone, ailienated [sic] and guilty. She might feel the way I felt when I first moved here. I had no friends and I felt like everyone was judging me. It's not the same exact thing, but maybe she felt the same way.

Alisha was able to transfer the way she responded personally to contemporary novels to her reading of a classic work without any formal lessons.

All the students had been given the same instructions to look for themes from their contemporary novels in the life of Hester Prynne. I encouraged those students who were having trouble making this connection to use a metacognitive strategy: I suggested they go back to an early entry in their log where they had summarized or made an initial comment about a book they were reading. When they found a passage that reflected guilt, alienation, or loneliness, I urged them to make a note in the margin of their response logs and think about those themes in relation to *The Scarlet Letter.*

Kristi was one of the students who complained about the lack of concrete instructions. She did not read for pleasure, but spent hours studying and practicing for the drill team. She was very goal oriented and grade oriented. Following my suggestion, she reread her responses to Ellen White's *Life without Friends,* focusing on the hunt for examples of guilt, loneliness, and alienation. A later journal entry shows her surprise at the personal connections she was able to make:

> First, Beverly shows signs of alienation when she says that everyone only took her father's side. Another example is when she asks her stepmother to leave her alone, Beverly is actually choosing to be alienated from others. Beverly's life in some ways reminds me of a friend of mine. This girl always complains that she had no friends but yet it is like she alienates herself from others by not talking and by always staying home, declining invitations to go out. I'm really enjoying this book because it is so different from any other book I've read.

Analysis of *The Scarlet Letter* was not nearly as difficult for her as it would have been had she not first read and responded to an easier-to-relate-to contemporary novel. She easily found examples of guilt and alienation in this classic, commented on Hawthorne's style, and used metaphor to relate to everyday life. She also challenged and encouraged herself as she read:

> Guilt is shown when Hester is thinking about her deed and the effect it will have on Pearl. The phrase is "She knew that her deed had been evil; she could have no faith, therefore, that its result would be for good. Day after day, she looked fearfully into the child's expanding nature; ever dreading to detect some dark and wild peculiarity, that should correspond with the guiltiness to which she owed her being." Loneliness and alienation are described in the following sentences: "Pearl was a born outcast of the infantile world. She was an example of evil and a product of sin, she had no right among christened infants." This goes back to the beginning of my journal when I described Pearl's friends.
>
> The book is really getting interesting, I love it. However, lots of the description is so confusing. I can handle it because I'm in an Honors class! One way of relating this story to school life would be if you have ever noticed when a teacher yells at a student, everyone turns and stares. This is like the emblem that alienates Hester, however this is done with language.

Seminar Discussion

The next step in my instruction was the seminar. I felt strongly that students should determine the points they wanted to discuss. Romano (1987) says that when "searching people interact in a classroom, ideas spark and learning occurs in countless ways" (p. 176). That's what I wanted our seminars to be: not a time when I talked and the students listened and parroted back my words, but a time for student-generated learning.

I set up the seminar as a graded discussion. Points would be awarded for topics raised, expanded on, answered, or extended; points would be deducted for speaking out of turn, interrupting, or insulting another student. I would participate when I felt something was being missed or neglected, but would try to keep my comments to a minimum.

Our first seminar consisted of a lively discussion. The students raised controversial questions about whether Pearl acted as she did because she was possessed or because of the environment in which she was raised; they argued about the point at which evil overcame Roger Chillingworth. Students dragged out books and journals to support the side they chose.

Discussion at first was dominated by the more extroverted students and it took several attempts for the students to rectify that situation. As a group, we finally decided that body language had a great deal to do with who was being called on. Handwavers, grunters, and people who all but fell out of their chairs seemed to command the most attention. At first I acted as moderator, but in the following days we appointed other moderators. We finally settled on appointing a student to raise the first question and call on people until each point was thoroughly discussed; then that person would call on

someone else to raise the next question, and that second questioner would act as moderator for the discussion that ensued. With this method, we had several moderators and involved more students in the seminar. However, the people who used body language still seemed to gain more than their fair share of attention. It was a problem we resolved to work on.

The response to the seminars was overwhelmingly positive. I was interested in how students felt these discussions compared to traditional teacher-led discussions so I asked them to make subjective evaluations. Julia wrote as follows:

> I have gotten so much more out of the seminars because, especially with a book that is hard to understand, when everyone pulls together and puts in ideas more things and symbols are clearer. Also, I feel like more of an adult in this situation and I think more mature thinking is encouraged with this kind of an atmosphere.

Stephanie said that she liked the seminars much better than questions:

> I have found out a lot more information in this seminar than I could ever learn from a worksheet. Some of these questions would not have even entered my mind without the seminar. I like hearing other people's views on those questions.

On the negative side, students mentioned that there were so many people in the seminar group that they often did not get a chance to comment. Many times what they wanted to say was expressed by someone else before they could be called on. Overall, however, the class and I felt the seminars were a success, and we looked forward to continuing these discussions.

Analytic Papers

The next step for me was to prepare my students for writing analytic papers. I felt students should choose their own topics so they could explore issues that were meaningful to them. As a class we brainstormed for issues or questions that were of interest. Many of the points that were raised had been discussed but not fully resolved in seminars; these were issues that seemed to depend on each reader's interpretation. One of the most popular issues was the question of who had committed the greater sin—Hester and Arthur or Roger Chillingworth. Scott chose this issue for his paper. In it he argued as follows:

> The sin of Chillingworth is far worse than that of Hester or Dimmesdale. He committed not only one sin, but two. His first one was against nature. He committed the first sin the day he married Hester. He knew she didn't love him and that he wasn't the man to marry her. Chillingworth's second sin is far worse than any other one. His sin is the subordination of the heart to the mind. He becomes willing to satisfy his fellow man for his own selfish interests.

Scott chose with this paper to take some risks. He made some assumptions about moral values and degrees of right and wrong. As a reader, I responded emotionally to his sensitive, idealistic assertion that Chillingworth's "subordination of the heart to the mind" was the far greater sin. As a teacher, I was delighted with his personal involvement with this composition. He was actively involved from the beginning to the end in a book that in years past had seemed so dry, sterile, and incomprehensible to students.

Marie also displayed a great depth of understanding and feeling in her analysis of symbols in *The Scarlet Letter*:

> A common object that many people see may mean nothing to most; yet to another person, it may serve as a reminder of his or her most sinful or regretted act. The sight of a playing child brings a smile to most faces along with thoughts of younger, happier days; in Nathaniel Hawthorne's novel, Pearl serves to remind Hester of her shame.... Pearl's attire reminds us of Hester first emerging from prison, when the letter was described as being "surrounded with an elaborate embroidery and fantastic flourishes of gold thread."

Marie clearly demonstrates her analytic skills in this passage. This was made easier for her because of the pool of resources she had available in her response journal. The relationships between the characters in the book and real-life situations that were mentioned in other papers were also inspired by the journals.

Evaluation

Evaluation of these projects was difficult for me in that it was subjective. On one hand, I was the students' biggest cheerleader, urging them to take risks and to believe in themselves; on the other hand, I had to be their evaluator and arrive at some numerical score that would indicate their efforts and performance for six weeks. Evaluation was (and continues to be) agonizing for me. It is difficult to reconcile my two roles and assume them in the classroom when they seem so at odds.

In the end, what I decided to do was give a modified completion grade on response journals. When I saw that a student had genuinely tried to become involved with the novel, I assigned "90-100 percent" as his or her grade and tried to give some type of written evaluation or response to indicate my reaction to the work. For essays, I used a composition profile that allowed for evaluation of content, organization, language use, vocabulary, and mechanics, with the most points available for content and organization.

Grades were generally high—mostly As and Bs. Lower scores occurred when work was turned in late; occasionally students failed to become personally involved with their books and response journals. At the end of the year I discovered that only one person out of 120 consistently showed little effort on his journal; he reported that this was because he was heavily committed to sports and other school subjects on which he placed a higher priority. All in all, I was extremely pleased with what I felt I had helped my students accomplish with my new approach to instruction.

Changes in Students' Writing and Thinking: Case Study #2

After the school year was over, I read pages and pages of the students' response logs to find some patterns. At the beginning of the year, many of the students began simply by recalling what they had read; eventually, with daily probing and encouragement, they progressed to deeper levels of understanding. Erin's progression was typical. Her first response to Cynthia Voigt's *Tell Me If the Lovers Are Losers* was simply a report of what she had read:

> It is about three girls who are attending Stanton Hall College. Neither knows the other and they find each other drastically different. Niki is energetic, loud, obnoxious, vulgar, and speaks her mind. She's very athletic and competitive. Hildy is serene, wise, and genuine. She is very sure of herself and intelligent about the world. Ann is a prep-good student, who searches to find herself, after given doubts by Niki. The three of them try to get along to make the

year go by faster, but can't see how they'll stand the next.

Erin analyzed little about her response to the book and did not share any personal association she may have made. Her responses followed this pattern for the next two books she read, *The Scarlet Letter* and *The Luckiest Girl* by Beverly Cleary. In writing about her fourth book, however, Erin showed that her responses were increasing in complexity. She analyzed and evaluated Sherwood Anderson's style in *A Storyteller's Story*:

> Overall I was disappointed in the author's style of writing. The book didn't hold my attention. It was hard for me to follow when he'd attempt to explain his ideas.... It is interesting in fact to note how such a dreamer and sightseer would evolve into a storyteller. He enjoyed the many chances and opportunities life had to offer. He fully indulged in this enjoyment of life and I'm sure this wealth of knowledge is visible in his art of storytelling. Not everyone finds it easy to talk their thoughts or even write what they are feeling. He's an extraordinary author who has accomplished and achieved what he's set to do, that's the extent.

This particular response involved some risk-taking on Erin's part. She stepped out of her familiar role of reporter and moved into the role of critic. This was a big step because, in her mind, that role had been reserved for writers of literary tomes in the library (or, in some cases, for teachers). Even though she felt a negative reaction to this author and his style, she was compelled to conclude with something positive. Her motives at this time, I felt, were a desire to please the teacher and, even more, to find something good to say about a published work.

Although Erin had started to evaluate what she was reading, her responses to the next book, *Unexpected Death*, still did not reveal any personal connection. I commented in her journal, "Great summaries, but for your continued growth as a critical writer/thinker/reader try to make personal comments and connections." Her critical comments increased with each book, but it wasn't until I wrote another note in her journal that I finally succeeded in eliciting this personal comment from Erin:

> In my last book, *Going Hollywood* by Marion Schulz, you write in a margin "how did I get interested in this book? Write back; let me know." Honestly, I chose this book at random, I had no idea it would pertain so closely to me. The reason I can relate so easily is because my parents are also divorced. The anticipation Mr. Todd felt for Christel and Polly's arrival is the same I see in my own father's face when I visit him.... I am not able to see my dad as often as I like and when our time together is up, and I have to go home, it's harder to say goodbye, because we know it'll be a long time till we see each other again.... Christie and Polly were fortunate to have a stepfather constantly around in their childhood, and to have loved him so much.

I was gratified by that tremendous personal connection and by the trust Erin revealed in me. I felt three factors contributed to this: first, this book presented a situation with which she was familiar; second, she was used to responding since this was the 15th book she had written about in her log; third, I had personalized my written comments to her.

That particular response was written in early March. From that point, Erin's journal revealed strong personal connections and high-level critical thinking skills. She

adopted a completely different tone, one that revealed confidence in her opinions. This was apparent in one response to *The Great Gatsby*, in which she compared the lifestyles of characters in East and West Egg to lifestyles in communities with which she was familiar. In later responses, Erin analyzed a section of the novel in her search for the author's overall purpose in writing this work:

> This meeting with Daisy will surely lead to the downfall of Daisy and Tom's marriage. I suspect Fitzgerald's overall theme of the book is definitely money and prosperity. I wonder why there's so much emphasis on this throughout. It's sad 'cause you see how hippocritical [*sic*] the wealthy are and then just look around [this town]—it's the same type of society.

Again she made a personal association based on a connection to the novel, and she applied a theme in the novel to her own experiences.

Erin became more deeply involved with books as the year drew to a close. She connected particularly strongly with Richard Wright's *Black Boy*, a book she chose to read during our African-American literature unit. It was clear to me that Erin (and, indeed, almost all of my students) had responded as I'd hoped to my new approach to instruction. She had succeeded in doing what students in previous years to my great disappointment had not: becoming personally involved in reading classic works of literature. This personal connection seemed not only to heighten enjoyment of reading, but to lead to the development of critical thinking skills.

Making a Personal Connection

I found that when students were led into a response-based study of classic literature with novels that were developmentally appropriate and appealing to them, they became capable of transferring insights and methods of response and analysis to their reading of the more difficult literature. Through response logs, students were given a place to verbalize and develop their thoughts. The act of writing helped them reflect on their reading and, ultimately, draw on higher level skills to make personal connections and comments. When students participated in the open, supportive environment of the seminar discussions, they were able to try out their opinions, theories, concerns, and questions. This, in turn, contributed to their growth as critical thinkers and built a base of thought processes that they could transfer to formal analytic writing.

Rosenblatt (1984) writes, "All the student's knowledge about literary history, about authors and periods and literary types, will be so much useless baggage if he has not been led primarily to seek in literature a vital personal experience" (p. 59) That vital personal experience had been missing in my classroom. By undertaking a research project to uncover and work to supply that missing piece, we were all able to learn from and connect to literature in new and exciting ways.

References

Alvermann, D., Dillon, D., & O'Brien, D. (1987). *Using discussion to promote reading comprehension.* Newark, DE: International Reading Association.

Atwell, N. (1987a). Building a dining room table: Dialogue journals about reading. In T. Fulwiler (Ed.), *The journal book.* Portsmouth, NH: Heinemann.

Atwell, N. (1987b). *In the middle: Writing, reading, and learning with adolescents.* Portsmouth, NH: Heinemann.

Bissex, G. (1990). Small is beautiful: Case study as appropriate methodology for teacher research. In D. Daiker & M. Morenberg (Eds.), *The writing teacher as researcher.* Portsmouth, NH: Heinemann.

Fulwiler, T. (Ed.). (1987). *The journal book.* Portsmouth, NH: Heinemann.

Romano, T. (1987). *Clearing the way.* Portsmouth, NH: Heinemann.

Rosenblatt, L. (1984). Literature as exploration. In R. Probst (Ed.), *Response and analysis: Teaching literature in junior and senior high school.* Portsmouth, NH: Heinemann.

Schon, D. (1983). *The reflective practioner.* New York: Basic.

Chapter 18

Teacher and Student Perceptions of the Value of the Computer for Writing

Mari M. McLean and
Christine M. Gibson

McLean, who wrote this article, and Gibson, who was the subject of the study it describes, are teachers in the Columbus (Ohio) Public Schools; McLean is also an adjunct assistant professor in the College of Education at The Ohio State University. Both are concerned with the issues facing teachers and students in today's urban schools.

C hris and I have been colleagues on the faculty of an urban public school and students in the same reading education program for several years. We also share an interest in the challenge of getting at-risk high school students to achieve at least some level of success in reading and writing. It seemed that in both Chris's English classes and in my Developmental Reading classes, students who rarely showed any inclination to read or write became especially motivated to write when word-processing programs and computers were available. We were interested in why these at-risk students had such a marked preference for writing with the computer rather than with pencil and paper, so we set out to conduct a study in Chris's "Writers' Workshop" (Atwell, 1987) course.

The Study

Writers' Workshop was designed to give grade 11 and 12 students who had failed one or more semesters of composition an opportunity to earn the composition credit required for graduation. At the time of the study, 28 students were enrolled in the class. These students had a history of failure in several high school subjects, and the majority had been characterized by the school personnel as having discipline and attendance problems. The class was racially mixed, and a third of the students were female.

Students divided their time between a regular classroom and the computer room next door. For each writing assignment, half the students worked with computers and half with pencil and paper in the classroom. New assignments were given approximately every two weeks and at that point students switched writing tools. Chris divided her time between the two groups.

Data for this study were collected over a 10-week period through observations, unstructured and structured interviews (modeled on Fetterman, 1989) with Chris and with selected students, and two whole-class surveys. Although I was the principal investigator and made most of the initial decisions about data collection, Chris and I were full collaborators on this study. We analyzed the data together and made joint decisions about how to proceed in light of our analysis. Our observations were made from two perspectives—that of teacher and that of general observer—and we designed the two surveys together. We had frequent professional conversations to discuss what we saw emerging from our research.

During the first month, observations of students working in the computer room were interspersed with interviews with Chris regarding her perceptions of the role of computers in the writing process of at-risk students. When the first writing assignment was completed, I conducted a formal interview with one student who had written the assignment with the computer and a second who had used pencil and paper. An unexpected finding from this interview was that the student who had written with pencil and paper had done significantly more content

revision (three complete drafts) than the student who had used the computer. The latter made only a few minor text changes involving single words or short phrases, despite his expressed enthusiasm for the ease of editing the computer afforded him.

Several days later, I conducted a structured interview with Chris regarding her beliefs and perceptions about at-risk students, the teacher's role in working with the students, the writing process, and the usefulness of computers as a writing tool. During the interview, Chris's own enthusiasm for writing with the computer was apparent, and she clearly believed that her students shared her enthusiasm.

After students had completed four assignments, Chris conducted unstructured interviews with three students whom our observations seemed to indicate favored writing at a computer. We wanted to know what it was about using the computer that motivated them in their writing. Contrary to our expectations and to what Chris had confidently stated to be true of at-risk students, two students expressed a clear preference for writing with pencil and paper.

Based on beliefs and perceptions that emerged from the various interviews, Chris and I developed a survey to be administered to all Writers' Workshop students. We were especially interested in whether other students shared a distinct preference for paper and pencil. If many did, that would signal that we may have misinterpreted the behavior we had observed not only in Writers' Workshop students, but in other students as well. In order to ensure that students would respond to each question with a level of agreement or disagreement, we used a 4-point rather than a 5-point Likert scale to eliminate the noncommittal middle response. The survey also allowed space for comments on each question.

Results

In interviews and conversation, Chris repeatedly stated her conviction (a conviction I shared) that the computer is a powerful tool for motivating at-risk students to write. Her feeling was that computers "take away the drudgery of writing by hand" and that students definitely prefer computer writing to pencil and paper writing. Since students often wrote longer compositions when they used a computer, Chris was convinced that using computers helped them "think about an idea." Other advantages to computer writing that Chris believed motivated students were the neatness of the resulting product, and the ease and speed of writing and revising it made possible.

Chris believed that the best thing about computer writing was that students seemed more willing to share their work with one another when they used a computer: "They talk to each other about their writing in the computer room, instead of always asking me.... When they're writing in the classroom, they're always asking me to read their stuff, but they hardly ever talk to each other. In the computer room, they hardly talk to me!" Chris seeks to establish in her classes a community in which she facilitates, rather than dispenses, learning. Consequently, she values peer collaboration; she believes that using computers promotes this.

Chris is a popular teacher and is especially effective at motivating at-risk students. In Writers' Workshop there were students who had failed other writing courses because they would not write, but who now wrote without complaint. There were students who posed discipline problems for other teachers, but who attended Writers' Workshop regularly, participated in discussions, turned in assignments, and were attentive, pleasant, and respectful. Chris modestly believed that it was the computers that motivated her students to write and to see themselves as writers.

The information we gained from our unstructured interviews with students provided our first signal that all of these perceptions might be wrong, that some students did not actually prefer writing with computers. The results of the survey, shown in the figure on the next page, seemed to show that our beliefs about the usefulness and popularity of the computer as a writing tool were indeed wrong. (However, it is important to note that due to absenteeism, only 20 of the 28 Writers' Workshop students took the survey.)

The survey did seem to confirm two of Chris's beliefs about computer writing. First, in comments accompanying survey questions 8, 10, and 11, students agreed that neatness was an advantage of using computers and that this neatness aided in editing because it allowed them to see mistakes more clearly. Twelve out of 20 students thought it was easier to draft and revise with a computer, although examination of one student's composition showed little evidence of editing or revision. (The phenomenon of students believing they were doing more editing and revising on computers than was actually the case is also noted in Hawisher, 1987, and in Daiute, 1986.)

Implications of the Research

The original intent of our study was to examine what it was about using the computer that led to positive attitudes toward writing among students who had failed previous composition courses. Our initial observations of Writers' Workshop seemed to bear out observations that Chris and I had made in other classrooms about the motivational effect of the computer for at-risk students. We had observed students writing without

The Survey

The following instructions and sample question show how the survey was conducted:

Instructions

For each statement, circle the one number that best matches how strongly you agree or disagree. 1 indicates that you agree *strongly*; 4 indicates that you disagree *strongly*.

Sample Question

1. When I work at the computer, I think better.

1 — agree strongly
2 — agree
3 — disagree
4 — disagree strongly

The Responses

1. When I work at the computer, I think better.

0 — agree strongly
5 — agree
9 — disagree
6 — disagree strongly

2. I am a good typist.

2 — agree strongly
8 — agree
5 — disagree
5 — disagree strongly

3. The computer limits my thinking.

4 — agree strongly
10 — agree
4 — disagree
2 — disagree strongly

4. For me, one disadvantage of writing at a computer is that I can't keep my work private.

3 — agree strongly
6 — agree
9 — disagree
2 — disagree strongly

5. I think the computer room is quieter than the classroom.

9 — agree strongly
4 — agree
2 — disagree
5 — disagree strongly

6. Writing with pencil and paper is boring.

2 — agree strongly
3 — agree
11 — disagree
4 — disagree strongly

7. I would rather write all of my papers using pencil and paper.

8 — agree strongly
7 — agree
4 — disagree
1 — disagree strongly

8. I would rather write all of my papers using a computer.

1 — agree strongly
6 — agree
7 — disagree
6 — disagree strongly

9. It is harder to draft and revise with a computer than it is with pencil and paper.

2 — agree strongly
6 — agree
8 — disagree
4 — disagree strongly

10. Writing with a computer makes me feel like a good student.

0 — agree strongly
9 — agree
8 — disagree
3 — disagree strongly

11. The computer helps me with my writing.

1 — agree strongly
6 — agree
9 — disagree
4 — disagree strongly

12. I write the same amount whether I use a computer or a pencil and paper.

2 — agree strongly
7 — agree
6 — disagree
5 — disagree strongly

13. I like to write.

5 — agree strongly
7 — agree
4 — disagree
3 — disagree strongly

complaint and with little prodding for entire 40-minute class periods, day after day. They expressed little if any frustration or dissatisfaction with either the assignments or the technology. Several instances of collaboration were observed. There seemed to be compelling evidence that Writers' Workshop students had all the positive attitudes toward writing with computers that we believed they had. The students' responses to the survey, however, showed us that we had some misperceptions. A surprising number of students did not, in fact, regard the computer as a valuable tool for writing and thinking. Many felt that pencil and paper were not only sufficient, but preferable for writing.

While it is tempting to conclude from the evidence that these at-risk students have a negative attitude toward the computer as a writing tool, we feel that limitations in the survey would make such a conclusion inadvisable. A number of factors should be taken into consideration when looking at these results. Poor keyboarding skills might be one reason for some of these negative responses, although admittedly most of these students have taken one semester of keyboarding; one student who expressed a preference for writing with pencil and paper had "strongly agree" to the statement "I am a good typist." Other factors that might have affected individual responses to the survey include (1) experience and comfort with technology, (2) the length of a writing assignment, (3) tendency to revise *any* writing, and (4) age and sex. Finally, the meaning of some terms may not have been clear: at least two students assumed that "think," for example, had to do with maintaining concentration rather than with developing and processing an idea.

The fact does remain, however, that students did not demonstrate an over-whelmingly positive attitude toward the use of the computer. One explanation might be that students disliked the lack of privacy they experienced: writing on a computer screen cannot be as easily concealed as writing on a piece of paper. This point was raised by two students during the interviews, and on the survey, nine students agreed or strongly agreed that lack of privacy was a disadvantage to writing with the computer. Self-consciousness is an attribute of this age group. Elkind (1984) says that the belief in the existence of an audience interested in everything that they do is characteristic of teenagers.

As we reflected on our results we kept coming back to the same question: *why* did students give the appearance of interacting positively with computers if they were not? The answer may have less to do with the appeal of technology than it does with students' appreciation for a teacher who supports the use of such technology as a learning tool. It may be that Chris's students would have written willingly for her anywhere, anytime, with any tool that she required because they were convinced she was interested in their ideas and that they could trust her to support, guide, and encourage their efforts.

Before school systems invest large amounts of money in computers with the hope that they will be a sort of educational cure-all, they need to seriously consider the role of the teacher in maximizing the effectiveness of technology in the classroom. A computer remains a gimmick of only momentary usefulness in the hands of an uninspiring teacher but becomes a truly effective and valuable learning tool—especially for promoting creative writing—in the hands of a masterful and supportive teacher.

References

Atwell, N. (1987). *In the middle: Writing, reading, and learning with adolescents*. Portsmouth, NH: Heinemann.

Dauite, C. (1986). Physical and cognitive factors in revising: Insights from studies with computers. *Research in the Teaching of English, 20*, 141-159.

Elkind, B. (1984). *All grown up and no place to go: Teenagers in crisis*. Reading, MA: Addison-Wesley.

Fetterman, D.M. (1989). *Ethnography step by step*. Newbury Park, CA: Sage.

Hawisher, G. (1987). The effects of word-processing on revision strategies of college freshmen. *Research in the Teaching of English, 21*, 145-160.

Part Four

Teacher Educators Are Researchers

Chapter 19

Teacher Research for Teacher Educators

Kathy G. Short

Short, who served as editor of this section of *Teachers Are Researchers*, teaches in the Department of Language, Reading, and Culture at the University of Arizona in Tucson. Her research interests include collaborative learning, children's literature, reader response at the elementary level, and professional development for teachers and principals.

Teacher educators are often involved in creating theories about education through their research and writing. While this research usually has as its ultimate goal the improvement of learning and teaching, it has focused almost exclusively on elementary, middle, and secondary school contexts; rarely have teacher educators directed their research and resulting theory at their own teaching in college classrooms (Wittrock, 1986). Teacher educators who do research in their own classrooms offer the profession both a different perspective on the learning environments of preservice and inservice teachers and a way to transform those environments.

Research undertaken at the university level has focused primarily on college students' behavior from a process-product paradigm of research that correlates teacher behaviors (process), with student achievements and attitudes (products) (Shulman, 1986). The teacher's experiences and perspectives are usually not examined beyond a description of that teacher's "treatment" for a particular group of students. Ironically, this research, which excludes the teacher's perspective, is often conducted by a researcher who is also the teacher involved in the study.

While teacher research has gained popularity in the last several years, the vast majority of that research has been conducted by elementary and secondary teachers (Cochran-Smith & Lytle, 1990). It is important to note that teacher research can add a new perspective about teaching and learning for *college* educators because it asks them to examine their own teaching and its implications for themselves as well as for the broader educational field. Teacher research at this and all levels needs to go beyond the examination of student learning to encourage critical reflection on the researcher's own beliefs and practices. For college teachers this involves taking a reflective stance on their own teaching in order to conduct planned, systematic inquiry aimed at examining and improving both teaching and learning in their own classrooms.

It is ironic that people who have been seen as competent researchers in other educators' classrooms have experienced difficulty in having the research they have conducted in their own classrooms accepted by the academic community. This community has excluded the perspectives of teachers at all levels from the research it considers valuable (Cochran-Smith & Lytle, 1990). This is particularly unfortunate because different types of research reveal different areas of interest, perspectives on problems, and aspects of events that together can only add to the depth of our understanding about teaching and learning (Shulman, 1986). Teacher research is not intended to replace other ways of researching but to provide the field with another perspective that will contribute to our knowledge base about education.

In addition, teacher research at the college level will help college educators to grasp more fully the potential of the theories and frameworks being implemented in public schools for transforming their own teacher-education programs and classrooms. While reading teachers have been moving toward interactive and transactional models of literacy learning (Harste, 1985), college classrooms have, for the most part, remained organized around transmission models. Teacher educators teach in a system of isolated and fragmented courses, passing on knowledge about teaching to frequently passive students. Many teacher educators seem to expect preservice and inservice teachers to teach on the basis of new models even though they operate their own classrooms on the old. While new perspectives on language and learning have affected *what* is taught in teacher-education programs, they are only just beginning to influence *how* that content is taught and learned. Teacher educators must start to explore ways to put their theories about others' teaching into practice in their own. Teacher research can play an important role in this process.

Constraints in the College Context

Teacher researchers at the college level face the task of reconsidering their beliefs within a context full of obstacles to change (Short & Burke, 1989). These constraints must be examined and transformed as teacher educators undertake research aimed at making their teaching reflect what they teach. The college classroom, for example, rarely encourages active engagement in or reflection on learning. Teacher educators primarily *talk* about reading, writing, learning, and teaching rather than actually involving learners in those experiences. One reason for this is that the usual college schedule does not allow the large blocks of time needed for reading, writing, and exploring ideas with others. Students are rarely asked or given time to reflect on their own learning processes, and their reflections on the content they are expected to learn often consists only of examining whether their answers match the professor's. Yet we know that learning is initiated by the learner's desire to understand, a desire that is not fulfilled when teacher educators set the agenda for their students with textbooks, syllabi, and tests. Learners often come out of teacher-education programs without a sense of themselves as educational decision makers. They have learned to rely on outside experts and prepackaged sets of ideas.

Learning involves a search for connections across experiences, perspectives, and people that will help learners make sense of the world (Harste, Woodward, & Burke, 1984). Both undergraduate and graduate teacher-education programs still consist primarily of distinct courses in which students are presented with isolated pieces of information, theories, and practices that are rarely connected to their own lives or to actual classrooms. Furthermore, students are expected to think in terms of "right" and "wrong" answers within those courses; the ambiguity that exists everywhere in the real world is artificially removed from the college classroom. Students are not encouraged to become risk-takers who live with the ambiguity and tension of knowing they must act on their current knowledge while realizing that these understandings are incomplete.

We know that real learning occurs within the complexity of learners' understanding about the past, present, and future, not through an orderly, prearranged sequence that focuses on one topic or idea at a time (Spiro, 1989). The very structure of most college programs keeps students from bringing a variety of perspectives and questions from different disciplines to the same topic and from interacting with others to find new ways of looking at things. Learning is a social process that is made more powerful when learners are encouraged to interact and think with others. Learners in college classrooms rarely feel that they are part of a collaborative community, either in terms of their own classmates or of the larger teaching profession.

Any learning environment—including that of a college classroom—must allow learners to be actively engaged in learning, to observe other learners around them, and to make connections to the demonstrations most important to them as learners (Harste, Woodward, & Burke, 1984). In teacher-education programs, students are seldom able to learn from observing their classmates or their teachers. Teacher educators rarely present or view themselves as learners because they focus on telling, not doing. Because class assignments are designed to elicit only predetermined "right" answers rather than encouraging open-ended discussion, collaborative learning is further discouraged.

Teaching and Learning through Teacher Research

The constraints found in most teacher-education programs have created a situation wherein *what* teacher educators teach is contradicted by *how* they teach it. Despite these constraints, some teacher educators are now attempting to "live" their theories and are using teacher research to understand what is happening in their classrooms. These teachers have begun applying insights from theory, research, and practice across teacher-education programs (Short & Burke, 1989). Some educators have modified the curricula of already existing courses; others have redesigned courses or entire programs; still others have focused on establishing more effective university-school collaborative projects and inservice programs.

In this section, teacher researchers share efforts such as these, all of which were designed to create more powerful learning environments for preservice and inservice teachers. In the first three chapters, teacher researchers explore the use of different types of learning logs or journals to understand how these logs can affect student learning and inform their teaching. Diane Stephens and Kathryn Meyer Reimer examine the use of dialogue journals in a reading practicum. While Stephens and her students all considered the journals to be an important part of the course, she wanted to look more closely at whether the journals were actually helping students become "reflective practitioners" (Schon, 1983). Because the students in the class were involved in practicum experiences, the relationship between journals and teaching practices could be investigated.

Laura Heichel and Tristan Miller were also interested in whether dialogue journals help teachers become more reflective, but they explored their questions with students who were preservice teachers. The dialogue journal kept by Miller, a student teacher, and Heichel, a university supervisor, is examined from both their perspectives to document the changes each experienced. Their article reflects the multiple perspectives that can emerge when students are research partners rather than research subjects.

Sharon Lee and Nancy Zuercher examine the dialogue between undergraduate students in two courses who exchanged journals. Their chapter on this exchange between students in different disciplines—education and English—focuses on writing as a tool for learning, the value of authentic audiences for writing, and the ways in which the journal exchanges did and did not extend student learning.

The next two chapters involve broader research on the broader learning environment and on course design. Kathryn Mitchell Pierce was concerned about creating a more powerful learning environment. Her research examines graduate students' approaches to inquiry and collaboration in small-group projects, with her own journal, student course evaluations, student reflection logs, and student and group self-evaluation serving as data sources. Ellen Brinkley was interested in knowing if her undergraduate students' attitudes toward writing and the teaching of writing would change, and, if so, why. To explore her questions, she examined the design of her writing methods course, collected data on students' responses to the course, and administered several surveys to determine students' attitudes toward writing and teaching.

In each of these studies, the questions asked by the teacher researchers grew out of their day-to-day professional experiences. They wanted to find out whether specific practices were effective and how to create more powerful learning environments. They were also concerned with broader questions of learning and teaching. They wanted to understand the "why" behind what went on in their classrooms and so planned systematic inquiries that would help them develop new ideas about both practice and theory. They share their ideas in these chapters, while at the same time showing other educators possibilities for conducting teacher research in their own classrooms.

While these articles are strong examples of teacher research at the college level, they also highlight the need for further investigation. Dialogue journals, for example, are only one type of tool now being introduced in college classrooms; others—such as literature circles, text sets, presentations in a variety of sign systems, expert projects, and self-evaluations—need further research. Research is also needed to investigate the effectiveness of new courses and programs and the collaborative projects currently being undertaken by universities and schools.

A wide variety of reforms in teacher education is currently under consideration. Teacher research offers teacher educators one powerful way to influence these reforms. Unless the reforms lead to ways of teaching and researching that are shaped by what we know about learning at all levels, they will be short-lived. Teachers and students both need learning environments that encourage active inquiry on questions that are significant to their lives. Teacher research can help us begin to establish those environments not only in our schools, but also in our colleges and universities.

References

Cochran-Smith, M., & Lytle, S. (1990). Research on teaching and teacher research. *Educational Researcher, 19*(2), 2-11.

Harste, J. (1985). Portrait of a new paradigm. In A. Crismore (Ed.), *Landscapes: A state-of-the-art assessment of reading comprehension research*. Bloomington, IN: Indiana University Press.

Harste, J., Woodward, V., & Burke, C. (1984). *Language stories and literacy lessons*. Portsmouth, NH: Heinemann.

Schon, D.A. (1983). *The reflective practitioner*. New York: Basic.

Short, K., & Burke, C. (1989). New potentials for teacher education: Teaching and learning as inquiry. *Elementary School Journal, 90*(2), 193-206.

Shulman, L. (1986). Paradigms and research programs in the study of teaching. In M.C. Wittrock (Ed.), *Handbook of research on teaching* (3rd ed.). New York: Macmillan.

Spiro, R. (1989). Knowledge acquisition for application. In B.C. Britton (Ed.), *Executive control processes*. Hillsdale, NJ: Erlbaum.

Wittrock, M.C. (1986). *Handbook of research on teaching* (3rd ed.). New York: Macmillan.

Chapter 20

Explorations in Reflective Practice

Diane Stephens and
Kathryn Meyer Reimer

Stephens teaches language and literacy
courses at the University of Hawaii-
Manoa. Her research interests include
university-public school collaborative efforts and assessment that informs instruction and teachers' learning. Reimer
teaches at Goshen College in Goshen,
Indiana, where she studies students' and
teachers' responses to and use of multiethnic literature, the use of literature in
reading instruction, and preservice
teacher development.

Every semester, I* ask
students in my reading methods courses to
write to me in dialogue journals. This en-
ables me to hear about how things are going
for each student; it helps me get to know the
students better and earlier. I consider the
journals an important part of the teaching-
learning process. The exchanges give me an
opportunity to address questions and concerns that individual students have and to
teach through my responses. Indeed, many
in-class discussions are continuations of
conversations begun in the journals. I hope
students learn through the journals that response is an important and valuable part of
teaching. I also hope that they see how their
own teaching can be informed by what they
learn from their students.

My students seem to share my positive
feelings about dialogue journals. They say
they like having an opportunity to "talk"
with me on a regular basis about particular
questions and concerns and to think on paper. As one student explained, "I've never
taken the time to write in a journal (part of

*Throughout this chapter, "I" refers to the first au-
thor; "we" refers to both authors.

my bad attitude toward writing) but in only two days of our dialogue journal, I can see a need for reflection on each day in class and on the readings."

Despite these positive responses, I began to wonder if the dialogue journals and other parts of my teaching were really helpful to my students as teachers. Liking the journals and knowing that the students liked them was pleasant and comfortable and informed my teaching, but I began to wonder if what I was doing in class really accomplished anything. I was supposed to be teaching students how to teach reading. Was I? Did taking my class help them become better reading teachers?

I was particularly concerned about my role relative to helping teachers become "reflective practitioners" (Schon, 1983). In various ways, educators have been calling on teachers to reflect on their practices, to engage in action research, and otherwise to function as decision-makers in their classrooms (see, for example, Bissex & Bullock, 1987; Calderhead, 1988; Dillon, 1987; Goswami & Stillman, 1987; Hansen, Newkirk, & Graves, 1985; Lester & Mayher, 1987; Newkirk & Atwell, 1986; Newman, 1987; Noffke & Brennan, 1988).

I agreed with these educators and with Schon's view that being reflective was a critical feature of being a professional, but I wasn't sure if my courses were really helpful. The dialogue journals did provide an opportunity for reflection; so did several other elements of the course. In these activities, I encouraged students to think through issues and to use what we were learning from one experience in another. But were opportunity and encouragement enough? Was I really helping students become informed, reflective decision-makers?

One of the classes I had been teaching was a five-week summer reading practicum.

As part of the class, teachers worked one-on-one with a student who was having reading difficulties and kept records of their interactions with and understanding of that child. The teachers, all of whom were working toward master's degrees, also had written to me regularly in dialogue journals. I wondered if examining those records would help me understand more about my effectiveness and determine whether these students were better reading teachers and more reflective practitioners at the end of the course than they had been at the beginning.

Reviewing the Literature

Kathryn Meyer Reimer joined me in pursuing answers to these questions. We began by reviewing the literature on dialogue journals. Staton (1983, p.6) argues that dialogue journals provide an opportunity for "the acquisition of reasoning and self-knowledge," but we found no evidence to support her claim. Most of the research on dialogue journals involved elementary and high school students and focused on developing writing competence; we found four interesting studies about the use of dialogue journals at the college level, but none examined Staton's assertion. Barbour and Holmes's (1987) content analysis of preservice teachers' dialogue journals showed that these students spent more time thinking about the affective aspects of teaching than the cognitive aspects. Yinger and Clark (1985) found that journal writing was a valuable planning and teaching tool for many teachers. Bixby (1989) concluded that students used six distinct modes of discussion in their journals: recording, conversing, reflecting, working through problems, deciding, and adopting a different stance to understand their experience from a different perspective. Newman (1988) reported that journals were useful for helping teachers understand language and learn about their role. None of these studies focused on change over time or considered the relationships between the responses in the dialogue journals and teaching practices.

We next looked at research on teacher change but found no studies in which reflection was related to teaching. Ross (1989), for example, examined "theory to practice" papers students had written over the course of one semester and found that there was no significant change in the preservice teachers' reflections on their reading and writing. Krogh and Crewes (1989) examined the nature and mode of student teachers' thoughts in their journals. At the end of each of two consecutive semesters there were changes in the frequency of certain responses but no clearly established pattern of responses.

It seemed that researchers had not collected the kind of data that would allow them to make connections between reflection and teaching practices. However, with dialogue journals and instructional records, we felt we had some access to what teachers were thinking about during the practicum and to what they were thinking about and doing with their case study child. We decided to look systematically at these sources of data to try to discover the relationship between teachers' reflections and their teaching practices, and how this relationship changed over time.

Analyzing the Data

To get permission to use the dialogue journals and instructional records, we wrote to the teachers and the parents of children involved in two summer practicum courses. Some teachers did not want their dialogue journals made public; some parents preferred that their children's records not be used. We ended up with permission to use 13 complete sets of data—5 from one summer (out of a possible 8) and 8 (of 15) from the next.

We began by transcribing and reading the dialogue journals to get a sense of what teachers had written and to begin to identify ways to handle the data. As we read and reread the journals, we became aware that there were both considerable similarities and differences among the writers and decided that categorizing the content of each remark would help us better understand what we were seeing. Our intent was not to impose categories on the data but to see if a categorization system would emerge from the data to help us understand the similarities and differences we were noticing.

Line by line, remark by remark, we—together and independently—noted what was discussed and began to see categories of responses. Once all the statements had been categorized (see Figure 1 for the categories we used), we began to look closely at the relationships among categories. Patterns in and between teachers' written response style and their approach to working with their case study subjects started to become apparent.

We then began reading and developing a coding system for the instructional records, which in this course were kept on sequential, ongoing "Hypothesis-Test" (H-T) sheets. In the first column of the H-T sheet, teachers were asked to state the questions or hypotheses that drove each tutoring session. In column two, headed "Curricular Decision," teachers listed the activities they had planned for the day that addressed their hypotheses. Under "Observations" teachers recorded what they saw happening during the instructional session, and, in column four, "Interpretation," teachers stated what they believed were the implications of their observations. Revised questions or hy-

Figure 1
Categories of Journal Entries

These codes were used to label the remarks made in dialogue journals.

1. Text related: comments related to course readings
   (a) summarizes text content
   (b) comments on text content
   (c) connects reading to the child she or he is tutoring
   (d) connects reading to her or his own classroom, previous experience, or anticipated experience
2. Teaching
   (a) tells—recounts events that happened in teaching
   (b) observes—comments on occurrences or interactions while teaching
   (c) interprets—analyzes child's abilities or makes judgments about activities or child's abilities
   (d) hypothesizes—raises possibilities
   (e) instructs—shares/reveals instructional decisions
3. Planning
   (a) discusses plans based on observation of the child
   (b) discusses plans determined independently of the tutoring session
4. Self as learner
   (a) projects uneasiness or confidence
   (b) provides background information about training or experiences
   (c) reflects on personal learning process
   (d) reflects on knowledge about reading or assessment
5. Talk about...
   (a) class—includes references to issues or topics discussed in class, reflections on comments made in class, and questions or comments about class procedure or expectations
   (b) the journal as a tool for thinking, reflection, questioning, or commenting
   (c) assessment used with children
6. Procedural comments or questions
7. Asides not related to the course

potheses were then entered in column one for the next day's session. In order to identify patterns in this data, we coded all comments as hypothesis (H), curricular decision (CD), observation (O), interpretation (I), statement (S), conclusion (C), or question (Q). These codes were used independent of the placement of the remark on the sheet. For example, the remark "At first Melissa saw no purpose for writing the letters on the cards, but when we began the game she saw the reason why the letters needed to match on the set of cards" was coded I, even though the teacher had placed the remark in the Observations column of the H-T sheet. Our analysis of this data source suggested that teachers' response style and approach to the case study experience in these documents was consistent with the patterns we had noted in the dialogue journals.

Response Style

The written responses of 4 of the 13 teachers were in a style, which we called "discrete," characterized by a simple telling about different experiences—texts read, experiences with the case study child, choices made, and so on. The following excerpts from Jessica's and Margaret's journals are representative of the entries they made over the five weeks, and of this response style:

> Reading *What Matters?* Easy, interesting, entertaining and yet informative reading. Nice illustrative examples. *(Jessica)*

> Seeing for ourselves...I really dislike reading about what teachers have done as research. It goes back to a U of Wisconsin course in which one text was full of research notes—BORING! See, I didn't even look in the book (just like the kids!)! I used to be in research projects and know how subjects are chosen or left out. I also do better when I can hear about them first hand and can ask questions. *(Margaret)*

Teachers with this response style often commented on what they were reading—as Jessica did—or answered questions that I had asked. Here, Margaret answered a question I had asked about the books she chose.

Teachers with the discrete response style also tended to focus in their journals on describing what had happened that day with the case study child. On the fifth day of teaching, for example, Margaret described what had happened that day with Steve:

> Steve seemed to get really involved yesterday. It wasn't until 1:25 that he wanted to play—he had been working through his tasks until then. He asked to make popcorn for today since one of the other lab kids did so yesterday and we missed out sharing it because we were in the library.

When we coded all the comments Margaret made that day in her journal, we found that the majority of her remarks (58 percent) "told" about what happened with the case study child, with the remaining remarks falling into six separate categories. This pattern held for all the teachers with a discrete response style.

We also noticed that teachers with a discrete response style made few explicit connections between observations of the child, hypotheses about the child's difficulties, and teaching plans. For example, in one journal entry, Jessica wrote as follows: "Handwriting was very frustrating for Melissa today. Most of our reading is shared by reading words together or by sharing pages. To be successful she really needs the very easy books." Neither this entry nor previous entries included observational data that would support Jessica's interpretation ("Handwriting was very frustrating for Melissa today") or her conclusion ("To be successful she really needs the very easy books"). Jessica did not provide any other information about or rationale for her current teaching plan ("reading words together" or "sharing pages"). In addition, Jessica did not make links between the three statements, leaving us uncertain about how the statements were related.

Similarly, teachers with this response style did not make explicit the relationship among comments on their H-T sheets. In particular, it was frequently unclear how the hypotheses, which were intended to be the rationale for the activities planned, were related to the activities, and how the observations and interpretations linked back to the hypotheses. For example, on Margaret's H-T sheet for day five (shown in Figure 2) there were no activities that "tested out" the questions Margaret had about Steve's knowledge of environmental print, and there seemed to be no observations that could lead Margaret to decide that Steve saw "little reading at home." Similarly, while Margaret described what Steve did with the books, only the third interpretation seemed to be related to this activity-

Figure 2
Margaret's H-T Sheet for Day Five

Hypotheses	Curricular Decisions	Observations	Interpretations
1. Besides suggesting we play, will Steve begin to make suggestions about reading and writing?		1. S/S relations "game"—I make sound, he says letter.	1. Beginning to take risks (changed picture).
2. What does he really know about books?		2. *Very Busy Spider*—repeated idea "She was very busy spinning her web." Did pick up on by second page.	2. Unsure of all s/s relations.
3. Will he need pictures to support comprehension?		3. Counts pages in book—chooses if short.	3. May not have comprehension, but done orally so may need picture support.
4. How can we help him see the value in reading?		4. Says sister reads to him but he'd rather play; also, Mom reads at home but said she's the only one (and reads catalogs).	4. Sees little reading done at home so probably doesn't see purpose (value).
5. What relationship does he see (understand) between oral and written language?		5. *Rosie the Hen Went for a Walk*—did not recognize the goat. At end of story only repeated parts where we'd looked at pictures (flour mill, bee hives) a lot.	5. May know general concept that there are "words" as put line between OR.
6. What environmental print does he know—McD's, cereals, etc.?		6. Worked 45 minutes then wanted to play. Taught me to play "Go Fish"—tie game.	6. Doesn't space between words so teacher inserted lines which Steve feels is part of writing.
		7. Read one more book—*The Tree House*. He picked up on pattern by second page and read with me. Mom says he says he's tired when he doesn't want to work. I ignored it today, he only said it once.	7. May know language.
		8. Drawing: started as his puppy "Sandy" (my idea). Asked if the head looked like a head, the body like a body. Added stripes to the body as "some dogs have stripes" then changed it to a *buttle bee*. Later said *bumble bee* (spelled Brttl B). Drew line between words.	
		9. Asks for help in spelling—I sound out words for him.	

Reflective Practice

observation-question sequence, although none of the observations seemed to support this interpretation.

We categorized the written responses of the other nine teachers as "intertextual." These teachers made explicit connections between themselves and the professor, between themselves and the case study child, among books and articles, and among past, present, and anticipated teaching experiences. An excerpt from Kristine's journal is representative of this response style:

> About the Newman and Toomes articles, you asked what specifically I found useful? Well both of these articles have altered my beliefs and strategies in working with students in content areas of reading. For instance, it seems so much less important that students read correctly word for word than for them to get the meaning from what they read. (Seems simple, huh? Not to me.) I found it useful to read how both articles drew particular conclusions about children's reading abilities based on their oral reading. For instance, the ability to identify what strategies children use in reading seems to be so useful. Yet this is something I had never heard before. When you think about it, we have strategies for studying (I realized this) and for writing (I realized this), but I had never thought to look at reading that way. Probably an avoidance of something I knew so little about. I think perhaps that is one of the greatest things I will take from these articles and this class—the confidence to address children's reading problems and help them to deal with them.

These teachers often commented on how an assigned reading affected or changed their ideas, as Geri does in this excerpt:

> I finished Calkins. Enjoyed it but am anxious to get on with Atwell to see how to set up a writing workshop and how to bring grades into this. I did like the way the teachers cooperated in Calkins—do hope I can have a similar experience with any coworkers at my school. It's really exciting to think about setting this up for my fifth graders. It will take them a while to get used to my new feelings about teaching. They may think I'm "nuts" when I tell them that their spelling is not important on drafts!

They also frequently talked about themselves as learners and used their learning experiences to help with their teaching, as shown in this excerpt from Elizabeth's journal:

> As I monitor my own reading behavior—especially when reading out loud with Sara—I noticed that I substitute or rearrange phrases (as I would say them)—not surprising. Can I point that out by asking if she noticed it? Explaining that it's O.K. with me and for her, too! Boy, this is complicated!
>
> As I think about today, it feels good to write it out. I am a very tactile learner and thinker. (Maybe Sara is too?)

Teachers with an intertextual response style spent far more time reflecting on their practice or on themselves as learners than telling about their teaching activities. For teachers with a discrete response style, it was just the opposite. A comparison of Margaret's and Elizabeth's day-five journal entries illustrates this. While 58 percent of Margaret's remarks for that day told about her teaching (as discussed previously), Elizabeth's were more evenly divided, with 38 percent related to herself, 20 percent telling about teaching, 12 percent related to course readings, and the remainder falling in the other four categories.

On their H-T sheets, teachers with an intertextual response style frequently made explicit links between hypotheses, curricular decisions, observations, and interpretations of the children's behavior, sometimes even drawing arrows to highlight the connections. Of the 268 connections Elizabeth made on her H-T sheets over the course of the practicum, for example, only 12 were between two areas (activities to observations); the remainder were links made from hypotheses to curricular decisions to observations to interpretations and on to a new or revised set of hypotheses. Elizabeth's H-T sheet for day five (shown in Figure 3) is representative of her entries and of the entries of others with this response style.

Approach to Task

From our analysis of the data, we identified two distinct ways teachers approached the case study experience: they either wanted to "fix" the child or to investigate the problem. Some teachers looked for what was wrong with their case study child and quickly drew conclusions about what the child could not do. Fairly early in the course, for example, four of the teachers drew conclusions about their students. On day one, Geri noted, "Brett has no knowledge about many of his letter recognitions. It's no wonder he is so poor in spelling and also reading some words.... I think his problems are mostly in writing, not reading." On day two, Margaret concluded that Steve had "no book sense" and that he needed "to focus on initial sounds when writing." On the same day, Jo decided that Samuel would not do tasks that required "stopping to think and plan." By the next day, Jessica had concluded that Melissa "still doesn't take risks involving reading independently...still doesn't have an interest in reading books in the lab...still does not seem to be sure of her own ideas

when it comes to writing them down independently."

Once teachers came to these kinds of conclusions, they focused their attention on "fixing" the problem. Geri began day two by asking Brett to "write some words I call out.... Read back what has been written and circle the mistakes." Margaret decided to try to get Steve to dictate stories but have him write the first letter of each word. Jo asked Samuel to do tasks that required the use of a diagram because she believed he needed activities that made use of "planning without obvious use of reading." Jessica took the position that if Melissa felt confident and successful, all would be well:

> Just looking at Melissa come through the door this morning I could tell that she was very proud of her cooking venture with her mom. The success is exactly what Melissa needs to encourage her in reading adventures....
>
> She wrote a shopping list today. She also understood that print in recipes was precise and that you needed to follow the directions. With the finished product, Melissa beamed with pride. High success really gets her going.

Nine of the other teachers took this investigative stance with their case study children. Elizabeth's remarks suggested that she wanted to find out what was causing problems for Sara and then use that information to help Sara improve her own reading:

> Nonattending to auditory stimuli:
> - is because of current hearing loss?
> - results in missed key instructional sequences during documented hearing losses?
> - contributes to inability to react correctly to complex conversation? or
> - is an established behavior pattern due to past inadequacies?

Figure 3
Elizabeth's H-T Sheet for Day 5

Hypotheses	Curricular Decisions	Observations	Interpretations
• Seems to look at difficult words as isolated stimuli—not linking it semantically with anything she's encountered before or within the context.	• *Check mail* for input on tie-dying from others.	• Mom came in with Tylenol for Jennie to take for an earache. Doctor's appointment today. She said she had had earaches for a long time. We talked about her hearing later today with her mom. She is getting her hearing checked. Seemed to be something that set off a "light bulb."	• History of ear infections and hearing loss may be answer to our questions regarding nonattending, lack of some phonetic decoding strategies, ill-at-ease behavior when lots of auditory stimuli around her.
• Not attending to auditory stimuli due to:	• *Read* Chapter 2—*Lion, Witch...* make sure to ask open-ended questions regarding interpretation of ideas, understanding of words, how ideas link with the story.		
•Physical difficulties?		• Checked our mail—read letter from Kate—cursive with rather difficult words. Read well, no errors.	• Evidence she did not really finish book and did not really enjoy it.
•Tuning out due to screening overload?	• *Share thoughts* on our weekend reading.	• Discussed books read over the weekend. She had not brought her book. She read her favorite part of *The Beast...*knew a part she liked beforehand, but chose the first paragraph to read to me. I chose the part about Matthew teaching him to spell. She got excited about the idea—obviously a new one to her. (She had read the book before.)	• Did not feel comfortable scanning for section—copped out and chose easy first page.
•Socially appropriate in her mind?	• *Ask her to read* her favorite part to me, give thoughts on story, how well written, who would enjoy this book.		• Strategy written about was a new idea? She got all turned on by the idea? Did not view this as teaching.
• Is non-risk-taking in recreational reading due to lack of commitment to reading for information or fun?	• Have her show me how to make origami frog.		• Evidence that she did not understand this part or did not really comprehend what they were doing or did not really read it.
• Only reads when required.	• Write out the steps to model my thoughts. Watch for her conceptualization of the steps.	• Looked through the craft book on tie-dying. Did not see any real information we could use that was new.	
• Has difficulty scanning to find main points on general organization.	• Plan for future tie-dying. Share my book and plan for next shirt. Watch for scanning techniques.	• Listened with Jim and Jennie regarding his interview for tie-dying. Jenny was very quiet, would not talk or comment.	• Tie-dying craft book was confusing and technical. Layout only interpreted the pictures' organization.
• Spelling strategies seem to be visual/shape of some words.	• Where does she get her clues?	• She showed how to make origami frog and opened up to the old Jennie. She dictated steps and wrote. Very clear steps and wording for directions.	• Very competent on things she does and participates in (hands-on). Difficult steps, extremely clear in her head.
• Phoneme/grapheme association in production weak.	• Ask mom about hearing.	• Jennie volunteered to take the tie-dying instructions home and recopy for the scrapbook. She also picked a book to take (a much harder one—third grade level) to continue our rating activity.	• Wants the book to be ours. Still committed to idea. Knew what we needed to do.
		She remembered to write her name and book on the checkout sheet (I had forgotten).	• Was this for me or will she really read this one? Will it be too hard?
		• She had written me a note—points of importance—very structured, well written ideas. Mixed up sentence constructions. Spelling together/SC (togethre); (agian) again/uncorr. Had my notes as a guide, as some book titles were repeated and spelled correctly.	• Don't think Mom helped. Cares about what I'd think. Wrote with her thought-flow. Not conscious of written print requirements in this instance (OK on note form).
			• Feels comfortable with me and will take social risks with me.

168   Stephens & Reimer

Seven-year-old Loreal frequently behaved in a way that made it difficult for Amy, her tutor, to proceed. In spite of these difficulties, Amy still consistently based her curricular decisions and interpretations on Loreal's verbal and nonverbal cues:

> Didn't want to write...perhaps writing itself is hard? Perhaps not motivated? Perhaps not interesting? Perhaps used to having others do it? Perhaps doesn't have strategies?

Indeed, Amy began keeping records of and thoughts about Loreal's behavior in order to better understand how to help her. On her H-T sheets, Amy included questions about Loreal's fear of being wrong, her lack of confidence, her nightmares and fantasies, and the violent stories she told.

Judith's work with Dan provides a third example of this investigative approach. Dan, a 12-year-old who was reading several years below grade level, had been labeled as having an attention deficit disorder. School records also indicated he could not follow through on tasks. Judith spent several days exploring what Dan could do and documenting the conditions under which he paid attention. Her intent was to understand Dan as a learner and then to design an instructional program that would help him be successful.

Teachers with this investigative approach to the case study experience did not draw conclusions about their student until fairly late in the semester, and when they did, they (1) left a "paper trail" of observations and interpretations that supported their conclusions, and (2) used their findings to design what they considered to be appropriate interventions. It was not until the last week of instruction, for example, that Elizabeth concluded that Sara had a history of hearing problems; it was not until the third week that Amy talked to Loreal's par-

ents about seeing a social worker. During the same week, Judith decided that Dan needed "to develop strategies for planning and dealing with difficulties." She had come to understand that Dan lost interest when he felt overwhelmed, but when he had a plan for managing what he wanted to do and had strategies for coping when things became difficult, he could succeed at the task. Under those conditions, the behavior that had caused some teachers to decide he had a "deficit" simply disappeared.

The Relationship between Response Style and Approach to Task

Our data suggest that teachers with an intertextual response style tended to take an investigatory stance, while those with a discrete response style tended to want to fix the child. The teachers enrolled in the practicum who had an intertextual response style made and tested hypotheses until they uncovered information about their case study child—information that was genuinely useful for making instructional recommendations to the parent and to the school. The teachers with a discrete response style often ended the five-week course knowing little more about their students than they had at the beginning. Elizabeth, for example, who had an intertextual response style, eventually found out that Sara had had a succession of ear infections that had not been reported or treated and concluded that many of her reading difficulties were related to hearing loss. On the other hand, at the end of five weeks Jessica, who had a discrete response style, reported information to Melissa's parent that paralleled the school's findings and were nearly identical to the remarks she had made to the instructor during the first week of class.

Based on these findings, we concluded that teachers who had a more intertextual response style were more effective at helping children with their reading difficulties. As a result of investigating hypotheses, these teachers learned new information that was useful for helping children progress in reading.

Answering Some Questions, Asking Others

We began this study with questions about the success of my teaching. I had wanted to know if I was helping my students become better teachers: Were they learning to better understand a child as a reader? Were they becoming more reflective? Our analysis of the data led to no definite answers but rather to partial answers and new questions.

We did find, as noted above, that over the five weeks of the course, having an intertextual response style was related to doing a "better" job with the case study task. We concluded from this that the course was helpful for those people who had that response style. We are not sure what this finding means or whether it is entirely accurate. Our data were limited. It is not clear if those teachers with discrete styles would have made more progress with their students had they had longer than five weeks in which to work with them. Furthermore, we categorized teachers through their writing, and the 13 teachers were not equally comfortable with writing as a mode of communication or reflection. It may be that our data revealed only the learning of teachers who wrote easily and quickly. If so, it is clear that different types of data would be needed to access the learning of all the teachers. It could also be argued that the teachers with an intertextual response style might have done just as good a job without the course.

We also wonder if our conclusion would be valid across all the courses I teach or across all courses taught in the same manner. If so, could it be generally true that people with different response styles benefit more from particular types of instruction and curricula? What type of curricula could be devised that would help all students become "better" at understanding children as readers?

I had also asked if teachers became more reflective over the five weeks of my course. Our data show that response style was consistent across the five weeks. We could find no evidence that the class, the dialogue journals, or the experiences with the case study children affected response style. This finding raised three concerns for us. First, we wonder if we would have seen changes had I used a different response style. I tended to respond to the points that the teachers made with affirming comments and then tried to "nudge" their thinking along by asking questions or suggesting further reading. Would we have seen changes in response style over time if my own response style had been different?

The second concern was alluded to earlier. We had only written texts—dialogue journals and instructional records—and we knew that some teachers were less comfortable with writing than were others. For instance, Margaret noted that she used the journal only to record initial responses:

> I found a journal was a good way initially to respond to ideas and events, but was not an effective way for me to develop a detailed analysis of the total picture. For me, a journal is talk in a stream of consciousness format, with the depth usually reserved for face-to-face meetings at a later time when all of the ideas have been fitted together into a cohesive whole. Therefore, I probably did not show the depth of understanding in my writing that had occurred within my brain. Synthesis occurs in such ways

that are difficult (or impossible) or too lengthy for me to convey in writing. My ideas exceed the speed of pen or processor and continue in a flux of fine-tuning through discussions with others and through continued readings.

Third, we know that shortness of the course affected what people wrote about and, indeed, what they thought about. One teacher, for example, kept her journal for a month after the course ended, and in so doing, provided a glimpse into the course's "aftermath." In her last entry of that month, she talked about her teaching experiences and synthesized new ideas from the course with her former practices and with what she hoped to accomplish in the future. In so doing, she appeared to make more intertextual ties than she had during the course. Her entries suggested that her thinking and learning did not end with the class and called attention to the fact that, in this study, we used only what teachers wrote during the course.

In order to better understand the relationship between what is learned in courses and what happens in practice, we would like to explore other ways of examining reflective teaching practice (interviews, observations, self-reports) over longer periods.

As is evident from the preceding few paragraphs, we ended this study with more questions than when we began. We did learn that some teachers made explicit links among all the experiences of the five-week course and that these teachers were better able to uncover new information about their case study children. We have begun to wonder, though, about other ways teachers might reveal what they have learned through experience. It could be argued that "reflective practice" is revealed in writing by the making of connections among experiences and by the making and testing of hypotheses about those connections. But how else can "reflective practice" be accessed? How else can it be defined?

We also learned that teachers with an intertextual response style appeared to learn more in the course than did those with a discrete response style. We are left wondering how to best meet the needs of all students.

Finally, we wonder about the current emphasis on "reflective practice." Many educators seem to have decided that reflective practice makes for better teachers. But do we know that? And, if so, just what is it that these teachers are "better" at? Our study indicates that teachers with an intertextual response style are better at quickly generating new information about students. But how important is this ability, particularly given that teachers almost always have longer than five weeks in which to work with students? Are there other abilities that are more important? If so, how do we identify those abilities and document success in them? If teachers should also be encouraged to see themselves as learners, how should pre- and inservice teacher-education classes be changed to accomplish this goal? And, once we have that figured out, how will we know if we have been successful?

This study represents the beginning of one attempt to answer those kinds of questions in one classroom in one course at one time. To answer these questions fully will require many studies in many classrooms. Those of us who teach, both in universities and in schools, will need to examine the effectiveness of our practices. What makes a "good" teacher? What does "better" mean? Are there similarities between doing a "good" job in a university course and doing a "good" job in the public school classroom?

Rather than providing the answers, our findings from this study suggest that if our goal is the professionalization of our field, we need to understand much more abut the teaching and learning processes. We also are coming to believe that we are going to need more than one course or set of courses, no matter how good or how long they may be, if we are truly going to achieve that goal.

References

Barbour, C., & Holmes, E.W. (1987). *Using journals and interviews to study the induction process of beginning teachers* (Rep. No. SP-028-565). Baltimore, MD: Towson State University. (ED 278 655)

Bissex, G., & Bullock, R. (Eds.). (1987). *Seeing for ourselves: Case study research by teachers of writing*. Portsmouth, NH: Heinemann.

Bixby, M. (1989). *Descriptive inquiry into pre-service journal keeping for teacher educators*. Unpublished doctoral dissertation, University of Missouri-Columbia, Columbia, MO.

Calderhead, J. (1988, April). *Reflective teaching and teacher education*. Paper presented at the annual meeting of the American Education Research Association, New Orleans, LA.

Dillon, D. (1987). Teachers learning. *Language Arts, 64*, 707-709.

Goswami, D., & Stillman, P. (Eds.). (1987). *Reclaiming the classroom: Teacher research as an agency for change*. Upper Montclair, NJ: Boynton Cook.

Hansen, J., Newkirk, T., & Graves, D. (1985). *Breaking ground: Teachers relate reading and writing in the elementary school*. Portsmouth, NH: Heinemann.

Krogh, S.L., & Crewes, R. (1989, March). *Determinants of reflectivity in student teachers' reflective reports*. Paper presented at the annual meeting of the American Educational Research Association, San Francisco, CA.

Lester, N., & Mayher, J. (1987). Critical professional inquiry. *English Education, 19*, 198-209.

Newkirk, T., & Atwell, N. (1986). *Understanding writing: Ways of observing, learning, and teaching*. Portsmouth, NH: Heinemann.

Newman, J. (1987). Learning to teach by uncovering our assumptions. *Language Arts, 64*, 727-737.

Newman, J. (1988). Sharing journals: Conversational mirrors for seeing ourselves as learners, writers, and teachers. *English Education, 20*, 131-156.

Noffke, S., & Brennan, M. (1988, April). *Reflection in student teaching: The place of data in action research*. Paper presented at the annual meeting of the American Education Research Association, New Orleans, LA.

Ross, D.D. (1989). First steps in developing a reflective approach. *Journal of Teacher Education, 40*(2), 22-30.

Schon, D.A. (1983). *The reflective practitioner*. New York: Basic.

Staton, J. (1983). *Dialogue journals: A new tool for teaching communication*. (ED 227 701)

Yinger, R., & Clark, C. (1985). *Using personal documents to study teacher thinking* (Rep. No. SP 026 230; Occasional Paper No. 84). East Lansing, MI: Michigan State University, Institute for Research on Teaching.

Chapter 21

The Importance of Reflection in Decision-Making

Laura G. Heichel and Tristan M. Miller

Heichel, who died before this book could be published, supervised and taught student teachers at The Ohio State University in Columbus, Ohio. She was a doctoral student in reading and language arts. Miller, who was Heichel's student, now teaches sixth grade at Hilliard Station School in Hilliard, Ohio. She is currently pursuing her master's degree in educational theory and practice at Ohio State.

We* are two educators, one a veteran teacher at the university level and the other a novice teacher who was enrolled in her course, who believe that teachers are professionals who should take an active role in educational change. Logic dictates that positive changes are based on perceptive, responsible decisions, grounded in theory and practice and tailored to meet the needs of the community. Sound decisions are clearly at the heart of educational reform.

Teachers need to be a dynamic part of the decision-making process within the profession rather than accepting the status quo without critique. One way teachers can become involved in change is to act as "reflective practitioners" (Schon, 1987), professionals who think about their actions and the consequences of those actions. Reflective practitioners examine their own practices in an effort to improve their teaching; they also know that teaching necessarily involves individual values, beliefs, and assumptions. Any call for educational reform should

---

*In the opening section of this article, "we" refers to both authors; "I" refers to the first author.

therefore carry with it the practical knowledge that reflective teachers have about their profession along with a clear understanding of the potential ethical, moral, and sociopolitical implications of that reform. Through a process of reflection and thoughtful decision-making, then, teachers can contribute to change that will result in more informed practice for the whole profession. As noted by Zeichner and Liston (1987):

> Learning, for both pupils and teachers, is greater and deeper when teachers are encouraged to exercise their judgment about the content and processes of their work and to give some direction to the shape of schools as educational environments (p. 24).

Many teacher-education programs, including the one that brought us together, have now implemented curricula that encourage their students to engage in reflection. As part of Tristan's 10-week student teaching experience, she was required to maintain a reflective journal. Her writing became for her a vehicle for thought, and Tristan found herself questioning her original beliefs and assumptions about teaching, children, and common school practices. I found that my own thinking about teaching was changing because of the use of reflective journals by the preservice teachers I was supervising. At the end of the student teaching experience Tristan and I joined together to investigate this change process. We were both interested primarily in how the journal might have contributed to Tristan's professional growth. After many hours of discussion we chose to focus on these three questions:

- How has journal writing helped us learn about teaching?
- How do journals indicate growth in student teachers' ability to reflect?

- What role do supervisors' comments in journals play in helping student teachers learn about teaching?

Student teachers' journals have been the focus of other studies. Bolin (1988) suggests that reflective journals can be a key to helping student teachers develop their own ideas about the teaching profession and their roles in it. Armaline and Hoover (1989) note that the student teachers involved in their study were better able to examine their own belief systems through journal writing. Key characteristics of these studies include analyses of the student teachers' journals and interviews between student and supervisor. Generally, findings from such research indicate that journal writing can be helpful in focusing student teachers' thinking.

We wished to focus on how journal writing might help student teachers become more informed about their practices. In addition, we hoped to gain insight on how supervisors can improve their practice by learning to use student teachers' journals more effectively.

Our Early Perceptions

Gitlin states that research involving data collected from preservice teachers "for the most part silences those studied, ignores their personal knowledge, and strengthens the assumptions that researchers are the producers of knowledge" (1990, p. 444). Because we believe this statement to be true, we chose to work together to analyze Tristan's professional growth with particular emphasis on how this growth was displayed in her journal. First we developed these questions for Tristan:

- Has the journal helped or hindered your thinking?

- Would changes have occurred in your thinking had you not kept the journal?
- Did you think there were definite right answers in teaching? Do you think so now?
- When you reread your journal, did your feelings about what you wrote change and, if they did, which feelings changed and why?
- How did you use the journal to learn about and reflect on teaching?

Then we came up with questions for me:

- How can journals be used more effectively as a means of assessment?
- How do journals change supervisors' views of their students?
- What can supervisors do to help student teachers maintain a high level of critical thinking about teaching?

A Student Teacher's Perspective

I [Tristan] began by giving considerable thought to the questions Laura and I had discussed. Because our inquiry required responses primarily from me, I knew I needed to clarify my thoughts and ideas. At the outset of my student teaching, I thought that there were certain practices and ways of dealing with children that applied in every situation. For example, I thought that if a child did not complete an assignment, the teacher should reprimand him or her and possibly begin deducting points after several missed assignments. Now I no longer think that there are right and wrong answers. In fact, my greatest frustration has come in learning that almost everything in teaching changes from day to day, that what is right one day may be wrong the next. For example, a child may miss an assignment for many reasons—a problem at home, illness,

defiance, forgetfulness, lack of comprehension—and these reasons may change for the same child from one occurrence to the next. A teacher's assignments and expectations may therefore need to be adjusted and readjusted for each child.

I think that many prospective teachers begin their student teaching believing in right and wrong answers. After all, our own elementary and high school teachers usually taught us that only one answer was right. Even the television game shows we watched as children taught us that every question had only one correct, prize-winning answer. I, and many of my colleagues, began student teaching with the aim of becoming "perfect" teachers who always had the right answers. We were disheartened when we learned this teacher was an illusion.

I think the journal was definitely instrumental in my growth process as a teacher and for my learning about teaching. My goal was no longer to become this nonexistent "super teacher," but to be the best teacher I could be. I believe that some changes would still have occurred in my thinking had I not written in a journal because my experiences would have remained the same, but the journal helped more changes occur more easily. Writing down my thoughts and troubles forced me to address them in a more complex manner. Instead of losing track of my thinking about an issue because of the day-to-day demands of my teaching assignment, I could refer to my original thoughts time and time again because I had written them down. Often while writing I would find one thought leading to another, and so, over time, I could note the progression in my thinking.

Being able to "see" my thoughts in this way helped me make changes in my teaching. For example, the children's scores on one test I gave were low, and my initial reaction to this was to bell-curve the scores up a bit. When I reread my journal entries about my teaching of the unit on which the test was based, I found myself coming up with a better solution: to review the material in class, allow those who had done poorly to retake the test, and average both test scores. I gained tremendous confidence from knowing that, through this writing process, I had used my ability to reflect on and solve problems in an actual classroom setting.

Although I could recall the feelings I had when I wrote in my journal, my reactions to the situations changed when I reread it. These reactions changed because I had changed, and I knew that I would not handle some of the situations I had described in the same way or hold the same expectations for my students. For example, one of my students lashed out at me after I had reprimanded him. His behavior hurt me deeply, for I had spent considerable time helping him with various assignments. On four occasions, I wrote in my journal about the situation and what I could do about it. Rereading my journal after that student teaching assignment had ended, I could still remember all my hurt and confused feelings and all the questions I had had at the time; yet I did not feel as hurt as I had previously. I was much less emotional and more able to reflect calmly as I considered the actions I had taken at the time and how I would react if a similar situation should occur in the future.

This situation illustrates how I used the journal as a means of expressing my feelings about significant occurrences at school. The process of writing helped me reflect and learn. In writing, I had time to think deeply as my hand caught up with my mind. I often became carried away with what I was contemplating and gradually, after many journal entries, I began to think

more critically. I gained a broader perspective and created possible solutions to my problems instead of expressing feelings. I did not make a conscious attempt to learn to reflect; it was through my writing that I became more reflective about the children in my classroom and my role in preparing them for the future.

Throughout this process I often found that I had more questions than answers, and Laura helped me examine my thoughts further. For example, in one entry I assumed that a student's failure to complete assignments was due to laziness. Laura wrote beside that entry, "What other reason could exist? Is he bored?" This question made me wonder if the real problem was with the student or with a failure on my part to excite him about learning. I then tried to improve my teaching by experimenting with a variety of methods to stimulate him. Laura wanted me not only to think about my students' needs, but about my own needs as well. What was I learning and how could I continue to grow? She wanted me to question myself, and her comments let me know that it was okay to take risks and try new things in order to develop as a professional.

Most important, just the fact that someone took the time to read my journal made me excited about what I wrote and eager to continue. Laura was concerned about whatever concerned me, and that made me feel my concerns were valid. Eventually, I had the confidence to determine the direction of my growth and my teaching. The process of reflection became a way to teach myself.

A Supervisor's Perspective

In addition to observing, my [Laura's] role as supervisor included helping student teachers think about their teaching. Rather than attempting to shape Tristan's thinking by imposing my values and beliefs on her, I attempted to respond to her journal entries with questions rather than suggested solutions. Occasionally my questions were rhetorical, but even these were intended as prompts for further thinking. Even though what I chose to focus on and respond to was grounded in my own beliefs and value system, I felt that by asking questions I could decrease this subjectivity. About half of my responses, which ranged in length from one word to a paragraph, contained several questions. The remaining remarks were positive comments—"A great way to involve the students"—or possibilities for action—"Start by setting realistic expectations for yourself."

There is no way to ascertain what direct effect, if any, my comments had on Tristan's learning and growth. My goal was to help her examine her values, beliefs, and assumptions about teaching. To that end, I feel the questions were successful, based on her responses both in her journal and during our conferences.

Tristan did admit that she sometimes found my questions and comments frustrating because she was uncertain about what I was looking for. She stated that at first she was not sure if she was doing the journal correctly. This response caused me to reflect on my own teaching: perhaps I did not explain myself or pose the questions well? The possibility does exist that Tristan's predominantly positive responses about my questions were simply her attempt to fulfill what was expected of her; her honesty about her strengths, weaknesses, and concerns, however, lead me to believe that this was not the case.

Although the purpose of the student teacher's journal is to serve as a vehicle for his or her process of reflection, I do feel that the importance of the supervisor's role should not be discounted. According to Cohn and Gellman (1988), "The role of the supervisor is akin to [that of] the teacher—asking probing questions to encourage students to see relationships, generate alternatives, and draw conclusions" (p. 4). This role can be enhanced by the thoughtful and judicious use of critical comments to guide beginning teachers toward higher levels of reflection.

Analyzing the Data

Before we began the process of formally analyzing Tristan's progress, we each reviewed her journal. Both of us noted the same patterns of growth. Tristan had progressed from being a teacher concerned with how to maintain a classroom of 28 children to becoming someone who questioned the implications of her decisions for society and for each child. Next we consulted Ferguson (1989) and Ross (1989) to determine how other student teaching programs incorporated written materials as part of their assessment of students' development in reflection. Although these studies were informative, their methodology did not meet our needs. We searched further and found studies by Zeichner and Liston (1987) and Lucas (1988) that described basing such assessment on Van Manen's (1977) three "levels of reflectivity." We found that Van Manen's levels best described the growth we saw in Tristan. The three levels address the technical, practical, and critical aspects of teaching. At the technical level, the primary concern of student teachers is the efficient application of their pedagogical knowledge—the art of managing time in the school day, planning lessons, teaching and reteaching, and evaluating students' work. At the practical level, teaching actions are measured based on personal values, beliefs, and assumptions. At the critical level, student teachers engage in a process of analyzing their decisions. At this highest level, an interior dialogue is maintained in which the student teacher asks discerning questions and evaluates actions.

Of the 22 entries in Tristan's journal, 10 could be classified at the practical level, 3 addressed both technical and practical concerns, 2 were entirely technical, another 6 discussed both practical and critical issues, and 1 was entirely critical.

Tristan's first journal entry gives a close-up view of the technical side of teaching and learning. Tristan was working with a group of students on some geometry concepts. In her description of the way the tutoring session progressed, her underlying belief that there were only right and wrong ways of teaching surfaced:

> Having the children explain their answers to the sample problems I gave them helped me learn exactly what needed to be retaught.... Thus, I knew what I needed to work on with him because I had asked questions and did not allow the students to guess without thinking about what they were doing.

Although this may have been an appropriate strategy for the particular tutoring session, Tristan arrived at it without reflecting on why that might be the case. She did not hesitate or express any questions or doubts. Reading this first entry, we realized that expression of doubt or questions in the other entries might be a good indicator of changes in her thinking.

In her fourth journal entry, Tristan began to question and try to solve problems. She was confronted with a discipline problem and was unsure about how to solve it. She thought about different approaches, expressed her feeling that the discipline problem might be masking some other deeper

problem, weighed her options, and finally settled on one. She referred to the same concern in her next entry and reaffirmed her feeling that the approach she had settled on was an appropriate one. In these entries, Tristan was moving toward the practical level of reflection. She demonstrates in them that she was not only concerned with efficiency but with incorporating her own beliefs about children, discipline, and teaching.

A strong indication of Tristan's functioning at the practical level was her eighth entry, which addressed the combined issues of grading, time, and planning:

> The more subjects I teach, the more I become inundated with a tremendous number of papers to grade.... I don't mind grading them for I love to make helpful comments and reward a job well done, but I am left with little time to plan lessons and get materials together for lessons.

Later in this entry she once again wrestled with finding a solution to a dilemma by listing several options and deciding on one course to follow. She elected to collect only some work and to grade the remainder in class with the students: "Although no system of grading students' work is perfect, I believe that mine will provide me with plenty of opportunities to check my students' work so I'll know how they're doing—without overloading me."

By her 15th journal entry, Tristan was moving from the practical to the critical. This excerpt reveals strong feelings about two students:

> How will this affect Alberto's progress in mathematics and his longterm career goals? As a teacher, I cannot accept the fact that I cannot help him now.... Jason's situation frustrates me for many reasons.... I think he could make a great deal of progress and im-

provement if he weren't so angry at the world. He has not had an easy life…. What does he have to take pride in at school? Who can blame him for feeling so angry at the world? After all, the world hasn't treated him very well. What can I, as his teacher, do to improve his situation? He is only one of 18 students in the class…so what can one teacher do to help all of them? Will Jason be just another statistic—a boy who was passed along through the grades without ever really knowing how to read or write?

We interpreted this entry as showing that Tristan was concerned about the outcome of the conferences she had held with these two students. Her writing indicates an understanding of some possible ramifications if students' needs are not met. She not only saw the problems at the classroom level, but demonstrated a genuine concern about a system of education in which a child might become "just another statistic." Tristan's move to the critical level is well illustrated in her second to last entry. Here she confronts the conflict between her feelings about the National Teachers Examination (NTE) and her beliefs about testing:

> I can't help thinking that the whole idea of taking such an exam [the NTE] is contradictory to much of what I have been taught in my education courses, though. First of all, it can't measure planning abilities or actual rapport with students, parents, and colleagues…. As of now, however, the NTE is like grading students' work—a necessary evil. I say this because I am required to take it in order to get certified in the state of Ohio, just as teachers are required to grade the work of their students and give them [standardized] tests even though the tests don't always accurately reflect the abilities of those students. I certainly hope that Ohio's legislators

don't continue to get so carried away with the testing craze currently going on in the U.S., for if they do, our students will end up spending more time filling out grids than learning!

Unlike some of the problems mentioned in the previous entries, for Tristan the NTE was a problem without an easy solution. Here she does not engage in the same style of problem solving as she had used in other entries. But clearly at this point in her development she was beginning to question what were once firm beliefs about teaching and to view common school practices as potentially problematic.

Although this brief overview suggests that Tristan's progression through Van Manen's (1977) levels was linear, it was not in fact as gradual and as smooth as we had expected. Instead of a slow but distinct progression toward becoming more reflective, we discovered Tristan's growth was neither continuous nor consistent. This was shown by the fact that many entries alternated between levels or included references to more than one level. At times Tristan's progress was interrupted by other technical concerns, as happened when she first became concerned about the National Teachers Examination. The NTE is an important part of becoming certified to teach in Ohio, and Tristan was worried about it. She described her technical concerns about this exam in one journal entry but followed that with the just-quoted entry that expressed her critical concerns about testing in general.

In sum, we believe our analysis of Tristan's journal provided some significant insights into her thinking and growth as a teacher. At first Tristan had as her goal becoming "superteacher" and believed this was attainable by way of a direct path. Now she realizes that no one is a perfect teacher and that the path to becoming a teacher doesn't end. Our data appear to confirm this: many of Tristan's journal entries were not at one specific level but overlapped. Problem solving can often involve thinking critically about technical and practical situations.

Implications

Tristan. When I first began writing in my journal, I saw the process as merely another assignment. I wrote because I was told to write—not because I wanted to—and my only goal was to fill the pages. As I began to teach more and assume more responsibility in the classroom, I faced more of the issues that all teachers must face. My journal forced me to slow down and think through these concerns. Soon I was looking forward to the times when I could sit down and write—and think. My journal was no longer just a notebook with empty pages, but rather a mechanism for helping me process my thoughts. I spent a lot of time thinking back to the incidents I had written about and reflecting on how I might react should a similar situation occur in the future.

Now as a first-year teacher, I know I will have little time to express my thoughts on paper, but that does not mean I cannot keep a journal in my head. Because of my experiences with Laura (my student teaching experience and, later, our work on this chapter), I learned how to think critically about my decisions. I realize that having the time and means to write my thoughts down was a luxury, but I have replaced that luxury by using the skills that activity helped me develop to evaluate my thinking. After the hectic pace of teaching becomes more routine for me, I think I would benefit from keeping some type of journal so my critical thinking skills will stay sharp.

Laura. This study not only confirmed my view of journals as useful for evaluating students, it also showed me that I could

make them a more effective means of assessment. Second and perhaps more important, I discovered ways in which I could help students reach a level of critical reflection and thereby make the student teaching experience and the journal more meaningful. As Tristan and I worked together, I began to realize that merely helping her reach the critical level of reflection was not all there was to my work with her. Like Tristan, up to this time I had treated critical thinking as a goal that all student teachers should attain by completing assignments in my class. I now know that I need to provide student teachers with a means to generate and maintain critical thinking on their own.

As I assessed Tristan's journal entries, I felt I understood her thought processes better than if I had simply observed her teaching. I did make comments in her journal for her to think about and we had discussions each week concerning her performance in the classroom and the contents of her recent journal entries. It was not until after Tristan's student teaching experience, however, that I realized how much I had underestimated the value of the journal as an assessment tool. When we began to work on this article and discuss her journal in more detail, I came to realize that the entries discussed only the beginnings of Tristan's reflective thought. I had assessed her on that reflection without providing her the opportunity to show me how her thinking developed. She would often bring up an event weeks, even months, after she had described it in her journal. I discovered that she reflected on her teaching while driving, eating, and getting ready for bed. For example, as Tristan mentioned, she had a discipline problem with one student. What I did not know until after her student teaching assignment had concluded was that she went back and reread her journal entries about this situation over a period of several weeks. She realized that she had reacted too emotionally and gradually was able to examine the child's behavior more objectively. This has all served to show me that I need to provide opportunities for student teachers to revisit their journals through further discussions or writing over time.

During my work with Tristan on this paper I also began asking myself how she would assess her own critical thinking when she became a teacher and no longer had a supervisor prompting discussion and urging critical reflection. Van Manen's (1977) three levels of reflectivity helped solve this potential problem. The levels offered a process through which she could examine her own growth and shape it as she worked. While we were analyzing Tristan's journal in preparation for writing this chapter, I saw that she was starting to look at her critical reflection through Van Manen's levels. When she was student teaching, however, her questions to me about critical thinking were along the lines of "Is this what you want?" At this stage she had not internalized the process of critical reflection, and, indeed, had it not been for our work on this chapter, she might never have accomplished this goal. I was forced to ask myself what the point of emphasizing critical reflection was if student teachers were to have no way of understanding it when they started work in their own classrooms.

I now see the need for helping my students discover a way to analyze their own thinking. For Tristan, Van Manen's levels offered a way to analyze reflective thought; there are undoubtedly other mechanisms that would help different teachers. Regardless of the method employed, this self-evaluation is crucial if teachers are to grow professionally throughout their careers. I am cautious, however, about discussing this

process too early during the student teaching experience. Early on, student teachers must ask technical and procedural questions in order to establish a solid foundation of pedagogical knowledge on which to build. If student teachers know that I am looking for critical thinking, they may "simulate" it in order to please me at a stage when they ought to be given a chance to discuss the more practical, basic issues they face in the earliest days of their teaching.

Weaknesses and Strengths

We did note some drawbacks to the use of the journal and some limitations to our analysis of its entries. Tristan felt she never had enough time to write thoroughly or respond to everything. For example, at the beginning of her experience when she was observing and teaching in a limited way, more entries were devoted to a single, focused issue; toward the end of her experience when she was teaching on her own, the entries became shorter because she had less time to devote to them. This was unfortunate because it was during this time that she had the greatest need to write.

We also acknowledge that journal writing does not provide a complete picture of a student teacher's growth. Through talking with me, Tristan could more fully examine and reflect on the significant events in her classroom. In addition, Tristan's first experiences in teaching had not provided her with an extensive enough knowledge base to express herself clearly in writing. It would have been helpful, both for the evaluation of Tristan's work and for the analysis of growth we undertook for this chapter, had we tape-recorded our discussions and analyzed them along with the journal.

Weaknesses may also exist in the process we used to analyze the journal. One drawback to our procedure was that we had to reconstruct the situations described in the journal. Although for the most part our recollections matched, we needed to rely on our memory of past events. Another drawback was that our analysis was conducted with the benefit of hindsight. Had we been able to engage in a thorough, ongoing examination of the journal while Tristan was student teaching, both our analysis and the practical assistance offered to her to guide her teaching might have been more effective.

Despite these weaknesses, we believe our study was beneficial in addressing our questions. Our work has aided us in developing these tenets, which we feel will guide our teaching in the future:

- critical, reflective thinking will help teachers grow and change;
- reflective journals can be a vehicle for helping teachers think critically;
- reflective journals are most effective as a means of assessment if they are discussed frequently to allow the student teachers an opportunity to reflect and expand on what they wrote;
- growth in critical, reflective thinking is an ongoing process and should continue after the student teaching experience.

Through Tristan's student teaching experience and our collaborative work on this study, we both grew in our knowledge of reflective writing in journals and, most important, we learned how to revisit and analyze that writing for signs of further growth in critical thinking. This process of analysis contributes to the development of the ability to reflect on teaching practice. We feel it is this ability that allows educators to grow on their own as professionals and to work to create a system that will meet the needs of every child.

Note: Laura Heichel died unexpectedly prior to publication of this book. I will miss her friendship and support as I begin my career in teaching. I salute Laura for her talent and her dedication to education and pray that her work in this chapter will inspire others to continue research in the area of student teaching.

TMM

References

Armaline, W.D., & Hoover, R.L. (1989). Field experience as a vehicle for transformation: Ideology, education, and reflective practice. *Journal of Teacher Education, 40*(2), 42-48.

Bolin, F.S. (1988). Helping student teachers think about teaching. *Journal of Teacher Education, 39*(2), 48-54.

Cohn, M.M., & Gellman, V.C. (1988). Supervision: A developmental approach for fostering inquiry in preservice teacher education. *Journal of Teacher Education, 39*(2), 2-8.

Ferguson, P. (1989). A reflective approach to the methods practicum. *Journal of Teacher Education, 40*(2), 36-41.

Gitlin, A.D. (1990). Educative research, voice, and school change. *Harvard Educational Review, 60*(4), 443-466.

Lucas, P. (1988). An approach to research-based teacher education through collaborative inquiry. *Journal of Education for Teaching, 14*, 55-73.

Ross, D.D. (1989). First steps in developing a reflective approach. *Journal of Teacher Education, 40*(2), 22-30.

Schon, D.A. (1987). *Educating the reflective practitioner*. San Francisco, CA: Jossey-Bass.

Van Manen, M. (1977). Linking ways of knowing with ways of being practical. *Curriculum Inquiry, 6*, 205-228.

Zeichner, K.M., & Liston, D.P. (1987). Teaching student teachers to reflect. *Harvard Educational Review, 57*, 23-48.

Chapter 22

Promoting Reflection through Dialogue Journals

Sharon Lee and
Nancy T. Zuercher

Lee and Zuercher both teach at the University of South Dakota in Vermillion. Lee's areas of interest include young adult literature, reading instruction at the middle school level, and teacher education, while Zuercher is involved in research on writing across the curriculum and English teaching in the secondary schools.

Although most teacher educators recognize that reflection is an important part of the teaching process, they do not always provide adequate opportunities for preservice teachers to engage in activities that promote it. Most students in teacher-education programs do little more than take a sequence of classes designed to certify them in particular areas and prepare them for a tight job market. Reflection about the teaching process, the teaching profession, and themselves as teachers happens only incidentally, if at all.

As teacher educators, Sharon in education and Nancy in English, we were interested in promoting reflection in our classes. We knew that writing could teach as well as test, and we began to wonder what would happen if students were expected to write their reflections on teaching and to think about their future roles as teachers. What kind of reflection would students do if they were given time to think and write in class? Would conversation between peers facilitate reflection? These questions became the impetus for a semester-long project undertaken in our classes.

The project was not particularly hard to organize. We simply had to agree to its terms and arrange our class schedules to include writing time, an accommodation that we easily made. But this project did have two unique dimensions: (1) it was interdisciplinary; and (2) it required considerable cooperation before it began. Dialogue between university departments is not always easy to arrange, and while research is emphasized at universities, it is seldom directed toward university teaching. Although our major goal was to give students an opportunity to discover their relationship with the teaching profession, as teacher researchers we also wanted to learn more about and ultimately improve our own teaching.

Writing is a powerful tool for active learning in any subject at any level. "Writing to learn" is the act of thinking on paper; this sort of writing does not have as its main purpose display or evaluation. When one writes this way it is primarily for oneself, so the language is informal. Correctness is not the point; the writer's internal dialogue is. When students write to learn, they construct knowledge by writing about a subject in their own words and connecting what they are learning with what they already know. Writing in one's own words rather than copying the language of another demands the use of higher order thinking skills and results in deeper understanding and internalization of learning. Britton et al. (1975) note that this sort of expressive (rather than explanatory) writing is the basis from which all other writing develops and can show how learning takes place as a person shapes ideas with words. Emig (1977) calls writing a "unique mode of learning—not merely valuable, not merely special—but unique" (p. 122). She identifies four major characteristics of writing that parallel effective learning strategies:

1. Writing involves hand, eye, and both sides of the brain simultaneously.
2. Writing allows for personal response.
3. Writing requires making connections and constructing meaning.
4. Writing is active and personal.

In addition, the slow pace of writing allows time for reflection and learning.

One strategy that promotes writing to learn is the dialogue journal, a journal that serves as a vehicle for an extended written conversation with another person, most commonly a teacher. In teacher-education classes, dialogue journals between a professor and students in field practicum courses are fairly common (see, for example, Brinton & Holten, 1988; Stephens & Reimer, 1990); preservice teachers and elementary students have also shared such journals (Ford, 1990). Like a personal journal or diary, a dialogue journal may cover a wide range of subjects or be restricted to a particular topic. Writing in a dialogue journal is comparable to writing and responding to personal letters. Our idea was that dialogue journals shared regularly between future teachers in different courses might serve to extend each participant's thinking. Because the teachers would be writing to peers, we thought their reflection might be freer and deeper and their learning therefore more internalized.

The Research Context

All secondary education majors at our university must take "Teaching Reading in the Content Areas," a third-year course that is often these students' first methods course. Students planning to teach secondary English must also take "English for Teachers." These two courses provided the setting for this project. Students in both courses often have an undeveloped sense of what it means to be a professional and few have a discernible passion for teaching. Some students seem detached and anxious to "get the course out of the way," while others are more enthusiastic about learning.

The content area course suffers many of the plagues of a required class. Students are frequently worried about its content since most know little about teaching reading. (Their apprehension increases when they learn that the course covers all aspects of literacy, including writing.) Many are resentful or apathetic because they see little need for knowing about reading instruction in their particular fields of concentration, which include subjects such as physical education, music, art, and physics. However, because the course is required, it is always full or oversubscribed; the semester of the project, there were 43 students enrolled.

The course is designed as an overview of reading and writing processes for students with little or no background in these areas. They are expected to read young adult novels and report on them, and the teacher reads aloud from a novel over the course of the semester. They evaluate content area textbooks and create an interdisciplinary teaching unit that incorporates reading and writing into a content area. There is always a writing component to this class: letters with younger pen pals, dialogue journals with another section of the same course, or dialogue journals with the instructor. Students write for authentic audiences and are given time in class to do so.

"English for Teachers" is required for all those seeking secondary teaching certification in English. It is designed as an experiential course in teaching English, primarily literature and writing. Students read professional journals, keep their own journals, plan and teach minilessons, and create and teach a portion of a unit that integrates reading, writing, listening, speaking, and thinking.

Although many students in the class share an eagerness to teach, at the beginning of the semester their notions about teaching are frequently overly romantic ("I'll have students sitting at my feet enraptured when I read poetry"), simplistic ("They just need to know the basics—you know, the rules of English grammar"), or based on their recollections of a favorite teacher ("She made grammar come alive with her stories; I want to be just like her"). Many were taught writing with the traditional product-over-process emphasis by teachers who saw writing class largely as instruction in grammar or who were overly critical. Some students enjoy reading and a few read regularly for pleasure; most, however, read little outside of assigned texts. Sometimes they believe from past experience that literature courses consist of learning names, titles, dates, and obscure methods of analysis.

The course enrollment in the semester of the project was 23. Almost half were Malaysian students preparing to teach English as a Second Language in Malaysia and were not native English speakers. Although we recognize that the educational and cultural backgrounds of these students were different from those of our usual American students, we did not treat their journals differently. Since we encouraged students to write about their past educational experiences in their journals, differences were expected and encouraged. The students all had in common two year-long literature survey courses—"American Literature" and "British Literature"—and other English classes; in addition, the native English speakers had completed the required 20 hours of practical work in schools. Many had completed "Reading in the Content Areas"; a few were enrolled in both courses in the semester of the project.

As language and literacy teachers, we share some common ground—we are both interested in whole language, we have both used journals in our classes (Sharon had used dialogue journals before our research project began), and we both were familiar with the work of researchers and educators such as Frank Smith, Janet Emig, and Toby Fulwiler. Each of us also had in-depth knowledge of a particular discipline, which we shared in many planning discussions. In addition, we spent considerable time discussing the growing field of teacher research.

When Sharon obtained a grant from the School of Education to purchase spiral notebooks for journals, we synthesized our discussions into a handout for both our classes that described the project and procedure (reproduced in the figure on the next page). Students in Sharon's class were to write every Thursday; their partners in Nancy's class would respond on the following Tuesday. The two of us also kept a dialogue journal. The students who were taking both classes were asked to write a journal in each; the unequal number of students (43 in Sharon's class and 23 in Nancy's) meant that some students ended up writing more than one journal. Absences sometimes disrupted the exchanges between partners.

Our intent was for all journal writing to occur during class (including our writing to each other), but the time devoted to it varied over the semester because of the demands of the rest of the courses' curricula. Often, writing time was the first 10 to 15 minutes of class when students were settling in; other days writing came at the end of class or served as a transition from one activity to another.

We debated giving the students prompts for their journals. We know that ownership of topic is an important dimension of journal writing (Kirby & Liner, 1988), and we know that students may not develop their own voices if given too many prompts. In the end, we decided that since these students did not know one another, it would create a more comfortable environment if we provided some prompts for the first four weeks of the course that would focus their writing on particular relevant topics. These were the prompts we provided:

Week 1: You probably had a teacher who made a lasting impression on you, perhaps someone who was instrumental in your decision to become a teacher. Describe that teacher and how he or she influenced you.

Week 2: There were many people, events, and experiences that worked together to help you learn to read and write. What do you remember about your own literacy learning? How did you learn to read and write? Concentrate on the elementary years and go beyond personal reflection. How does what you remember relate to some of the things you are learning in these classes?

Week 3: Now that you have had some time to reflect on your own elementary school education, what do you remember about your secondary school experiences? (You may include your college years also.) What did your teachers do to help you become a better reader and writer?

Lee & Zuercher

What have you done to improve your literacy skills?

Week 4: Think about the textbooks you used in secondary school. What do you remember about them?

How did your teachers use the textbooks? From which ones did you learn the most? Were textbook readings discussed in class or merely assigned? Are

The Introductory Handout

A dialogue journal is a learning tool that allows students to write reactions to classroom instruction and methods. The main idea behind a dialogue journal is that the act of writing about what goes on in class helps students reflect on and internalize the concepts and ideas presented. The main goals of a dialogue journal are increased learning and increased fluency in writing and thinking. Students can write about present or previous experiences that pertain to classroom instruction, ideas or questions that are raised during class time or in preparation for class, reactions to certain methods or assignments, or simple descriptions of what is going on in the classroom. All are important in a dialogue journal.

There are a variety of ways to organize and structure dialogue journals. The dialogue may be between individual students and the teacher, two students in the same class, or two students in different classes. Teachers may give students writing prompts or they may simply allow students to write on any topic they choose. As long as students are writing about what they are learning and are getting responses from another journal writer, the dialogue journal is accomplishing its purpose.

A dialogue journal is a partial requirement for this class this semester. By taking this class, you have displayed your interest in becoming a teacher, and it is assumed that you are interested in professional matters considered essential to teaching. Your dialogue journal will focus on professional concerns of teaching through your communication with a peer. You will be keeping your journal with a student enrolled in a similar class required for preservice teachers.

Responsibilites:

1. You must write on a weekly basis to your partner. Time will be given in class each week for writing your journal entry. This is one reason that class attendance is so important.

2. Your journal entry should deal with professional concerns of teaching and learning. Personal matters are a natural part of any dialogue, of course, but they should not be the central focus of the journal.

3. Your journal entries should be one page in length. You will be given credit for a full page of writing. Your instructor will be strict about this standard.

4. You should demonstrate "good faith" effort in your writing. You will want to respond to the assignments and to respond to your partner.

5. The instructors from both classes will have access to the dialogue journals and will read and respond to the journals on a regular basis.

6. At the end of the semester you will be asked to discuss the merits of dialogue journals and their effectiveness in helping you learn and internalize material presented in class.

these experiences different from those you have had since beginning college?

Analysis

After the semester was over, we met and discussed the project. We read the journals and discussed what we thought we were seeing. At first, we anticipated that the journals would reveal our students' growth through increased use of the language of the profession, progress in thinking as teachers as well as students, and more references to what they expected in their future teaching. Although our first reading and analysis did yield some information, we felt we were not addressing the journals as a whole. We decided to reread and allow themes and categories to emerge. Here we were engaging in reflection *on* action, "reflection on practice and on one's actions and thought, undertaken after the practice is complete" (Killion & Todnem, 1991, p. 15). Although our students were gone, our own learning and reflection were continuing.

As teachers, we wanted to find some general trends in the journals in order to make decisions about whether this practice had been valuable for our students and ought to be continued with future classes. Our analysis did reveal that the journals included some genuine dialogue with connections from one entry to the next. Students seemed comfortable with writing to a peer. Learning is a social activity, and even though not all the journal entries were related to the sharing of thoughts about education and course content, we thought initially that the relaxed exchanges we noted in the journals might have had a positive influence on how students responded to the courses in general. Nevertheless, school was still separate from life for most of these undergraduates. Reading for school was often described as something to avoid. Some students' comments in their journals showed their lack of interest—"I'm supposed to talk about something in class, we talked about learning strategies, well that's enough of that," for example—while a few did express enthusiasm about some of the required readings. Classes and assignments tended to be mentioned as being "hard" or "easy," but not discussed for the ideas they presented; teachers were described more in terms of personality than in terms of the content of their classes or their teaching abilities.

Most students also focused on personality in response to our prompt about former teachers. Encouragement, caring, patience, and understanding were frequently mentioned. One student's entry was typical: "I believe that [she] taught me that school can be personal as well. Good teachers, I feel, are those who are willing...to share, not simply instruct." His partner responded to this entry as follows: "A good teacher has students that learn. Learning is the main point in this field. To have a person that you like teaching you seems to me to be a big plus."

Some students did show that they were beginning to think like teachers. One wrote that as a seventh grader she had felt that one teacher's assignments were "dumb things, [but] now the dumb things don't seem so dumb." Another wrote, "Teachers have the power to influence the lives of many kids. Far too many teachers take this idea lightly. When the issue of influencing the lives of students in the most beneficial way no longer becomes important, it is time to get out of the profession." Still another wrote, "Today we talked about trying to draw high school kids' thoughts on a subject out of them and not just standing in front of the class and spitting endless information at them. For some reason I kind of took this topic to heart. I hope I'm not developing a

Lee & Zuercher

level of maturity toward education! What a concept."

Students also began to question the discrepancy between theory and practice, as shown in this excerpt: "A professor said that teachers are wrong when they try to teach middle and high school students in preparation for the real world. The students are in the real world right now. It's just that their real world is that of an adolescent. [But what about] when professors say 'Just wait until you're in the real world'?" Other students, although not thinking as teachers, did begin to see that the responsibility for learning was theirs. One wrote, "I never read anything until last year when I was a junior. I just decided that I was sick of just getting by and I wanted to be a little smarter. So basically, it is on my own that I'm coming to be a really good student—finally."

Even as students began to think in professional terms about issues of teaching and learning, the language of the profession still did not appear very often. One wrote, "So maybe I do get off the track a little too much when I write to you, but this is too much fun to throw in something as mundane as actual school topics in these letters. I always feel these letters give me the opportunity to 'brainstorm' with you. (How's that for tying in some actual 'Education' jargon?)"

A Case Study

While these general findings gave us some insight into our students and some sense of how they had approached the process of journal writing, they do not illustrate the full nature of the dialogue that grew between many students over the semester. We felt that a case study might yield a more complete picture of how the dialogue journals worked in our classes.

We considered Laura and Carol, both English Education majors, to be among our top students. Laura, a third-year student enrolled in "Reading in the Content Areas," was also pursuing a minor in speech; Carol, a fourth-year student in "English for Teachers" was completing a mathematics minor and had already taken the reading course. They wrote to each other regularly over the 11-week semester, and their journal shows clearly the differences between prompted and unprompted writing, recalling and reflecting, and replying and responding.

Laura and Carol took our four writing prompts seriously. Their entries were insightful and full of reminiscences about their own schooling and teachers. Overall, Carol responded more to Laura than vice versa; Carol also frequently used questions to extend the dialogue. Laura's first entry, which began the dialogue journal, shows the level of her commitment to the assignment:

> The topic we are to write on in today's class is an influencing teacher of the past that inspired you to teach. One of the greatest influences I had was from a high school teacher of mine. His name was Bruce Smith...a quite shy, strong man. He was very attentive in the classroom.... I don't remember how or why I bothered to talk with him outside of the classroom, but I did. He turned out to be someone you wouldn't expect to find behind that "lecturing-silent" teacher.... He was the final decision maker on my choice of entering the education field.

Carol responded to Laura with "It sounds like you really admired Mr. Smith," and then discussed an influential British literature teacher:

> [He] treated his students with respect and in turn we had a lot of respect for

him. That was my first exposure to British literature and it was a positive experience. Although I never talked to him outside of class like your conversations with Mr. Smith I think he still influenced my decision. He gave us a lot of freedom in the classroom but it was always in control. It sounds like Mr. Smith was not only your teacher but also your friend. Have you talked to him recently—does he know what an influence he was on your decision? Maybe you should let him know. I'm sure he'd appreciate it.

Not only had Carol addressed our prompt, she had also genuinely responded to Laura in a personal way and prompted further dialogue. In contrast, in her reply Laura simply answered Carol's questions:

> Before I start on today's topic, I just wanted to let you know that I did write Mr. Smith a letter last fall to thank him for his influence. I found out that he has returned to graduate school at a private college in Minnesota and has his first child, a son. He seems to be doing extremely well.

She then confessed, "There isn't really much I can remember [about learning to read]," in response to that week's prompt, and said she had felt inferior when she was in fourth grade and couldn't read as fast as others. Rather than expanding on this, she then wrote a half page about herself, ending with "Tell me more about you." She seemed more interested in Carol than in our prompt.

Carol responded with greater reflection: "I can't remember much about learning how to read either. I think that's because I didn't realize I was being taught the actual process of reading." She recalled books she had read and ended with news that she had worked in Laura's hometown.

In her next entry, Laura stayed solely on the topic of our third prompt. She re-

called observing a class during her paraprofessional experience: "The teacher allowed the children every day to either read or write for 10-15 minutes alternating the days. The kids kept a journal Tuesday and Thursday and read the remaining days." And then she reflected, "I wish [my teachers] would have done more for me and my peers.... I feel that in my own literacy skills that I, myself, have made the improvements.... The work in [that school] is much like this class." Carol responded, "Sounds like that high school is well on its way to improving the reading and writing abilities of its students." She recalled that everyone read for 15 minutes each day in her high school. She then reflected on this recollection:

> I think it was great that they started it, however, I think favorable attitudes toward reading need to be started at a much younger age, even having a teacher read to very young children for 10 minutes each day has got to create a favorable attitude towards reading. The reading and writing that you wrote about—was that every class and all levels or just one particular class? Did you find out if students like it—is it improving their reading and writing skills?

Laura ignored Carol's questions in her next entry but wrote convincingly about textbooks, the fourth prompt. After over a page, she apologized to Carol for not having more to say about textbooks and said, "I have too many other things on my mind." Carol uncharacteristically did not respond to Laura in her entry, but focused only on the prompt.

When they ran out of prompts, Laura and Carol's—and their classmates'—conversations changed in nature. In the next seven weeks of unprompted writing they talked of school activities, boyfriends, families, weekends, and anxieties about tests. While we expected and encouraged a certain amount of that in the dialogues, we were surprised to see how the personal writing increased and the professional writing decreased over the course of the semester. Though we had stated that the journals should focus on "professional concerns of teaching and learning," our students rarely applied their writing to a teaching situation. For example, Laura wrote about a class activity in which students had to ascribe a value to certain situations and defend their positions. While she commented on how much she enjoyed and learned from the activity, she never mentioned it as a teaching tool or how it might be adapted in her own classroom one day. When she and Carol mentioned teachers from their pasts, they made no connection between them and their future teaching. (The only exception was a comment about one of the discussions in "Teaching Reading in the Content Areas." Laura wrote, "Today we discussed instructional strategies. When you are in the classroom—all you think that those teachers are doing is lecturing. I hope to institute a lot of those strategies in my classrooms.")

Their dialogue did nourish a friendship and a sense of collegiality, spurred, ironically, by the one week Carol did not write an entry. For the first time, Laura responded immediately and personally: "Hi! Alright what is up? Why didn't you write to me? Were you absent? I hope things are okay with you." From this point on, Laura attended more to Carol. There were also two examples of assistance and encouragement. Carol, after a visit to the school where she would student teach, became concerned about discipline and teaching writing. Laura responded, "I bet you are nervous about student teaching. Don't be—knowledge reduces anxiety! That's what I keep hearing. You'll do fine. What grades and subjects will you have?" Laura, concerned about writing a thematic unit on aging, asked the more experienced Carol for her experience and help, especially about incorporating literature. Carol responded as an expert:

> You seem to have picked a fairly hard theme. Aren't they [the units] supposed to be one word titles or did it change? You could also pick something about how elderly are treated in different types of literature like some works that treat them with a lot of respect and that they are a source of wisdom while others treat them like a waste to society and that society isn't responsible for them. Multicultural literature would be an interesting area—Native American especially—their ideas are considered the wisest of the people. Just some thoughts for you—hope they help.

The 11th week saw the pair complaining about their workload and reassuring each other that they would "make it through the semester."

Student Impressions

Our reflection *on* action through our reading of the journals and the case study helped us see the range of topics students wrote about, their commitment to the assignment, their level of writing sophistication, and the beginnings of their viewing themselves as teachers. We did have another source of information available to us for our analysis, however: what we thought of as the reflection *in* action—"reflection on phenomena and on one's spontaneous ways of thinking and acting in the midst of action" (Killion & Todnem, 1991, p. 15)—of our students. We had asked the students to evaluate the dialogue journal experience during the semester. Students evaluated their partners' writing on a scale of 1 to 10 in a memo to their partner's professor. Comments about those who received 10 points emphasized enjoyment and understanding of the dialogue journal concept:

- "He seemed very committed to the project, seemed genuinely interested in what I had to say, and always responded with professional, personal comments and suggestions."
- "She always had something to say that was worth reading. The content wasn't just hello, goodbye, etc. The content had meaning and always left something to think about and respond to."
- "I even cried on her shoulder during a couple of discouraging times."

In contrast, one student who awarded her partner only 8 points wrote, "Sometimes, I felt he was writing just to get done. A little more effort could be put into the work."

Students in "English for Teachers" were also asked to evaluate the dialogue journals as part of the final exam. Their comments were mostly positive. Students enjoyed the experience as a "a quiet time to collect my thoughts," "a perspective on what I've already learned in other classes," "a good place to practice," "an opportunity to write about something that I feel right, wrong, sad, or angry about," and "a comfortable writing pattern." Providing more prompts was frequently suggested as a means of improving the assignment in the future. Some students felt they needed direction or valued learning only when topics pertained to the course content. Others, however, praised the process of making friends on paper. One student suggested that the dialogue journals be used in one class only as "a more accurate way to gather information and ideas, as well as clear up questions which related to the class." Another, objecting to the spiral-bound journals, suggested writing "in-class letters" on notepaper. Two students realized they had not written on appropriate topics. One wrote, "If I had to do it over, I would write more about education issues and classroom discussion so the dialogue journals would be a beneficial learning device."

While these comments were helpful in our thinking about how to make the project more meaningful in future classes, we realized it took place too late in the process to be considered real reflection in action because it did not allow students to redirect and refocus *during* the process. When we do this project again, we will allow more discussion and evaluation along the way.

Our Own Dialogue

Killion and Todnem (1991) also describe something they term "reflection *for* action," a process by which thinking is focused to accomplish certain goals. As our written and oral conversations developed over weeks and months of discussions and analysis, it became fairly obvious to us that our understandings and interpretations were being guided by our own personal experiences and perceptions. While we certainly agreed on a number of points, we were forced to recognize that our different backgrounds affected much of our understanding. Because we were learning so much from each other, we decided to include our dialogue as part of our analysis. The sort of conversation that follows helped us formulate ideas for how we might change the journal assignment in the future, stretch our thinking, and sharpen our insights into our own teaching.

Sharon: Time to write is not the same as time to reflect. I knew that before, but I didn't put it into practice in this assignment. I guess I thought I was doing my part by giving students ample opportunity to read their dialogue journals and then to write to their partners. I know that the writing process can have powerful results, but were our students actually engaged in the writing process? There was no time to revise, meet for conferences, or edit. The entries were basically first drafts, attempts to get some thoughts on paper in a fixed amount of time. I knew better!

Nancy: But dialogue journals are basically writing to learn, not writing to publish. The best comparison is to personal letters where we might "revise" by crossing out, adding a P.S., or inserting stuff. They are "first drafts" in a sense—first drafts that aren't intended to be published. We don't usually have conferences to discuss personal letters.

Sharon: I understand the differences and know the power of writing to learn. But can true reflection come from 10 minutes of writing on an assigned topic? Maybe we need to reinforce our description of what the journal is all about if we do this again. We should remind students of the intended nature of the conversations. Making sure they have own-

ership is not enough if they don't have a clear understanding of the focus.

Nancy: Reinforce is a good word. Now we know what to emphasize.

Sharon: The response should be from a person who clearly understands the conversation's focus and is able to respond to the comments as an insider. We had two novices reading and responding to each other. They couldn't very well ask questions of each other since neither of them had the answers. None of the students had the expertise necessary to answer questions about teaching.

Nancy: I know the literature on dialogue journals demonstrates success when one partner is an insider, but I think we're on to something new here that is still in process. Rather than answering questions, we could have a sort of mutual addressing of questions; our dialogue journals might be more effective for our purposes if we emphasized inquiry as a way of learning. That may be something else we need to reinforce—an active, questioning attitude rather than a passive, receiving attitude. Calkins, Berthoff, Mayher, and Graves all talk about this sort of thing.

Sharon: I think in a way they did have a questioning attitude. They were questioning themselves and each other in order to find answers. But they were not always *responding* to each other. We gave them no direction in how to write a true response.

Nancy: I'm interested in your idea of "true response." To me, a true response is something that seeks discovery, turns over the earth rather than just describes its surface. In any journal I look for some movement, some trial and error—not necessarily all in one entry, but in the course of the conversations. I'd like to see students challenge each other rather than stating something as truth. Perhaps we need to teach them to question. Then these journals might have a better chance of being effective as you say.

Sharon: Exactly. In order for this to be effective, the students need to learn how to write responses that probe and extend the conversation instead of starting it fresh with every entry.

Nancy: We could model on handouts and an overhead transparency the passive stuff and the inquiry, and ask them after two or three writings to try and show how their thoughts are progressing in the conversations. But I'm creating another problem: 10 minutes is not enough to read and write this way.

Sharon: Maybe a field component would be helpful. If they had more practical experience first, they would have more of the background knowledge necessary for thinking like teachers.

Nancy: I use guided imagery in class with good results. For example, I ask students to imagine their first day of teaching. Descriptions are full of reality and feeling and perspectives that they haven't yet thought about.

Sharon: You know that vicarious experiences are not as powerful as concrete ones. Imagining yourself as a teacher is not nearly as real or as scary as standing in front of a group of kids and being expected to teach them something.

Nancy: You know, we are having a better dialogue now than we could in the dialogue journal because we have time to concentrate and more than 10 minutes to write.

Sharon: So, how do we apply this to the project if we do it again?

Implications

Written conversations like this one pushed our thinking in new directions but it wasn't until we sat down together to write the manuscript for this chapter that we began to find answers to our research questions and to come up with ideas to improve our teaching practice. We were experiencing the power of writing to learn, the very thing we had tried to demonstrate to our students.

Would we do this project again? If so, what would we change? Our research, analysis, and reflection led us to these answers:

1. We need to have an equal number of students participate in the project from each class. Asking some students to write two journals is too much to ask. A possible solution would be for the teacher with the larger class to include this project as an option in a list of possible writing-to-learn activities.

2. We need to be more explicit about the focus of the journal. We thought that the prompts and the assignment sheet would be enough, but obviously they weren't. A solution might be to write a letter to the students at the beginning of the semester and outline not only the nature of the assignment, but also state explicitly the direction the journals should take. This letter might also eliminate the need for prompts.

3. We must demonstrate the process by providing examples of journal entries and responses. We could show our dialogue on overhead transparencies and talk about the differences between replying and responding.

4. The journal must be a priority. While we gave time in class for the project, we did not devote a lot of time to talking about what the journals were meant to help the students learn. We gave credit for the journals, but they did not constitute a large part of the overall grade. Since we know that these preservice teachers still have at least part of their student perspectives, what is seen as valuable to the teacher is what will "count" most with them.

5. More evaluation of both process and product is necessary. This assessment would provide us with information to help students refocus and to give students feedback we know they need during any learning process.

6. The final change we would make in the future relates to something we thought was clear in this project. We have to help students understand the purpose of this assignment. For some students, the journals remained simply a teacher-assigned project. We need to spend much more time discussing what we perceive as the journals' function and allow students to work within that function for their own purposes.

With these ideas firmly in mind, we were able to address the more important issues. Did the process of writing in and responding to dialogue journals benefit our students' abilities to reflect and, ultimately, lead to greater learning? While many students reported it had been a wonderful experience, significant learning was not seen. Does that mean our research project was not worthwhile? Certainly not. Would we use dialogue journals in this way again? Definitely. Do we have a better idea of how to organize and monitor the dialogue? Absolutely.

This knowledge was not, however, the only benefit of our work as teacher researchers on this project. The two of us also renewed our interest in writing as a learning tool and reminded ourselves of the value of writing for authentic audiences. The project also opened our eyes to the value of response in writing. A response that does not make a writer want to delve further, to ask more questions, or to pursue new thoughts does not extend learning. We entered this project knowing that it would be an exploration of our own teaching. We learned how to modify this project—and other aspects of our teaching—based on what we learned. And that, after all, was the true focus of the project—to learn how to make our own teaching and the learning we hope it will facilitate more effective.

References

Brinton, D.M., & Holten, C. (1988). *Dialogue journals: A window on the act of language teaching.* Paper presented at the 22nd annual meeting of the Teachers of English to Speakers of Other Languages, Chicago, IL.

Britton, J., Burgess, T., Martin, N., McLeod, A., & Rosen, H. (1975). *The development of writing abilities.* London: Macmillan.

Emig, J. (1977, May). Writing as a mode of learning. *College Composition and Communication, 28,* 122-128.

Ford, M.P. (1990). Reflecting on learning about teaching—glimpses of a child's mind: Journaling beyond the campus to the classroom. (ED 324 681)

Killion, J.P., & Todnem, G.R. (1991). A process for personal theory building. *Educational Leadership, 48*(6), 14-16.

Kirby, D., & Liner, T. (1988). *Inside out: Developmental strategies for teaching writing.* Portsmouth, NH: Heinemann.

Stephens, D., & Reimer, K.M. (1990). *Explorations in reflective practice.* Cambridge, MA: Bolt, Beranek & Newman. (ED 324 692)

Chapter 23

Collaboration and Inquiry in a Teacher-Education Classroom

Kathryn Mitchell Pierce

In addition to teaching courses in children's literature and language arts methods at the University of Missouri in St. Louis, Pierce helps teachers in local public schools explore the uses of literature in the classroom.

The following excerpts are taken from two students' evaluations of their work in and response to my graduate course in children's literature:

> You have definitely helped me outgrow as well as maintain things that I learned last semester. I'd like to experience the peer evaluation—even commenting in each other's logs—more. Keep your expectations high and don't back down because students feel disequilibrium. That's what helps them learn more. Keep working on the timeline thing. We all need to continue to grow.
>
> I want to use [self-evaluation] in my [elementary] class. I am going to use your suggestion from my log—I will have students give their input along with mine to develop a rubric for self-evaluation. Maybe you should try this with one of your own classes at the beginning of a semester.
>
> Set dates and stick to them [for the inquiry-group projects]. We can work well under a little more pressure and if we had had a tighter time frame my group would have met sooner and proofread our paper with the "cold eye" you mentioned.... This was my group's weakness last semester—

remember? We need to change this somehow.

The emphasis on "we" in these passages is significant to me because it shows that these students clearly recognized the value of our collaboration, our search for ways to support learners and create more effective learning communities within our classrooms. I have been trying over the past several years to create in my college classroom a learning environment based on what we know best supports learners of all ages. During this time I have been working with elementary teachers interested in creating more inquiry-oriented, collaborative classroom environments. Together we have explored the use of various strategies—such as text sets, discussion groups revolving around literature selected by either the teacher or the students, writing workshop, and methods of evaluation (including self-evaluation) that are consistent with our changing perspectives on curriculum.

With each step my colleagues and I have taken toward creating supportive learning environments in elementary classrooms, I have looked for ways to make parallel changes in the college courses I teach. For example, I now use text sets of related books and provide time during class for small groups to discuss readings and collaborative projects. Students have an active role in determining course content and in evaluating their own work as well as the course itself. I have also instituted something I call an "inquiry project" as a regular assignment. In it, students select a question, issue, or topic related to the course content that is of particular interest to them or reflects a lack they have identified in their own professional development. Students with similar interests then organize into small "inquiry groups" that serve as support or study groups. Group members

meet during each class to talk about their progress, discuss readings, and plan ways to share their inquiry experience with the rest of the class, usually through a written paper or presentation.

The inquiry project was based on an outline for a similar strategy created by Mary Ann Rankey, a sixth grade teacher with whom I have worked for several years. Our collaboration, along with our work with other classroom teachers and teacher educators, has enabled us to make use of each other's expertise in order to revise the procedures and the class experiences that support the inquiry process. The environment Mary Ann's sixth graders and my college graduate and undergraduate students encounter when they enter our classrooms differs significantly from most of their other classroom experiences. Admittedly, many students are uncomfortable when they discover that most of their strategies for dealing successfully with school will not be well suited to our classrooms.

At the end of each semester I review the course evaluations the university requires students (anonymously) to complete, along with students' self-evaluations and evaluations of their inquiry group experiences. In these materials I look for insights into students' perceptions of the course and ideas of things I might do to provide a more supportive learning environment. The teacher-research study described in this chapter shows how I analyzed students' individual and inquiry group evaluations from one recent course. Over the past few years I have been intrigued by the different ways in which students respond to the usually unfamiliar course design and have grown increasingly concerned about those students who express frustration and confusion even at the end of the course. I am also particularly interested in the ways students describe the inquiry group project. To address these concerns, I developed these initial questions to guide my research:

- What topics do the students talk abut in their self-evaluations?
- How do they describe the inquiry group process?
- What specific references do they make to "collaboration" when they describe their work in the course?
- What can I learn through this analysis that will help me improve the design of future courses?

The Research Context

This research was conducted using student work from a graduate-level children's literature course that I taught at an urban, midwestern university. The students enrolled in the course were in various stages of completing their master's degrees in elementary education, some with an emphasis in early childhood education. Most were classroom teachers or teacher aides in preschool or elementary classrooms near the university; one student was a library science major and one was a school librarian who was taking the course for professional development.

Major course experiences or assignments included a review of current children's literature and discussions on such topics as the use of literature discussion groups in the reading program and the incorporation of literature across the curriculum. Students also participated in literature discussion groups about an adult novel and about readings from professional literature that I assigned or that were selected by inquiry group members. Students responded to these readings in reflection logs and used excerpts from these logs to initiate weekly discussions of the readings. Students also

used the logs to record classroom experiences related to the readings and reflections on course activities.

During the second and third weeks of the course, students identified topics, issues, or questions relating to the use of children's literature in the elementary or early childhood classroom that they wanted to explore. They then formed groups of two to six members who shared similar interests to conduct a collaborative inquiry project focusing on the shared topic. These inquiry groups met each week for 45 to 60 minutes during class to plan and evaluate the steps they would follow in completing their inquiry, work together on a paper, plan a 30- to 45-minute class presentation on some aspect of their inquiry, and compose a final group evaluation of the experience. These meetings generally consisted of discussions about the inquiry process and related professional readings and classroom experiences. Notes from weekly meetings were recorded in a group log. The aspects of the group project that were undertaken by individual members—library work, explorations within those members' own classrooms, and readings—were conducted outside class time. Most groups met once outside class near the end of the inquiry project to finalize work on their presentation, paper, or evaluation.

Finally, students submitted an individual evaluation of their experiences in the course as a whole. These generally included additional comments about the group inquiry assignment, thoughts about the reflection log, and discussions of changes in the way children's literature was being used in the students' own classrooms.

I discussed my interest in the collaborative nature of the inquiry projects and the role of self-evaluation openly with students throughout the course, frequently sharing my perceptions of the similarities between process-centered classrooms at the elementary and university levels. I invited students to offer comments and share experiences in class. During one such discussion, several students commented on how essential collaboration is for successful inquiry group experiences. These students encouraged me to focus my research on the role of collaboration because, as they pointed out, it is as important in elementary classrooms as it is in college classrooms. At this point I asked students for their permission to keep copies of their individual and group evaluations for the purposes of this research project. I also invited them to respond to the research while it was in progress (several of them did so).

The Research Process

Sources of data used in this study were university-maintained course materials (course syllabi and students' anonymous course evaluations); samples of student work produced during the course (individual and group evaluations, group papers, group logs, and individual reflection logs); my own files (course planning notes, overhead transparencies, handouts, etc.); and my research journal, which included my reactions to professional readings, course experiences, and conferences and workshops attended, as well as notes for ongoing staff-development activities and other research projects in which I was involved. During the analysis of the group and individual evaluations, comparisons were made with similar documents created by students enrolled in some of my other graduate and undergraduate courses in language arts, children's literature, and reading. Of these numerous sources, the group evaluations were my primary focus because they were most directly related to the topic of collaboration my research was designed to investigate.

Data analysis occurred in four main phases: first, I collected and organized the group and self-evaluations; second, I categorized, described, and analyzed the topics addressed in these evaluations; third, I developed "strategy memos" to describe the insights I gained; and fourth, I developed the final report of my process and findings. Throughout all four of these phases I read related professional literature on teaching, teacher-research strategies, and qualitative and naturalistic research procedures. I also frequently referred to sets of evaluations from other courses to verify emerging patterns. In addition, I discussed my progress with elementary and university classroom teachers. These discussions served to focus my thinking on process and patterns, assisted me in identifying my unexamined assumptions and premature leaps to conclusions, and offered opportunities to compare my experiences with those of others interested in creating supportive learning environments. These colleagues and I shared a great deal: they knew what kind of classroom I was striving to create, they recognized self-evaluation as essential to student-directed learning, they were knowledgeable about collaboration, and many of them came to know my students well enough through my sharing of my research to identify inconsistencies in my interpretations.

Analysis

Some of the ways I organized and analyzed data were more useful and productive than others. The least successful strategies were those I used early in the analysis, although even these played a role because they contributed to the development of more successful strategies. These initial strategies also helped familiarize me with the content of the group and self-evaluations because they gave me an "excuse" to read and reread these pieces of the students' work.

The initial analysis of self-evaluations was made to highlight their common topics and themes. This was accomplished through "data briefs"—summary comments for sets of data (Gilles, 1991). The data briefs of the group evaluations included title of group, randomly assigned group number, size of group and number of student members whom I'd taught in previous semesters, group goal(s) and focus, an outline of the content of the evaluation, and any criteria for evaluation stated in concluding remarks. I used these data briefs extensively in developing and interpreting the patterns that emerged from the data, but they did not replace the complete evaluations. After I completed this initial analysis, I began some more intensive work with the data. The following sections describe in detail three of the most successful strategies for analyzing the data: topical analysis of the group evaluations, creation of inquiry group "portraits," and examination of the key characteristics of highly contrasting groups. After completing each strategy, I took stock of the insights I had gained and established the next steps I would take in the analysis.

Categorizing Comments on Collaboration

My initial topical analysis of the group evaluations indicated that "collaboration" was a frequent topic of discussion for all the inquiry groups and seemed to be related to discussions of "transactions" and references to work with "others" outside their groups. To examine discussion of these related topics further, I prepared a chart with columns to record statements from the evaluation that related to "collaboration," "transaction" and "reference to others." The completed chart enabled me to make comparisons among groups. (The figure on the next page gives an example from my chart.) I developed similar charts for other topics common to the group evaluations and for the criteria students set for evaluation of the group experience, which often included reference to group- or syllabus-established goals.

My analysis of the information recorded under "Collaboration" demonstrated that many students had heard about or tried cooperative learning or other small-group experiences in their own classrooms, and a few had worked in small groups themselves in other university courses. I acknowledge that all the groups undoubtedly talked about their members' collaboration in large part because experiencing collaborative group work was listed as a course outcome, and successful collaboration was a criterion for evaluating the inquiry group activity. Each group, however, had different degrees of success in working collaboratively, as shown by the way group members described their collaborative experiences.

Some groups equated collaboration with cooperation in working toward shared goals. These groups talked about sharing responsibilities and work equitably (usually deemed to be equally) and successfully accomplishing group tasks (the paper and the presentation). For example, members of Group Two wrote in their evaluation that "many, many times we reminded ourselves and each other what we wanted to gain from our group.... We worked very well together and we met our goal of becoming more familiar with children's books." In her self-evaluation one member of this group wrote, "I liked sharing the responsibilities of the work so that I didn't feel so stressed out." Group Five reported that "we all agreed that we would have never accomplished these goals on our own. During each weekly meeting, our collective efforts and

Excerpts of Topical Analysis Chart

Transactions

Group 1: no mention

Group 2: "The more we read the more interested we become with the awards."

Group 3: "We were immersed for a semester in drama and literature and we see ourselves changed because of it."

"Many transactions took place between the group and the literature, the literature and the drama, and the drama and the group."

Group 4: see Collaboration for extensive examples

Collaboration

Group 1: "Next we divided the organizational responsibilities according to the strengths and weaknesses within the group in regard to writing and presenting."

"...peer-edited our paper and presentation within the group."

"Our goal was reached through a group collaboration of ideas."

Group 2: "We shared, disagreed, talked out our problems, and thought through our goals."

"We backed each other up and helped each other with ideas and gave suggestions for other book titles and resources."

Group 3: "We learned collaboration techniques."

"There is a strong chance the collaboration begun will continue."

"We melted two minds into one. We expanded our own viewpoints and horizons—not only from what we did but what we found possible. We became enlightened to the possibilities of collaborative effort."

"Using skills learned in collaboration with [group members]."

"We [benefited] a great deal from our collaboration."

Group 4: see entire evaluation which was devoted to their collaborative experiences—includes discussion of topics such as:
- communication in group;
- accepting unique perspectives of individual group members;
- developing a shared history and spending time getting to know one another;
- time involved in genuine collaboration;
- prior experiences with cooperation vs. collaboration;
- realization that roles shifted throughout their work as a group.

"Talking over and discussing our material helped us understand diverse perspectives. We could not have had that working individually."

Others

Group 1: no mention

Group 2: "We received much positive feedback from our classmates."

"The information we presented was what educators are always glad to learn but not likely to look up for themselves."

Group 3: "We had to revise only slightly, and that was the decision to develop a single unit based on one play which we changed to giving curricular ideas for all the plays. We felt that an entire unit would take us off track of our initial goal. Many teachers can develop a unit but few can be playwrights, so we feel this was a good decision."

"[One member] will continue to develop plans for her children's theater group."

"[One member] will use this in curriculum development and unit planning with teachers."

Group 4: "We wonder if we left the class with a desire to learn more or if we presented too much information and overwhelmed our audience. It would have been beneficial to get feedback from the class."

successes helped us renew our enthusiasm to achieve our goals." Accomplishing the assigned tasks appeared to be the ultimate goal and criterion for success (defined as receiving an A for this section of the course) in these groups.

Other groups described collaboration more in terms of using the group experience to work through and create new understanding and to support individuals in the group, in both the group project and in teaching in general. These comments from members of Group 1 illustrate this perception of collaboration:

> As we decided on how to take our knowledge to our classrooms to start literature discussion groups, I found it very helpful to share experiences each week.... I felt comfortable with the relationships that developed in our group, where I wasn't afraid to come into class and say, "Hey, guess what I did today!"

> I feel very comfortable working in small groups. I think it's a great opportunity to really get to know some students well and share ideas more in depth. I also think it's a wonderful opportunity to get into a subject that you feel will benefit your own growth as a teacher.

These students seemed to go beyond the amicable and cooperative atmosphere described previously, and their groups strove to move beyond compromise to consensus. Members occasionally talked about experiences in which the group worked together to solve particular inquiry problems. These comments from Group 6 illustrate this process:

> We then shared [our research findings] with each other. We then collaboratively discussed, refined, reworded, and corrected together until we were satisfied.... Our paper was a cooperative and collaborative effort.

I attended each session eagerly, wanting to find out more about authors and how to use some of their books in my classroom through inquiry groups.

I have never done a group project with five people before. I was absolutely amazed that it worked so well. The five of us actually accomplished so much more than I had expected. Even though I sensed exasperation (really I think they were wanting to strive and really learn) by some members of the group, they grew so much. Being older I could say, "Look how far you've come—we're doing something so useful for us."

Still other groups described their collaboration in terms of creating a supportive community of learners. Most of these groups included at least one member who had completed another of my graduate courses that required a group inquiry project and self-evaluation of coursework. These students were frequently sought out as resources by other students who were struggling to understand the course design or to make sense of my expectations. These comments from members of Group 4 show this type of collaboration:

> We found the job of collaborating to be difficult. One of the first obstacles we had to overcome was communication. We had a lot of verbal exploration. It was time consuming but necessary for us to get to know each other before we could get to work. Each of us came to the group with our own personal history...but the shared history helped us develop trust in each other which we recognize to be an essential part of a successful group experience.... We think that all group members would benefit by reading each group member's log. Reading the same articles and discussing them before writing the paper

would also be beneficial. Doing this would help us gain perspective about each other and establish a common history, and we feel it would have made writing the paper easier.

When I try to step back to visualize my role in the group process, I see myself as the "disturber." Every time the group moves toward consensus, I am jumping in to mess things up! Sometimes I can do it—and sometimes not. I can't honestly evaluate my intentions as selfish or altruistic. Do I want my own way? Or has the group failed to consider this additional point?

I have truly been enlightened on the value of talk in constructing knowledge. The group needs to build trust in order to create an environment where it is important to share thoughts and create ideas. Competitiveness needs to be set aside.... This process has to be explored—it can't be taught.

The topical analysis chart highlighted the different ways the groups discussed collaboration and helped me explore the reasons their views and experiences were so dissimilar. My next step was to construct charts to examine group and individual comments regarding the evaluation process, along with specific responses to the course structure. When I looked at my charts together, I was able to see the topics that were discussed in each of the group evaluations. While I was in the process of identifying these common features, however, I realized that I was more intrigued by the unique features of each group. At this point I began to reread the group and individual evaluations as well as my data briefs to identify these features. I then decided to create "portraits" of each group to capture the ways in which the groups differed.

Developing Group Portraits

Each of the groups included the same general information in its evaluation: the overall goal or focus of the group, references to inquiry procedures, comments about the paper or class presentation, and concluding remarks that generally made mention of the criteria group members were using to evaluate the quality of their work. Even with these similarities, each group was unique in its approach to the process of working collaboratively, the insights expressed in the evaluations, and the feelings shared about the relative success of the course. I created a summary sheet to highlight the two or three distinctive features of each group. Here are several examples:

- Group 1: "excited to find" and "most exciting discovery was"; great summary of process, presentation, and paper.
- Group 2: defensive tone—"our paper and presentation overlapped but," "didn't meet our original goals but," "because of our topic..."; heavy emphasis on goals—"thought out our goals."
- Group 4: focus on insights gained about and from collaboration; photo log to document collaboration.
- Group 5: focus on getting organized in classroom, then working with parents; met and exceeded goals—"would never have done this on our own."

This way of looking at the groups led me to organize them into three related sets, based on the patterns that emerged on my summary sheet. The first set (groups 2 and 5) I labeled the "goal-oriented" groups. These focused on completing the assignment by producing the required material (the paper, the presentation, and the group evaluation). Throughout the course I worried about these groups because they concentrated on doing what I wanted rather than on finding out about something they genuinely cared about. Early on in the group work they divided their topic and assigned equal amounts of work on the resulting subtopics to each member. I frequently commented in my planning notes that I needed to meet with these groups to see if I could help them work *together* rather than as a collection of individuals.

Groups 1 and 6 I labeled the "process-oriented" or "journey" groups. These groups defined success in terms of the journey they made in producing the paper, presentation, or evaluation. Members described their group experience positively, frequently commenting that the collaboration had helped them discover new things about the inquiry process or about their topic. These groups were exciting for me to watch because they were actively involved in the inquiry process itself. Their discussions and logs showed that they changed procedures and developed understanding on an ongoing basis. While they did divide up the work to be completed before the next group session, they used those sessions to share and evaluate what each member of the group had been able to accomplish and to establish an agenda for their next meeting. In addition, each group member concentrated on subtopics and aspects of the group experience that reflected his or her strengths; as a member of Group 1 said in her self-evaluation, "The one thing that I could have improved on would have been to increase my input into the paper, but as we looked at our group's strengths and weaknesses, I did not choose to be involved in the organization of the paper, but instead in the organization of the presentation."

Groups 3, 4, and 7 I labeled the "transactive" or "inquiry-oriented" groups. These

groups seemed to have an outstanding collaborative experience. I wrote in my planning notes and reflections that they achieved the full potential of collaborative group inquiry as I understood it. From their initial meetings, these were the groups that excited me as a teacher. During the fifth week of class, for example, I wrote that Group 4 was "taking this assignment and running with it. They're using the course structure to pursue their own interests and needs."

Like the journey groups, these groups described their inquiry process in detail, frequently explaining how discussion sessions had led them to revisions in both procedures and understanding. However, the transactive groups went on to examine their thinking on the design of the course and to relate it to the process-oriented classrooms they wanted to create for their own students. They used terms like "transaction" to refer to their group experiences and described their understanding of collaboration in detail, again referring to their own experiences as both students and teachers. Group 4 included photographs of a "marathon Saturday" session in its log; the pictures were introduced with the caption, "The following pictures do not quite capture the tone of the day we [got together] to practice our presentation and write our paper, but [they do] give you an idea of what our group collaboration looked like."

The group portraits enabled me to focus on the essential characteristics of the most and least successful groups. The successful groups—that is, sets two and three—were those that seemed to understand and feel comfortable with the process-centered, inquiry-oriented learning environment I was striving to create. They clearly articulated what they had learned as a result of their inquiry and were genuinely excited about the unanticipated learning that emerged during the process. These groups were also able to describe the collaborative nature of their work and to make connections between their learning experiences in my course and their goals as classroom teachers.

Highlighting the unique features of each group had been so successful as a data analysis strategy that I decided to compare and contrast two of the groups. I wanted to understand *how* these groups were different in the hope that I would be able to identify ways I might have enhanced their experiences or could improve the experiences of future groups.

Consideration of High-Contrast Groups

Group 4, a transactive group, and Group 5, a goal-oriented group, provided the strongest contrast. Group 4 had five members, four of whom had completed a graduate course with me the previous semester; Group 5's four members included no "repeat" students. The number of repeat students was not, however, sufficient to distinguish the transactive groups from the goal-oriented ones, since some groups with repeat students had not been particularly successful. (Interestingly, though, all of the inquiry-oriented groups did have at least one group member who had taken my graduate language arts course the previous semester.)

I began this stage of my analysis by rereading the group and individual evaluations for groups 4 and 5, looking for their distinguishing features. This led to the identification of several patterns that I verified by considering the data for all of the groups. I then compared the patterns I found with those that emerged from the group evaluations prepared by students in the previous semester's language arts course and the graduate literacy course I was then teaching.

The goal-oriented groups were the least successful. They consistently described their work as cooperative and supportive and identified the primary value of the group as providing motivation, encouragement, and opportunities to share. They talked about sharing concrete resource materials such as reproducible masters, children's literature titles, and "new and creative activities to enhance learning." They rarely connected their own classroom teaching experiences to the design of this course, and, when they did, they emphasized the differences in levels of responsibility adult and child learners are capable of handling. Members of these groups limited their group evaluations to descriptions of the work they had completed or the goals they had accomplished and seldom offered examples or elaborated on topics. The group *and* individual evaluations by members of these goal-oriented groups included descriptions of their discomfort with the course design and with my lack of clarity in establishing objectives and goals for their learning in the course. These students were also uncomfortable with the self-evaluation process and wanted more frequent feedback from me on the quality and effectiveness of their work.

The transactive groups, on the other hand, had clearly been the most successful. They described their work as "collaborative" and frequently gave examples of the benefits of their collaboration. Their discussions included references to members' own prior experiences with group learning strategies (such as cooperative learning) both as teachers and as students. Members of these groups who had not worked in collaborative groups and who were initially uncomfortable with the course design talked of their discomfort fading as the course progressed. These groups described and evaluated their inquiry process and summarized the key points group members learned through inquiry. During discussions members offered suggestions for ways future groups might proceed as well as ideas of ways I might be able to better support my students in the inquiry group component of the course.

For many students, the self-directed, small-group inquiry experiences in this course were unfamiliar and, for some, this meant they were threatening. This course violated the way they thought a college course should be organized. If students (or, for that matter, teachers) expect teachers to be the single source of authority and knowledge, they become uncomfortable if their expectations do not match reality (Anders & Richardson, 1991). My analysis of student perceptions suggests that students must resolve this discomfort and come to understand the structure of the course in order to make the most of self-directed learning. One member of Group 1 described this process of resolution:

> At the beginning I felt frustrated not knowing exactly what or how much was expected of me. Then I realized that you were allowing me to set my own goals for my needs. After I realized that, then I felt much better.

Becoming comfortable in the course was made easier for those students who relied on their group's members to share ideas, work through course expectations, and learn. The transactive groups talked of the time they spent early on in their group experience getting to know one another and building a "shared history" by responding to one another's journals, describing how they were implementing new ideas in their classrooms, and discussing shared readings. The development of a suitable shared goal was also helpful in creating a successful group experience. While all the groups focused on accomplishing the overall course goals, the

transactive groups worked toward inquiry-oriented rather than task-oriented goals—that is, at least some of their goals focused on collaborative inquiry rather than accomplishing a task simply to get it out of the way. The transactive groups recognized the ongoing and generative nature of inquiry, often commenting that the inquiry could never be complete; the goal-oriented groups found satisfaction in accomplishing each goal in turn and seldom talked of new goals for learning or questions that emerged from the inquiry process.

Members of transactive groups were comfortable enough with one another to move beyond polite cooperation to argue, debate, and disagree about issues. These groups' members outgrew their established thinking through the inquiry process and fully understood the advantages of learning collaboratively. These were the students who spoke about basing activities for their elementary classrooms on those of the inquiry group project. In addition, these students were willing to take a "vulnerable stance" (Watson, Harste, & Burke, 1989) in relation to their own learning. They successfully engaged in reflection, identified areas of strength and accomplishment, and suggested ways of improving their inquiry processes for "next time."

Implications

The efforts of teacher researchers should yield ideas for new instructional strategies, insights into current practices, questions for further inquiry, and suggestions for improving research processes (Myers, 1985). I considered each of these areas when I reflected on the implications of my research.

Throughout the inquiry I relied on my own collaboration with other teachers—both teacher educators and elementary classroom teachers—and with former students. All have helped me identify effective classroom practices and productive ways of viewing the experiences that took place in my class. My students were often direct in their suggestions about how I could create a more supportive and successful learning environment. I agree with their assessment that the groups must have considerable time in the beginning of the course to build a sense of community.

Each year, Mary Ann Rankey and others with whom I share my teaching experiences talk of how quickly this year's students seem to "gel" in comparison to last year's group. We seem to be getting better at helping learners feel a sense of membership in and responsibility to the community they are creating. During some semesters I do feel more successful in this endeavor than during others. I celebrate when students comment that they could not have completed the course without the support of their classmates, but my pleasure is tempered by the fact that they do not always feel that this is positive. I need to know more about the process of creating a learning community, particularly within the constraints of a traditional university system.

These days I vacillate between attempts to offer too much and failure to provide sufficient support for groups and group members. The students want support and feedback from me as well as from their classmates in selecting, focusing, and accomplishing their goals. Students' comments suggest that I should provide this support by sharing the goals of former students, some sample inquiries that captured the "best" of what is possible, and excerpts from evaluations that illuminate collaboration and the evaluation process. Discussing the course design explicitly with the support of these examples may help students who are uncomfortable with it

come to understand, if not value, it. My analysis of the student self-evaluations made me conscious of the criteria I was using intuitively to evaluate students in my courses. This should allow me to articulate my values to students more clearly. I am hopeful that discussing these criteria openly with students will help more of them clearly understand my objectives and intentions for their work in the course.

Encouraging students to explore collaborative, inquiry group experiences in their own classrooms may also be beneficial. Many successful students discussed having done so. Whether their understanding and valuing of collaborative inquiry made this connection to classroom teaching possible or whether the connection facilitated understanding needs further exploration.

In addition to things I learned from my research, I also established some questions for further inquiry. I continue to be concerned about the difficulty some students and groups have in resolving their discomfort over the unfamiliar course structure. While my research permitted me to examine my own thinking about successful course experiences and student learning, I still feel the need to identify the ways in which my decisions support or inhibit students' efforts to comprehend and value the role of collaboration and self-evaluation in the learning process. Discussions with former students have helped me identify the more successful actions I have taken; interviews with these students coupled with a systematic analysis of my own log might help me better understand this complex issue.

I tried to examine the group logs for further insight into how the transactive groups functioned in comparison to the goal-oriented groups, but they did not provide enough detail to support such an inquiry. Analyzing the transcripts of tape-recorded group discussions might be a useful way to find such insight. At the heart of the learning found in an inquiry-oriented class-room is often the sort of "exploratory talk" (Barnes, 1976) the transactive groups engaged in, but the written documents I analyzed failed to provide a complete picture of its nature.

My research was based on two beliefs: first, I believe that what we know about the "best practices" for elementary classrooms provides insight for creating more supportive college classroom environments; second, I believe that collaborative, inquiry group experiences reflect the best of what we now understand about supporting learners of all ages. Based on my data analysis, I now believe that for students to be successful in my courses, they must understand and come to value the inquiry group experiences. As a result, my work as a teacher researcher will continue to be focused on the search for ways to support students, particularly those in the less successful goal-oriented groups described in this chapter, move in this direction.

In trying to understand these goal-oriented groups, I recognized and began to question another belief that was guiding my work. I believe that a teacher can create a single learning environment that will support all learners. I am therefore looking for ways to extend my support of the more successful groups while helping the less successful groups appreciate what I value. This search has involved me in extensive discussion with elementary teachers who are also working to create collaborative, inquiry-oriented classrooms. They, too, are working to help struggling students understand and come to value this type of learning environment. While they seem to begin the school year with students like those in my goal-oriented groups, they report successes (of varying degrees) with all their students by the end of the school year. These teachers know something about supporting the goal-oriented groups that I haven't figured out. I hope to use these teachers' input to explore strategies for supporting students in my classes. At the same time, I would like to explore an emerging concern: I am asking my students to work within something I, without consulting them, have defined to be "a supportive learning environment." Perhaps students views of what makes up such an environment are different from my own.

Classroom teachers, and their students, have already taught me that I should ask my students to enter into a collaborative inquiry with me to find answers to my questions. While the invitation has been extended to all students in the past, only members of the transactive and journey groups have accepted. My next goal is to formulate an invitation that successfully leads to collaborative inquiry *with* members of goal-oriented groups, rather than *about* them.

References

Anders, P.L., & Richardson, V. (1991). Research directions: Staff development that empowers teachers' reflection and enhances instruction. *Language Arts, 67*(4), 316-321.

Barnes, D. (1976). *From communication to curriculum*. Portsmouth, NH: Heinemann.

Gilles, C. (1991). *Negotiating the meanings: The uses of talk in literature study groups by adolescents labeled learning disabled*. Unpublished doctoral dissertation, University of Missouri-Columbia, Columbia, MO.

Myers, M. (1985). *The teacher-researcher: How to study writing in the classroom*. Urbana, IL: National Council of Teachers of English.

Watson, D., Hartse, J., & Burke, C. (1989). *Whole language: Inquiring voices*. New York: Scholastic.

Chapter 24

Passing on the Joy of Literacy: Students Become Writing Teachers

Ellen H. Brinkley

Brinkley, who teaches in the English Department at Western Michigan University in Kalamazoo, is currently engaged in research on writing assessment and on issues of censorship and intellectual freedom.

Becoming a teacher is a lot like reliving adolescence: there's the impatience that comes with having parent-like administrators, who claim to know what's best, prescribe a seemingly endless number of rules and requirements; there's the constant advice about what should or should not be done in the classroom; there's an eagerness to get on with it, coupled with a nagging fear of not ever really being ready; and there's the struggle to find a new identity. Over the course of several semesters in my "Writing for Elementary Teachers" course, I observed—or thought I observed—that many students began the semester feeling "student-like" but by the end of term they seemed to feel like professionals, eager to teach and fairly confident of their ability to do so effectively. At first my observations were based on impressions and hunches, and I decided I needed to explore them in more detail through classroom research. I initially had two research questions:

- Do my students in fact experience this shift in attitude?

- If they do, why does it happen?

What I discovered over two semesters was that while there was increased confidence about teaching, there was an even greater shift in my students' attitudes toward writing and toward themselves as writing teachers. It was from their own experience of becoming "joyfully literate" (Calkins, 1986, p. 102) that my students became eager to pass on the joy of literacy to their own students.

Research Context and Process

Students usually take this 15-week course during the semester or year before they begin student teaching. Although most have taken reading pedagogy courses, very few have had courses focused on writing pedagogy and, in fact, many have had no writing-related courses since their first-year composition class. My course is designed to help preservice teachers learn about children's writing development and how to foster their future students' growth as writers. We write and share our writing throughout the semester, starting in the first class, and students are encouraged to reflect on and consider the implications of their own writing experiences for their future classrooms. Class sessions are supplemented by readings, journal writing, and study of children's writing samples. Near the end of the course students complete two major assignments: they teach two hour-long workshops in an elementary classroom, and they conduct a 30-minute in-class workshop in which they present individual or collaborative research on a writing-related topic of their choice.

In the first semester of my research project I used materials that were already part of the course—students' written comments made in the first and last class sessions and excerpts from their journals—as my primary sources of data. These were supplemented by my own notes written after class sessions and other written materi-

als produced by students throughout the semester. During the second semester of my study, I focused more narrowly on students' apprehensions about writing and on confirming or correcting particular impressions gained during the previous semester. To what extent were my students apprehensive about writing? To what extent did they overcome their apprehension during the course of the semester? The 26-item version of the Daly-Miller Writing-Apprehension Scale (Daly, 1985, p. 46) helped provide data to answer these questions. I hoped that all the data I collected would enable me to determine if lowered writing apprehension would affect my students' attitudes toward teaching.

Starting Out

On the first day of class in the first semester of my study, I asked students to tell me briefly about their hopes and fears for the course. I had done this in previous semesters as a way to determine students' interests and needs, but in the past I had only read through the replies casually. When I actually categorized and counted the responses this semester, I was surprised by what I saw. Almost half of those who mentioned teaching already seemed confident and eager to teach. For example, one student wrote, "I am excited about the practical work in elementary classrooms"; another wrote, "I find working with young children exciting and stimulating." I was wary that these positive comments might be "teacher-pleasers," and thought that the comments from the other half of my students—those who discussed teaching in terms of "fear"—might be more sincere. One such student wrote, "I don't want to get into a teaching situation and not know what to do," and another expressed what I thought was probably an unspoken fear of many others when he wrote, "My fears are that I will get into a classroom someday, and everything I have learned will be irrelevant to the real world (God, I hope that doesn't happen)."

In addition to comments about teaching, I discovered an unexpected number of comments about writing and about how my students saw themselves as writers. Again, some comments were positive: "I have always enjoyed writing" and "I love to write myself and hope I can get others to enjoy writing, too." However, for each student who expressed such enthusiasm, two or three expressed dissatisfaction and apprehension about writing and about themselves as writers. These students wrote, "I'm not very good at writing," "I always find it hard to express my thoughts in writing," and "My fear is that I will not be able to measure up as a writer."

When I compared these reactions to those of inservice teachers in writing workshops with which I had been involved, I found some striking parallels. Although inservice teachers have overcome their classroom jitters, they often admit that they don't like writing and explain that their own preservice training did not include information on how to teach writing. Once when I was planning for a workshop, a teacher told me that her colleagues had insisted she ask that any writing they were called on to do be extremely brief since writing was *not* what they expected to do in an inservice workshop. It seems clear that writing apprehension affects inservice and preservice teachers alike.

I then turned to the professional literature and was glad to discover that several studies described in journals focused on writing apprehension. For example, Daly (1985) explains that an individual's attitude about writing is just as basic to successful writing as are skills; indeed, a positive *atti-*tude about writing is associated with and may even be a prerequisite for the successful development and maintenance of writing skills. Research on practicing classroom teachers' attitudes toward writing gave me even more to think about. When Claypool (quoted in Daly, 1985) assessed how often high school teachers assigned tasks that required writing, she found "a significant difference between highly and less apprehensive teachers in the number of assignments they made. Highly apprehensive teachers on the average reported making only seven assignments yearly compared to the annual average of 19.9 by low-apprehensives" (p. 52). Bizzaro and Toler (1986) showed that writing center tutors (and, by extension, classroom teachers) who were apprehensive about their own writing emphasized lower order, sentence-level concerns, seldom waited for students to make discoveries about their writing, and avoided mentioning students' strengths.

Reducing my students' writing apprehension certainly seemed to be a goal worth striving for. In fact, I began to believe that it was absolutely essential if my students were to become effective teachers of writing.

Students Share Reflections

Through my experiences in earlier semesters I had come to realize that my students came to class possessing beliefs about writing and writing instruction based on the past instruction they had experienced. Consequently, each time I taught the course I tried to pull out of students' long-term memories any recollections of experiences that had led them to develop certain assumptions about writing. I asked them to write about and share their early memories of writing. When they did, their stories were met with nods and smiles from classmates as they each told in turn stories that ranged from dutifully making circles on paper to carving a name in an antique desk, from having a poem displayed on a bulletin board to learning as a fourth grader that writing was used as a punishment. Students' implicit assumptions about writing began to emerge: the belief that writing is hard and discouraging work; that it requires primarily attention to form, grammar, spelling, and punctuation; and that it often results in feeling bad about oneself. "Struggle" was a word that seemed to sum up many students' beliefs about writing, and it did not take long to discover that many of these negative feelings came from past school experiences. One student's story provides an example:

> When I was very young, I loved to write stories.... I was very proud of them and I wrote many until one of my teachers laughed at me and said I was silly. After that I still wrote every day but only for myself in a diary.... I realized that my whole attitude toward writing changed because of that comment by a teacher I really liked. Since then, I've always felt that I was not a good writer, even though I usually got good grades.

If this incident sounds extreme, consider Bishop's (1989) relating of the sad tale, told by a college writing center tutor, of a student who brought a graded paper to his writing conference:

> The instructor had written the words "ultimate failure" on this, the first graded paper by a student who had been out of school for a year and a half, [who] had written on something that concerned him, and [who] was not confident of his abilities to begin with (p. 7).

Perhaps it is surprising not that our students have so many writing insecurities and apprehensions, but that they don't have more.

I believe there was a kind of catharsis at work in our sharing sessions as past experiences and beliefs were acknowledged, shared, and finally accepted. Graves (1991) recommends that teachers do this kind of reflecting in order to answer questions such as "How much does your personal history contribute to your use or nonuse of writing?" (p. 60). These group sessions also allow students to learn from one another. As they hear others describe their beliefs and experiences, students begin to sort out for themselves what they want for their own teaching. Such activities help students become aware of what they already know and so nudge them toward trusting their own judgment. I hope that by encouraging this sort of reflection, I am also pointing my students on the path of thinking about their work, being open to learning from their experiences, colleagues, and students, and, perhaps, becoming teachers who might someday conduct their own classroom research.

It was during a second such sharing session that I became aware of Jenny. Here is what I wrote in my log:

> Jenny shared her writing with the whole class, apparently having been chosen by her small group (not by me). She started reading very fast...so much so that I interrupted her (politely, I believe) and said I was missing part of what she was saying—so could she start over and slow down. The second time I still missed most of what she was saying, so (again politely, even gently, I think) I asked her to repeat what I—and surely the class—had missed. At that point she slowed down enough that we heard the rest. After class she told me that she had a great fear of speaking in a group though she recognized that as a teacher she'd have to do it.

I realized that because of her fears Jenny might be a particularly important student to observe as part of my study. Could the extra attention to attitudes somehow benefit someone as shy and insecure as she seemed to be?

Learning from My Students

Early in the semester I asked students to write about a personal experience and explained that we would be thinking and talking about their writing process as they experienced it. I gave them copies of personal narratives written by a former student and by a professional writer, and then asked them to search their memories for their own stories to tell. I had designed what I considered to be a nonthreatening assignment, one that I felt they could all succeed with.

On the day they brought drafts to class, I asked them to respond to prompts about their writing experience. From their responses it was clear that several students felt considerably less comfortable with my "nonthreatening" assignment than I had anticipated. For example, in response to the prompt "When I heard the assignment, I thought or felt...," they wrote such things as "I felt confused and frustrated because I didn't have any ideas," "I felt like I was doomed; the thought of writing anything makes me tense up," and "I thought, why is she doing this to me?" Such comments taught me just how intimidated students can feel when faced with the prospect of beginning to write after reading polished, revised, "finished-product" models—even models from previous students.

Fortunately, several students were more positive when asked to discuss later phases of the writing process. Some seemed to experience a breakthrough, saying, "I felt like things were falling into place. I could remember detail after detail even to the point of

refeeling some of the emotions that I had felt at the time of the event" and "Eventually—after hours of pacing—the words started to come." When asked how they felt about their writing when they reread it in class, however, some seemed very uneasy—one said, "I feel sick. It looks awful," while another said, "I think I should throw it out." It was clear at this point that several of these third- and fourth-year college students felt unsure and vulnerable as writers and therefore couldn't welcome the prospect of teaching writing. Fortunately, discussing and conducting writing conferences soon provided not only suggestions for improving writing but new confidence as well.

In a sharing session later in the term each student was asked to read to the class a polished piece of writing. I would not have insisted that students participate if I had been teaching strictly a writing class, but I felt strongly that these future teachers of writing needed to know how vulnerable some student writers feel, to be willing to take risks themselves, and to understand the value of receiving responses to their writing. In spite of all my good intentions, however, I sensed a lot of anxiety from my students as the day for this session drew closer. Here are my log notes for that class:

> Today when I came into the classroom, I saw just 3-4 students. Since it was very close to 9:00, my heart sank. The sharing session seems so important, in part as a way to model sharing sessions that we recommend for elementary classrooms.... It was foggy outside but not enough to seriously delay anyone. My greater fear was that they had had so much anxiety that they had decided not to show up! Not to worry...soon a steady stream of students poured in. One carried two big boxes of donuts, announcing as he came in, "I decided if we're going to have a celebration, we need food."

In the end, every student attended that day's session. Later, students said that they had felt considerable anxiety followed by relief and even elation that day. One said, "Before we shared I was extremely nervous. I worried about it all week long. I thought people would think my story was stupid. But no one did." Another commented, "I felt that my story wouldn't compare to anyone else's...but everyone was so receptive and made me feel good about my writing." Attitudes seemed to be shifting in a positive direction. These comments about the session suggest why: "[This session] has brought us as a class closer together. We are people, not just bodies sharing a class" and "People's stories were different from what I expected. I had planned on hearing a bunch of cutesy stories, but these were deep and meaningful both to the writer and the listeners."

I learned from students' comments that this session was indeed a turning point in the course, a time when students experienced—some for the first time—the joy of having their own stories heard and accepted. Furthermore, they were beginning to understand and experience the satisfaction that comes from pushing through the struggles in order to share a part of themselves in a way that their peers would respect and appreciate. As they wrote and shared their stories, we came to recognize that we had become a learning community of writers.

I have to admit I was especially concerned about how Jenny might handle the session. She was the last to volunteer to read and did so very quickly, with paper shaking and her head down. She has given me permission to quote excerpts from the piece she read, a very personal narrative indeed:

> I've always had this need to go back to school and finish my education.... I went down to the college one evening to take a GED test. I was sure that I

would not pass the whole test, but thought that I could pass a couple of parts and then I would know which parts to study.... [The test administrator] said he would quickly grade all of the tests and give me an unofficial score.... I was so close to tears and I did not want to cry in front of him.... When he finished he looked up and said, "You passed." I just could not believe it. That day was the beginning of a whole new outlook.

Jenny had not finished high school, had married young and had children, and then entered college after passing a high school equivalency test. She certainly had had far different experiences from those of her classmates. Yet, after her reading, her younger colleagues put into practice what they had learned from our reading and in-class discussions about the responses writers need. They offered affirming comments, to which Jenny smiled and replied, "I'm glad I did it."

Jenny taught me time and again not to underestimate what she was capable of. From this point on, she offered her insights during whole-class discussions and volunteered to participate in class sessions; at the end of the term, she confidently gave a well-researched presentation for her classmates.

Student Writers Becoming Writing Teachers

Each student was required to lead two writing workshops in an elementary classroom as a practicum assignment. Though not all the classroom sessions were roaring successes, most students seemed to find in them the confirmation they needed that all that we had experienced in our classroom would work in an elementary classroom as well. Barb expressed well the shift in attitude that many felt:

> At the beginning of my second day when we were gathered together and

I was getting ready to read a story, a little boy asked, "Are we going to be authors today?" I asked him if he liked being an author, and the whole class answered "Yes!"... I thoroughly enjoyed both days—it came quite naturally for me to talk in front of the class—I thought I might feel awkward. This type of classroom participation was very valuable to me—instead of observing at the sideline, I was in charge—what a great feeling!

(Readers will notice that Barb's final comment doesn't sound very student-centered. When more experienced teachers recall their first teaching experiences, however, I believe we remember how important it was to our fragile confidence levels that we feel in charge. More important though, was that after so many semesters of coursework, Barb was able to appreciate the classroom interaction that energizes new and experienced teachers alike.)

Unfortunately, unlike Barb's, Jenny's second practicum did not go very well. She said that the students groaned when she mentioned writing and that the classroom teacher whispered to her, "They hate to write." When I heard this, my first impulse was to curse the bad luck that Jenny had found herself in such a negative classroom setting. What seems remarkable for Jenny, however—and surely represents progress in her effort to become more confident in herself as a teacher—is that when she explained this to me she was obviously not pleased about the way things had gone, but neither was she devastated. Clearly her experiences in a class that I believe nurtured her confidence helped her get through a difficult time.

Confirmation of Positive Attitude Shifts

At our last class session before final exams, I asked students to respond anony-mously to a few prompts. I hoped this would help me determine more clearly how and why their attitudes had changed. My first prompt, for example, was "When I registered for English 369, I thought to myself..."; responses ranged from "I wondered if it would be about teaching handwriting or if it would be about writing stories" to "I hear Brinkley is hard" to "This is going to be a hard class for me because I am not especially strong in grammar." The second prompt was "Now that the class is almost over, I think...." In this case the responses were confident and enthusiastic. One student said, "I feel more prepared to teach. I am ready, whereas I wasn't at the beginning of the semester"; another said, "I feel I gained a lot from writing in this class.... I discovered a lot about myself and that I can write!"; and another said, "The class was nothing like I had expected and has gotten me really excited about writing and the writing processes of children." I acknowlege that the phrasing of the prompts suggested that I was looking for positive change, but the evidence still seems persuasive: of 36 respondents, *all* reported that their attitudes had improved, with 50 percent mentioning a change for the better in their attitude toward writing, 25 percent mentioning a positive change in their attitude toward teaching, and 44 percent mentioning a positive shift in their attitude toward teaching writing.

The final prompt was a question: "If your attitudes have changed, what specific factors have been involved in the change?" I analyzed and charted the factors mentioned into the following categories:

- Course content/activities (readings, practicum, class discussion): 24 students, or 67 percent;

- Instructor (support, enthusiasm, knowledge, as model): 20 students, or 56 percent;
- Classmates (small-group sharing, peer writing conferences, student presentations): 10 students, or 28 percent;
- Other (attitudes reinforced rather than changed, attitudes changed but no reason given, journals): 6 students, or 17 percent.

The process of identifying the categories from the data my students provided was enlightening. As I went through the responses the first time, it was difficult to extract discrete items, but eventually a list emerged and it became easier to see connections and categories. My prior experience with the course had already told me how much students appreciated a core text (we used Calkins's *The Art of Teaching Writing*) that taught by sharing classroom stories and reflections; now I could also see how important the class's support had been in allowing students to express their uncertainties and to come to believe they could succeed.

The Next Semester

During the second part of the study in the next semester, I used a measure of shifts in attitude that I had not used originally. The 26-item version of the Daly-Miller Writing-Apprehension Scale (Daly, 1985, p. 46) was given as a pretest during the first class session and again as a posttest during the last class session. The results, shown in the table on the next page, provide overwhelming statistical evidence of reduced apprehension about writing among students over the course of the semester. (I have separated the items which express attitudes negatively from those that express attitudes positively.)

Clearly, by the end of the semester far fewer students reported avoiding writing (statement #1), experienced initial writer's block (#7), reported being nervous about writing (#13), and reported being "no good" at writing (#26). Curiously, however, responses to two statements—#4 about writing evaluation and #18 about expecting to do poorly in a writing class—did not show clearly a positive shift. I can only guess at the reasons—perhaps these responses indicate the depth of feelings about previous negative experiences with composition and evaluation, or perhaps they indicate unhappiness with the grades the students had earned in my class.

I believe what is even more interesting, however, are the responses to statements that express attitudes positively. Here every item without exception indicated a positive shift, and the shifts were statistically more significant. A tremendously increased number of students reported looking forward to writing (statement #3), said they would enjoy submitting writing to a magazine (#9), claimed they liked to write (#10, #15, and #17), felt others enjoyed their writing (#14), liked seeing their thoughts on paper (#19), and found it easy to write good compositions (#23). The number of students who reported that they liked friends to read what they had written (#12) and enjoyed discussing their writing (#20) doubled between the pre- and posttests. Although I had tried throughout the semester to emphasize each part of the writing process, these numbers led me to reconsider the potential positive effects that sharing could have on students' attitudes.

Implications

I believe my students were sincere when they told me their attitudes had changed—although not everyone demonstrated the dramatic change that I saw in

Results from Daly-Miller Writing-Apprehension Scale

Note: for the pretest, n=58; for the posttest, n=61. Posttest results appear in parentheses.

Negatively expressed items:

	Agree	Uncertain	Disagree
*1. I avoid writing.	12 (3)	6 (6)	40 (52)
4. I am afraid of writing essays when I know they will be evaluated.	16 (19)	10 (5)	32 (37)
5. Taking a composition course is a very frightening experience.	20 (12)	7 (9)	31 (40)
*7. My mind seems to go blank when I start to work on a composition.	20 (10)	11 (8)	27 (43)
8. Expressing ideas through writing seems to be a waste of time.	2 (2)	0 (1)	56 (58)
*13. I'm nervous about writing.	20 (14)	15 (7)	23 (40)
16. I never seem to be able to clearly write down my ideas.	18 (12)	10 (13)	30 (36)
18. I expect to do poorly in composition classes even before I enter them.	8 (11)	7 (5)	43 (45)
21. I have a terrible time organizing my ideas in a composition course.	23 (15)	8 (10)	27 (36)
22. When I hand in a composition I know I'm going to do poorly.	4 (3)	10 (8)	44 (50)
24. I don't think I write as well as most other people.	24 (21)	16 (18)	18 (22)
25. I don't like my compositions to be evaluated.	20 (16)	15 (18)	23 (27)
*26. I'm no good at writing.	2 (1)	14 (6)	42 (53)

Positively expressed items:

	Agree	Uncertain	Disagree
2. I have no fear of my writing being evaluated.	19 (23)	10 (15)	29 (23)
*3. I look forward to writing down my ideas.	31 (46)	16 (9)	11 (4)
6. Handing in a composition makes me feel good.	29 (36)	17 (15)	12 (9)
*9. I would enjoy submitting my writing to magazines for evaluation and publication.	12 (26)	20 (22)	26 (13)
*10. I like to write my ideas down.	40 (54)	11 (5)	7 (2)
11. I feel confident in my ability to clearly express my ideas in writing.	29 (38)	16 (17)	13 (5)
*12. I like to have my friends read what I have written.	21 (40)	15 (9)	22 (12)
*14. People seem to enjoy what I write.	24 (40)	31 (20)	3 (1)
*15. I enjoy writing.	36 (49)	12 (11)	10 (1)
*17. Writing is a lot of fun.	25 (40)	20 (17)	13 (4)
*19. I like seeing my thoughts on paper.	36 (51)	17 (6)	5 (4)
*20. Discussing my writing with others is an enjoyable experience.	16 (41)	28 (9)	14 (10)
*23. It's easy for me to write good compositions.	9 (22)	22 (21)	27 (17)

*Indicates a shift in the attitudes of at least 10 students.

Jenny. Yes, they were more confident and enthusiastic about teaching and, what was more striking, they felt more positively about themselves as writers and about teaching writing. Based on my students' comments, I believe this change was due primarily to what we did and studied and discussed and how this all suggested to them things they could do as teachers— writing, reading, sharing, reflecting, and learning in a community.

Several times during my research, students revealed how deeply they had personalized what they were experiencing and learning. When they reflected on their own past experiences, they said such things as "I wish I had been encouraged to write on my own topics," "I wish I had been encouraged to take writing risks," and "I wish I had had the chance to sit in an author's chair." One student's comment describes the kind of shift in attitude I would welcome any time: "I had a really negative attitude about writing before I came into this class, but now that it's over, I will walk away with the most wonderful gift—enthusiasm to write and the ability to pass that down to my students."

This study has shown me how much more apprehensive about writing my students are than I had thought, that students benefit from being invited to monitor not just their learning but also their attitudes, that classroom environment plays an important role in shifting students' attitudes, and positive attitudes toward writing free students to feel more positive and more professional about teaching. Brooke (1988) explains that students' "stance" toward writing is often developed by observing their teachers. If so, then not only must I model a positive stance for my students, but they will have to model a similar stance for their future students.

I have begun the process of applying all I learned from this study to my other classes. For example, I recognize that some students in my "Reading as a Psycholinguistic Process" course have negative attitudes toward reading (though my hunch is the number is not as large as it is for those with negative attitudes toward writing). I recognize the need for students to think about and discuss their attitudes toward reading and toward the teaching of reading. I select texts and classroom experiences that I hope will produce an environment that will nudge students toward finding the joy in reading. I'm looking for ways to allow students to share their reading…. In fact, as I write this paragraph, I find myself thinking that the time may be ripe for a new study. Teacher research is like that—new discoveries lead to new questions and to new learning. Perhaps through my modeling of what it means to engage in reflective practice, my students will be better equipped to model and pass on to their own students the joy of learning.

References

Bishop, W. (1989). We're all basic writers. *Writing Center Journal, 9*(2), 31-42.

Bizarro, P., & Toler, H. (1986). The effects of writing apprehension on the teaching behaviors of writing center tutors. *Writing Center Journal, 7*(1), 37-43.

Brooke, R. (1988). Modeling a writer's identity: Reading and imitation in the writing classroom. *College Composition and Communication, 39,* 23-41.

Calkins, L.M. (1986). *The art of teaching writing.* Portsmouth, NH: Heinemann.

Daly, J.A. (1985). Writing apprehension. In M. Rose (Ed.), *When a writer can't write* (pp. 43-82). New York: Guilford.

Graves, D.H. (1991). *Build a literate classroom.* Portsmouth, NH: Heinemann.

Author Index

Subject Index

Note: An "f" following a page number indicates that the reference may be found in a figure; a "t," that it may be found in a table.

ASSESSMENT: 96, 177; comparative, 65; of literature studies, 139, 143-44; reader response and, 64, 65, 72; of reading workshop, 118-20; self- (*see* Self-evaluation[s]); whole language and, 38, 71-84. *See also* Evaluation forms; Examinations; Gates-MacGinitie Reading Test; Grading, paper; Progress reports; Quizzes; Surveys; Tests

ATWELL, NANCIE: 22-23, 61, 96, 97, 115, 116, 117, 124, 137-38

AUDIOTAPES: as teacher resource, 9, 38, 62, 64, 123

AUSTRALIA: teacher research in, 72-84

AUTHORS: 118, 122; student letters to favorite, 119

AUTOBIOGRAPHY OF BENJAMIN FRANKLIN, THE: 137

AUTOGRAPH BOOKS: 48

AVERAGING, TEST-SCORE. *See* Bell curves

AVI (author): 100

BANK STREET COLLEGE OF EDUCATION: 14

BARBARA (Langston Hughes Intermediate School teacher): 89-90

BASAL READERS: 62, 63, 65, 115; inadequacy of, 121; manuals for, 95

BEAM, KATHY (LDOS teacher): 43, 49

"BEAR, THE" (Faulkner): 131-32, 133

BELL CURVES: 176

BERTHOFF, ANN E.: 193

BIAS: teacher researchers and, 32, 39. *See also* Prejudice

BIOLOGY: prereading for students of, 133

BLACK BOY (Wright): 145

BODY LANGUAGE: as class-discussion element, 142; teacher use of, 49

BOOK REPORTS/REVIEWS: 139, 143; in teacher-education program, 185

BOOKS: assigned reading of classic, 97; for hearing-impaired students, 46-50; physical appeal of, 33; resistance to, 30-31, 33 (*see also* Readers, reluctant); student promotion of favorite, 62; student response to, 117,

118-21; student selection of, 29, 82; war-related, 52-59. *See also* Authors; Basal readers; Characters; Journals; Library; Literature; Reading; Reference books; Textbooks; Trade books

BRAINSTORMING: class, 143; teacher, 24

BRITAIN: action research in, 15

"BUILDING A DINING ROOM TABLE" (Atwell): 138

BUNTING, EVE: 52

BUREAU OF EDUCATION EXPERIMENTS (BEE): 14

BUSH, GEORGE: 103

BUTTER BATTLE BOOK, THE (Seuss): 52, 56, 57

BUZZ WORDS: *See* Jargon

CALKINS, LUCY: viii, 61, 100, 108, 193, 217

CALL IT COURAGE (Sperry): 67

CALL OF THE WILD, THE (London): 134

CAMBRIDGE INSTITUTE OF EDUCATION (CIE): 15

CAMPBELL, JACK: 21, 22, 23

CAMPBELL, KIMBERLY: 20, 21, 23

CATCHER IN THE RYE (Salinger): 134-35

CHARACTERS: maps of book, 123; reaction to book, 64, 117, 118

CHEMISTRY: prereading for students of, 132-33

CHERYL (LDOS teacher): 48

CHILD ABUSE: as classroom reading/discussion topic, 54; as writing topic, 103

CHOSEN, THE (Potok): 128

CLASSROOMS: collaborative, 198-209; process-oriented, 205

CLEARY, BEVERLY: 144

CLOSE ENOUGH TO TOUCH (Peck): 140

COLD WAR: as classroom discussion topic, 54

COLLABORATION: 202f, 203, 205. *See also* Classrooms, collaborative

COLLEAGUES: research results shared with, 33

COMENIUS, JOHN AMOS: 13

COMPOSITION: ix

tural aspects of, 11. *See also* Teacher educators; Teachers; Teaching

EDWARDS, ANNA CAMP: 14

EDWARDS, JONATHAN: 137

EIGHTH GRADERS: reading assignments for, 135-36; and reading workshops, 20, 116-21. *See also* Jo (Wood student)

ELEMENTARY CLASSROOM: teacher research in, 37-41

11TH GRADERS: and literature, 138-46

ELIE WIESEL: MESSENGER FROM THE HOLOCAUST (Greene): 52, 56

ELLIOTT, JOHN: 15-16

EMILE (Rousseau): 13

ENGAGEMENT: reader response and, 64

ENGLAND. *See* Britain

ENGLISH AS A SECOND LANGUAGE: 185

ENVIRONMENT, CLASSROOM: importance of, 29; least restrictive, 20

ERIN (Hirtle student): 139, 144-45

ESSAYS, STUDENT: 139, 143-45

ETHNOGRAPHY: whole language and, 16

EVALUATION. *See* Assessment; Self-evaluation(s)

EVALUATION FORMS: 80, 81f, 83

EVENTS, SEQUENCE OF: 61

EXAMINATIONS: 134; final, 136. *See also* Assessment; Tests

EXPERT PROJECTS: 159

EYE OF THE STORM (film): 135

FAITHFUL ELEPHANTS (Tsuchiya): 52, 54, 56

FAULKNER, WILLIAM: 131, 132, 133

FICTION: current events vs., 52, 53-54; patterns of, 73. *See also* Literature; Novels

FIELD NOTES, TEACHER'S: 9, 53, 72, 87, 96, 200. *See also* Teacher journals/logs

FIFTH GRADERS: assessment of, 72-84; reading programs for, 62-65; reading response of, 70; writing workshops for, 166

FITZGERALD, F. SCOTT: 145

FLOW EXPERIENCE: prereading and, 133-36

FRANK, ANNE: 135-36

FREE-CHOICE TIME: 48

FULWILER, TOBY: 138, 186

GAMES: science teaching enhanced by, 89

GARDINER, JOHN R.: 66

GATES-MacGINITIE READING TEST: 115, 116, 120

GENRES, LITERARY: student preferences among, 122, 123. *See also* Fiction; Poetry

GIVING TREE, THE (Silverstein): 120

GOING HOLLYWOOD (Schulz): 145

GOSWAMI, DIXIE: viii

GRADES. *See* Assessment

GRADE SHEETS: 116

GRADING, PAPER: 178, 179

GRAMMAR: 185, 213; books on, 114. *See also* Words

GRAVES, DONALD: viii, 61, 193, 213

GREAT DIDACTIC, THE (Comenius): 13

GREAT GATSBY, THE (Fitzgerald): 145

GREENE, CAROL: 52

GROUP STORIES: 20

GUIDED IMAGERY: 194

GULF WAR: as classroom reading/discussion topic, 51-55, 58-59; glorification of, 58; as writing topic, 103

HANDWRITING: 164; Jo (Wood student) and, 113

HAVE YOU SEEN MY DUCKLING? (Tafuri): 47

HAWTHORNE, NATHANIEL: 139. See also *Scarlet Letter, The*

HEARING-IMPAIRED CHILDREN: 39, 169; books for, 46-50; learning problems of, 44; teacher research among, 38; teaching of, 44-50. *See also* Louisville (KY) Deaf Oral School

HERBART, JOHANN FRIEDRICH: 13

HIGH SCHOOL STUDENTS: prewriting activities for, 134; reading assignments for, 131-36. *See also* 11th graders; 10th graders

HIROSHIMA: as classroom reading/discussion topic, 53, 54, 55

HISTORY: prereading for students of, 133-34

LISTENING: 105. *See also* Hearing-impaired children; Language arts

LITERACY: ix; joy of, 211. *See also* Reading; Writing

LITERATURE: African-American, 145; children's, 199; study of, 38; teaching, of, 137-46. *See also* Books; Fiction; Genres, literary; Poetry

LITERATURE CIRCLES: 159

LOGS: group, 199, 200, 208; learning, 158; observation, 20; photo, 204; reading, 116, 118, 136; reflection (*see* Reflective journals); research, 38 (*see also* Field notes); response (*see* Student journals/logs). *See also* Journals

LONDON, JACK: 134

LOUISVILLE (KY) DEAF ORAL SCHOOL (LDOS): 43-50

LOWRY, LOIS: 63f

LUCKIEST GIRL, THE (Cleary): 144

MAGAZINES, CLASS: 102

MAIN IDEA: 61; of dialogue journal, 187f

MAIRNEY (LDOS teacher): 48-49, 50

MAPS: reading-related analytical, 123

MARIAN (teacher-research facilitator at Langston Hughes Intermediate School): 90

MATHEMATICS: language skills and, 20, 49

MATRONE, HARRY: 24

MAYHER, JOHN S.: 193

MAYHEW, KATHERINE CAMP: 14

MAZER, NORMA FOX: 120

MEANING: language and, viii; words vs., 166

MEMORIZATION: Progressivism vs., 14

MERRIAM, JOAN: 22, 23

MESSAGE BOARDS, CLASS: 20

METAPHOR: 24; student use of, 141

MINILESSONS: planning of, 185; as reading workshop element, 116, 117, 118-19, 123, 126

MINORITY STUDENTS: underachieving, 86, 87, 88-89

MITCHELL, LUCY SPRAGUE: 14

MODEL BUILDING: 15

MODELING, TEACHER: 113

MONTESSORI, MARIA: 13

MORIMOTO, JUNKO: 52

MULTIPLE-HANDICAPPED CHILDREN: 50

MY HIROSHIMA (Morimoto): 52, 54, 55-56, 58

MYTHS: hearing-impaired students and, 44

NATIONAL TEACHERS EXAMINATION (NTE): 179

NAZIS: class discussion of, 53, 54. *See also* Frank, Anne; Hitler, Adolf

NEWSPAPER(S): class-produced, 48; as writing-topic source, 103

NORTHERN VIRGINIA WRITING PROJECT: 89-90

NOTES: from reference books, 83; student-to-student, 123, 124; teacher's (*see* Field notes); teacher researcher's (*see* Field notes)

NOVELS: as reading assignments, 115, 121, 130, 138, 139-46, 185, 199; as whole-class project, 121. *See also* Fiction; Literature

NUCLEAR WEAPONS: class discussion of, 55. *See also* Hiroshima

OBSERVATION, NATURALISTIC: 13

PARAGRAPHS: 118

PARAPHRASE: student use of, 64

PARENTS: of hearing-impaired children, 49; input of young readers', 72, 78; literacy portfolios shared with, 126, 129; student correspondence with, 126-29. *See also* Jo (Wood student)

PARKER, FRANCIS W.: 14

PAULSEN, GARY: 120

PECK, RICHARD: 120, 140

PEERS: as resource, 20, 67

PERCEPTION: reader response and, 64-65

PERSIAN GULF WAR. *See* Gulf War; Hussein, Saddam

PESTALOZZI, JOHANN HEINRICH: 13

PHONICS: hearing-impaired students and, 44

PIAGET, JEAN: 13

PLATO: 72

POETRY: Jo (Wood student) and, 110, 112; student, 123; writing inspired by, 23

PORTFOLIOS, LITERACY: 122-29; assessment using, 96

POSTERS: 48, 103

POTOK, CHAIM: 128

PRACTICUMS, READING: 161

PREDICTION(S): 82, 116, 118; shared reading and, 73, 75, 76

PREJUDICE: and bias contrasted, 32; as classroom reading/discussion topic, 135

PREQUESTIONS: 134-35

PREREADING: 96, 130, 132-36

PRESERVICE TEACHERS: 20, 155, 156; dialogue journals of, 161. *See also* Student teachers

PREWRITING: 134

PRINT: 49

PROBLEM SETTING: 8

PROCESS APPROACH: 20

PROFESSIONAL DEVELOPMENT SCHOOLS (PDS): 16-17

PROFESSIONAL JOURNALS: IRA, 12; politics of publishing in, 2; teacher-research results in, 16. *See also* Articles, journal; *Journal of Reading*; *Progressive Journal*; *Reading Research Quarterly*; *Reading Teacher, The*

PROGRESSIVE JOURNAL: 14

PROGRESSIVISM, EDUCATIONAL: 14

PROGRESS REPORTS: and reading workshops, 126

PROMPTS: dialogue journals and, 186-88, 189-90, 192, 195; journal responses as, 177; for preservice teachers, 216-17; teacher use of, 66; writing, 214

PRONUNCIATION: 96

PSEUDONYMS: ethical rationale for student, 33; use of in volume, ii

PSYCHOLOGY: ix; teaching and, 10-11

PSYCHOLOGY AND PEDAGOGY OF READING, THE (Huey): 16

PUBLISHING: of Cynthia's article, 104; of student writing, 77. *See also* Professional journals

PUNCTUATION: 125, 139, 213

QUESTIONS: classroom, 19; commerical reading program, 61; "piggyback," 62; reading-related, 57-58, 66, 68, 117; reflective journal-related, 175; student-developed, 62-63, 63f; teacher researcher, 19-34, 37, 52, 73, 88, 90-91, 199, 210; teacher self-, 8-9, 19-20. *See also* Prequestions; Prompts

QUINCY SYSTEM: 14

QUIZZES: reading-related, 130, 131, 133. *See also* Assessment

RANDALL, CHRISTINA: 20-21, 23

RANKEY, MARY ANN: 198, 208

READERS: engaged/nonengaged, 80-82; reluctant, 121

READING: collaborative, 52, 61, 62-69, 70 (*see also* Reading, paired; Reading, shared); dislike of, 27; hearing-impaired children and, 44, 47; invitations to, 28, 29-30, 30f, 33; language development and, 48; literature as aid in teaching, 38; paired, 65; remedial (*see* Language therapy; Speech therapy); round-robin, 67; shared, 65, 73, 76; silent, 61, 67, 73-74, 76-77, 78, 80, 82, 116; student response to, 123 (*see also* Portfolios, literacy); writing and, ix. *See also* Authors; Book reports/reviews; Books; Language arts; Prereading; Print; Reading aloud; Reading workshops; Speed reading

READING ALOUD: 116

READING BEGINS AT BIRTH (Doake): 47

READING PROGRAMS: 123; commercial, 61

READING RESEARCH QUARTERLY: 2

READING TEACHER, THE: 2

READING TODAY: 2

READING WORKSHOPS: 61, 65-69, 115-21, 123-29; benefits of, 121; eighth graders in, 20; in upper grades, 121

REALITY: Aristotle on, 13

RECITATION: and discussion contrasted, 138; of memorized facts (*see* Rote)

RECORD-KEEPING: ix

REFERENCE BOOKS: taking notes from, 83

REFLECTION(S): 28, 34, 39, 75, 161, 162, 170, 183, 213; action and, 14, 84; for action, 192; in action, 32, 191, 192; on action, 32, 139, 188, 191; on classroom practices, 73-77; decision making and, 173-82; dialogue journals and, 161, 170; discrete response style and, 166; importance of, 8, 10; intertextual response style and, 166; perils of solitary, 72; student, 73, 74-75, 79, 124-29. *See also* Reflective journals

REFLECTIVE JOURNALS: 158, 174-82, 199, 200, 203; purpose of, 177, 180, 182; weaknesses of, 181-82. *See also* Dialogue journals

RESEARCH: and context, viii; ethnographic approach to, 9; experimental approach to, 7, 9; medical, 9; naturalistic approach to, 7; observational, 14; pre-, 39; process-observational, viii; qualitative, 19, 23; qualitative vs. quantitative, 14-15; by teachers (*see* Teacher research; Teacher researchers). *See also* Action research

RESPONSE LOGS. *See* Student journals/logs

RESPONSES: dialogue journal, 163-67. *See also* Discrete responses; Intertextual responses

REVISION. *See* Editing

RIGOR: academic fascination with, 9-10

RILKE, RAINER MARIA: 25

RITA (Langston Hughes Intermediate School teacher researcher): 87, 89-91

ROBINSON CRUSOE (Defoe): 68

RONDA (LDOS teacher): 49, 50

ROSE BLANCHE (Innocenti): 52, 54, 55, 56, 57

ROTE: Progressivism vs., 14

ROUSSEAU, JEAN JACQUES: 13

RUNNING LOOSE (Crutcher): 140

SALINGER, J.D.: 134

SCARLET LETTER, THE (Hawthorne): 137, 139-43, 144

SCHULZ, MARION: 145

SCIENCE: games as aid to teaching, 89; vocabulary of, 90

SEATWORK: 95

SELF-CONFIDENCE: hearing-impaired students and, 45; reading workshop's development of, 126

SELF-EVALUATION(S): 159; student, 122, 124-29, 198-208

SEMINARS: literary-appreciation, 139, 142, 143, 146; student moderating of, 142

SEUSS, DR. (Theodore Seuss Geisel): 52, 56, 57

SEVENTH GRADERS: and prereading, 133; reading self-assessment by, 124-28; and reading workshop, 115-21. *See also* Cynthia (Whitin student)

SHERRY (Langston Hughes Intermediate School teacher researcher): 87-89, 90-91

SIGN OF THE BEAVER, THE (Speare): 60-61

SIGNS: educational use of, 159

SILVERSTEIN, SHEL: 120

SIMONS, GRETCHEN: 134-35

"SINNERS IN THE HANDS OF AN ANGRY GOD" (Edwards): 137

SLANG. *See* Vernacular

SMITH, FRANK: 186

SOWERS, SUSAN: viii

SPACE SCIENCE: as preschooler "hook," 42-43, 45

SPARKS, BEATRICE: 31

SPEARE, RACHEL GEORGE: 60

SPEECHES: 103

SPEECH THERAPY: 21

SPEED READING: 124

SPELLING: 74, 125, 126, 139, 213; engaged/nonengaged writers and, 82, 83; as unimportant, 166

SPERRY, ARMSTRONG: 67

STENHOUSE, LAURENCE: 15

STONE FOX (Gardiner); 66-67

STORY MAPS: 123

STORY PYRAMIDS: 123, 125

STORYTELLER'S STORY, A (Anderson): 144

STRATEGY MEMOS: 200

STUDENT JOURNALS/LOGS: 9, 23, 29, 31, 38, 69f, 70, 78, 80, 83, 90, 91, 97, 135, 138, 139, 140-41, 143, 146, 211; evaluation of, 140, 143-44; and literature assignments, 139-40,